ASK THE WINE DOCTOR

ASK THE WINE DOCTOR

All the Questions You Had About Wine
But Were Too Busy Sipping to Ask

EDWARD FINSTEIN

(a.k.a. Dr. WineKnow)

Published simultaneously in the United States of America by McClelland & Stewart Ltd., P.O. Box 1030, Plattsburgh, New York 12901

Library of Congress Control Number: 2002107049

National Library of Canada Cataloguing in Publication Data

Finstein, Edward, 1949-
    Ask the wine doctor : all the questions you had about wine but were too busy sipping to ask / Edward Finstein.

ISBN 0-7710-3112-2

1. Wine and wine making – Miscellanea.   I. Title.

TP548.F.55 2002   641.2'2   C2002-902500-1

We acknowledge the financial support of the Government of Canada through the Book Publishing Industry Development Program for our publishing activities. We further acknowledge the support of the Canada Council for the Arts and the Ontario Arts Council for our publishing program.

Illustrations throughout by Visutronx
Typeset in Minion by M&S, Toronto
Printed and bound in Canada

McClelland & Stewart Ltd.
The Canadian Publishers
481 University Avenue
Toronto, Ontario
M5G 2E9
www.mcclelland.com

1 2 3 4 5   06 05 04 03 02

To Pooky, who had faith

CONTENTS

ACKNOWLEDGEMENTS

Words of thanks are a lot like flyers. You often distribute many, but only some are actually appreciated. I don't know any other field where gratitude is more respected than in wine. Whether it's gratitude to a grape grower or winemaker who grows and turns the fruit into this glorious nectar, or to the consumer – without them, wine would simply not matter – saying thanks means so much.

To the diligent people who grow grapes and make wine, I tip my hat. Without you folks, the world would indeed be a "drier" and less enjoyable place.

To my editor, Pat Kennedy, who believed in my idea.

To my friend and fellow oenophile, Tony Aspler, whose support over the years and invaluable advice about the ins and outs of the publishing world were greatly appreciated.

A special word of thanks to my wife, Jo Ann, who proofread the manuscript and provided insightful, constructive input.

Last but not least, my heartfelt gratitude to wine consumers everywhere. It's your inquisitive minds and fascinating questions, over my last twenty-five years in this business, that prompted and gave rise to the material for this book.

To all of you, I raise a glass and say "à votre santé."

INTRODUCTION

*W*ith the vast amount of wine available in the world today, you might find yourself overwhelmed and confused about many aspects of the juice of the grape. And for good reason! There's a mountain of information to scale: how wine is grown, made, aged, stored, served, and matched to food. The input overload never seems to end. Well, take heed. You can conquer this potable Everest and enjoy doing it, too.

I'm Dr. WineKnow. You may remember me from such pictures as "The Grape Wine Robbery" and "How Grape Was My Valley." Well, in fact, I'm mild-mannered Edward Finstein, wine guru. I wasn't always the shy oenophile who is penning these liquid words. I come from rather humble beginnings. As a post-graduate psychology major at university in 1972, I thought I was going to set the intellectual world on its head. Wow, did I have impressive ideas and the "chutzpah" to carry them off. My part-time job as a professional musician, which financed my schooling, took me around the world. I was in and out of musical groups and recording studios like nobody's business. In fact, so great was my love of music that it soon became my full-time gig, and I left university behind. Then it happened . . . disco. My aspirations were crushed. All I had to drown my dreams of musical success were memories of what might have been and a decent glass of wine here and there. While I was looking for some way to continue my studies, a friend asked if I would be interested in working part-time at a wine store over the Christmas season. Well, against my better judgement, I agreed. After all, I had only a passing interest in vino but, on the other hand, the job would provide the much-needed funds to finance a renewed assault on psychology. Boy, was I wrong. This innocent little job changed my life.

I became smitten with the grape. My voracious appetite for wine knowledge led me to intensive reading, wine courses, wine tastings, and travels to wine regions worldwide. It's as if Bacchus had taken me under his wing. One thing led to another, and before you could say "trockenbeerenauslese," I was a senior wine consultant and part of the buying team for the world's largest liquor monopoly, the LCBO. But alas, feeling somewhat stifled by the Crown corporation after about nine years, I decided to branch out on my own and set up a wine business, catering strictly to the dissemination of wine knowledge. I have not looked back.

Having dedicated the last quarter-century to writing, judging, teaching, consulting, appraising, and travelling, all for the pleasure of the grape, I've learned a few things. Wine is great and it's fun. Now I wish to share this with you.

This is a light-hearted, entertaining, informative, useful look at the problems, concerns, and questions that plague wine lovers the world over. Yes, the good doctor is here to handle your vinous needs, diagnose the problems, and to answer your queries via a prescription of sorts. Consider this book a reference source, somewhat like a medical, home-remedy volume. This book is for all wine lovers everywhere, whether beginners or experts. I'm sure you'll find something between these covers that's beneficial. Wasn't it the great American story-teller Mark Twain, who said "my books are water; those of the great genuises is wine. Everybody drinks water"?

Hopefully, this one is both. Drink these words and enjoy. If your particular problem is not listed here in some form, please feel free to e-mail Dr. WineKnow for advice at wineknow@globalserve.net. I also have a Web site at www.drwineknow.com.

Cheers!

CHAPTER 1

GRAPE EXPECTATIONS
Growing It

*I*t is said that wine is made in the vineyard. If this is the case, who needs wineries? We do, of course. What this saying refers to is the fact that the grapes themselves dictate what the finished wine will be like. They are the soul and expression of the resulting product. Although this applies to some grape varieties more than others, you can only make as good a wine as the raw material you start with. Ripe, high-quality grapes usually result in great wines. Now that's not to say that poor-quality grapes can't make decent wine, or are not used. It's just much harder to end up with something drinkable. Winemaking becomes more challenging and the chances of greatness are drastically diminished. If you think you can't tell good from bad wines, think back. Have you ever tasted a wine and said, "God, this tastes terrible?" Of course you have. You may not have known why, but the taste expressed it. Not only was the winemaking poor, the grapes utilized were probably not great. Quality of fruit is what it's all about. The importance of this cannot be emphasized enough. If you make use of vintage charts, you will see this reflected in them. These charts, usually produced for each wine region, rate the quality of the fruit, and ultimately the wine, from each year. The better the quality of fruit for a specific year, the higher the quality of wine.

Over the years, though our understanding of grape growing and viticulture technology has evolved, some things still remain the same. The way a grape vine grows, produces fruit, and flourishes really remains constant. More importantly, we always have been and most probably will continue to be at the mercy of Mother Nature. She holds all the trump cards. No matter how advanced our grape-growing panache, Mother Nature has a way of keeping us in our place. Perhaps this is a good thing. It keeps grape growers humble and on their toes and initiates and stimulates many viti-culture innovations. Without her fickle ways, every growing season would be exactly as the one before. Fruit character would not differ. In other words, the wine would taste the same year after year. How boring! After all, part of wine's appeal and excitement is the fact that every vintage year is different. Herein lies its pizazz.

Location, Location, Location

These are the three most important words to real-estate agents, but could easily apply to wine producers, as well. Where grape vines are planted will obviously determine how and what they produce. If you are a home gardener, you know the trials and tribulations of finding just the right spot to plant that perennial or annual. Certain parts of your garden may be too shady or sunny, hotter or cooler. The soil might contain more clay on one side than the other. Maybe a certain part has better drainage. Ultimately, where the plant goes in the ground will determine what it produces.

Specifics aside, when it comes to wine growing, one must think on a broader scale. Climate and soil play the biggest roles and are part of what defines the whole character of the wine known as "terroir." Most grapes need reasonable sunshine, heat, and rain to produce. Reds, especially, need hot, dry, long growing seasons to be prolific. However, not all grapes are created equal. Some are not winter hearty, or have thin skins and won't work in regions that have severely cold weather. Other grapes need temperatures to cool down at night, so they have a chance to rest. If there is too much constant heat, the vines become stressed and the fruit over-ripens. Still others, because of their tight clusters, require a certain amount of wind to blow through them, to dry up moisture and prevent rot. Maybe a location closer to the sea would work better for them. Understanding specific grapes and their structures will ultimately enable a wine grower to pick the correct grape to grow in a specific site. Then a simple climate analysis of a potential region will give a very detailed picture of what will best work there.

As for soil, it is the other most important aspect of grape growing. Often a finished wine is a direct reflection of the soil it is grown in, and can even possess characteristics of it in the taste. Grape vines do not like rich, dark, soil. These dense soils tend to retain moisture, and are not good for wine grapes. They're great for other fruits and veggies, but not these guys. There is an old saying that "the poorer the soil, the better it is for wine grapes." Although not entirely true, there is some validity to this. Thus, soils composed of gravel, sand, broken rock, and other loosely structured dirt work best. Furthermore, every grape variety requires a little something different from the soil. Some require more phosphorous and nitrogen, while others require less. By simply doing a soil analysis of a potential site, one can come to a pretty good understanding of what grapes will best suit that site. If the site does not contain the appropriate nutrients for a specific grape, it will lack varietal character and perhaps not be as affluent as it should. It may also not be as resistant to disease and the elements.

Dear Dr. WineKnow:
I need you to settle a battle between me and my Dad. He says that grape vines grow everywhere in the world except the North and South pole, and I say it's not true. Who's right here?

Diagnosis: Indeed, grapes can and do grow most places in the world where temperatures rise above 50°F and remain there for a while. In warmer climates grapes are very prolific and produce massive amounts of fruit. In cooler climates they are a little more restrained and produce less, mainly because of a shorter growing season.

Grapes for wine are usually grown between 30° and 50° north and south of the equator. It's simply too hot or cold above and below those latitudes to produce grapes with enough structural components to make wine. Sure, you can grow grapes that are great for eating, but not for wine.

Dear Dr. WineKnow:
The world is the world when it comes to grape growing, isn't it? "Old World," "New World," what's the difference?
Diagnosis: Well, hold onto your wineglass, it's going to be an eye-opener. Surely you've heard Europe and the Mediterranean referred to as the "Old Country." No surprises here; this area is also the "Old World" when it comes to grape growing. Therefore the "New World" is everywhere that's left over, that is, those colonies established by European exploration. So places like Australia, New Zealand, North and South America, and South Africa are considered "New World" wine-producing countries.

Dear Dr. WineKnow:
How do grapes differ if they're grown in different temperatures? And can grapes get sunburn from intense heat or frostbite from the cold?
Diagnosis: There is a huge difference between grapes grown in hot and cool climates – known as warm-climate and cool-climate viticulture. The resulting grapes differ in the following ways. In hot climates there is never a problem ripening grapes, because of the heat. Sugar levels are generally high, resulting in higher potential alcohol. That's why wines from places like Australia often possess very high alcohol levels. However, warm-climate grapes often lack

acidity, the sour component of wine. On the other hand, cool-climate grapes never have a problem with acid levels because of the lower temperatures. However, they may have trouble ripening and producing higher sugar levels. Also, heaven forbid, they might be lower in alcohol.

As for sunburn and frostbite, they are real concerns. Sunburned grapes tend to produce over-jammy or cooked character in wines. Grapes hit by frost are basically shot and useless for wine.

Prescription: For low acid or insufficient ripeness due to low sugars, things can be done by the grape grower to solve these problems. In a warm climate the vines might be planted at a higher altitude, or nearer to a body of water where the air is cooler to avoid too much heat. Or the ripe grapes can be harvested earlier to avoid massive sugar levels. This way alcohol can be kept to a reasonable amount. In a cool climate, grape growers can manage the vines' canopy so as to expose the grapes to maximum sunlight, thus obtaining higher sugar levels. They may want to let the grapes hang on the vine longer to increase sugar levels and harvest them later (late harvest). So certain things can be done in the vineyard to affect the grapes' juice and ultimately the wine – and protect them.

Dear Dr. WineKnow:

There's an old story about the grapes being planted on "the south side of a hill." I sort of understand the "south side" aspect, but why "on a hill"? This question is giving me a case of the bends.

Diagnosis: Put plainly and simply, vines do not like "wet feet." Aside from giving an interesting "slant" on things, a slope of some sort is a good idea for grape vines. If water is retained around the roots, the vine will get root-rot and die. They require good drainage at all times. The grape vine is better off extending its roots deep into the soil to look for water. This creates a solid, strong root structure.

Avoiding the "erosionous" zone is key. Just keep in mind that too much of a slope can be bad, as nutritional run-off and erosion may be a problem.

> ## GRAPE FLASH
> "Luck" be a grape vine tonight. Did you know that this little four-letter word can make the difference between life and death for a grape vine, no matter where you plant it? Planting grapes is sometimes likened to a Las Vegas crap shoot. Sometimes the odds are on your side, and sometimes they're not. You could decide to plant your grapes in an area that is susceptible to nature's wrath. One season you decide to harvest your grapes the day before a killer frost hits, while your neighbour opts to leave them on the vine with hopes of riper fruit. Ultimately, he would get nailed and you wouldn't, all due to luck. Grape growers have to check weather reports and daily news to prevent being unlucky in case a killer storm, frost, or other current event should affect their crop and business.

Dear Dr. WineKnow:

I'm in a constant state of "terroir." In my reading, I've seen this word used in reference to grape growing. Can you tell me what this means?

Diagnosis: It's a kind of earthy package deal. Very simply put, "terroir" is the natural environment of a piece of land that grows grapes. This reflects all aspects of climate, soil, and topography. Climate accounts for temperature, rainfall, wind, and amount of sunshine. Soil involves all the chemical components and the drainage of surface soil and subsoils. Topography refers to the lay of the land, the degree and direction of any slope, affecting when the vineyard gets sun (morning, afternoon, etc.), and all of these give the wine from that area its character.

Prescription: Get the dirt on wines. Read up on areas and the characteristics of the wines they produce. The concept of "terroir" is so important that many wine-producing regions, worldwide, use it as a basis for demarcating, delineating, and regulating wine zones. Appellation systems, sub-wine regions, and "cru" systems are based on this.

Dear Dr. WineKnow:
I went out in my backyard and planted some grape seeds but nothing sprouted. Where did I go wrong?
Diagnosis: Let's face it, a Johnny Appleseed, you're not. Grape vines need to be procreated from cuttings of other vines. Simply putting seeds in the soil does absolutely nothing. Believe me, I've tried it. That's why there are nurseries where dedicated agriculturists create new vines to sell to grape growers for planting. The more you buy, the cheaper the cost. Cuttings are usually kept in a nursery for about a year before they are ready to be sold. At this point they can be transplanted to the vineyard. Immature vines like these are extremely susceptible to the elements and need tender, loving care until they are hearty enough to prosper.
Prescription: Get thee to a nursery. If you are in the market for grape vines, contact a winery and find out who they purchase vines from. However, be aware of what you are buying and what factors are required for the vines to be prolific.

The Noble Vine

"To vine own self be true." Grape varieties are an incredible lot. It's hard to believe that their fine little berries can become the liquid treasures they do. Interestingly, they differ in size, shape, bunch formation, colour, density, skin thickness, susceptibility to disease and the elements, and taste. It never ceases to astonish me just how different each grape vine is and how unique its resulting wine. Although they all differ, there are certain aspects of their productivity that apply to most. Grape vines, like people, have a life cycle. They start out as saplings, mature to a peak production period, and then decline.

Ask any dedicated grape grower his favourite place in the world and you'll always get the same answer: standing among the rows of vines while the grapes are ripe and hanging. Having spent endless hours, myself, strolling through vineyards at this time, I can attest to the pleasure. There's really something special about being in a vineyard laden with fruit. All you can hear are the birds chirping and the wind rustling through the leaves. You can almost hear the grapes growing. It's positively Zen-like.

Dear Dr. WineKnow:
Grapes for the table and those for wine are grown the same way, aren't they? Just some you eat and others you turn into wine.
Diagnosis: To the average person, grapes are grapes. Very profound. In a manner of speaking the above is true. But, although both evolve the same way in the vineyard, there are significant differences. They all bud, flower, ripen, and are harvested. To a farmer, though, growing them is a whole different game. Just try getting a farmer to switch over from growing grapes for food to grapes for wine.

If you are growing grapes for food, it doesn't matter how prolific a vine is. Since most grape growers get paid by tonnage produced, the more a vine produces the better. However, for wine, the vines need to be stressed. Less, but better-quality, fruit is required. These smaller yields from vineyards are what make better wines. So vines are treated very differently when grown for wine. They are trellised differently, pruned back, and wine growers use different canopy management.

Dear Dr. WineKnow:
How long does a grape vine take, after planting, to start producing grapes for wine?
Diagnosis: Since most grape vines are started in a nursery first and not really transplanted to a vineyard until the second year, they are already small plants, as opposed to a saplings. They will probably produce fruit the first year.

But – and this is a big but – although a young grape vine will produce fruit almost immediately after it is transplanted to a vineyard, the quality of the fruit and, ultimately, the wine made from it, is usually not very concentrated. Most wineries will not use this fruit in their higher-end wines but assign them to blends or more commercial offerings. Once the vines achieve more maturity, the fruit will be utilized for better wines.

Dear Dr. WineKnow:
What is the ideal age for a grape vine that is producing fruit?
Diagnosis: A grape vine, as you probably realize, is a living thing and has a life cycle. There is a period when it is young, when at its peak, and finally when it is in decline. Most producers ideally like to use a vine's fruit when it is at its peak, because the quality and quantity is decent.

The ideal age for a grape vine is somewhere between fifteen and twenty-five years, on average. It varies somewhat from species to species.

GRAPE FLASH

Did you know that a nasty little bug called "phylloxera" nearly destroyed all the grape vines worldwide, back in the 1860s? This scourge affected all pure *vitis vinifera* (traditional European vines), except in a few very isolated places like Chile and South Africa, or those grown in sand. The little louse (I love that term) would burrow into the vine's root and slowly suck the life out of it. It would move from vine to vine by digging tunnels under the ground. The main noticeable effect was the fact that, each year, the vine produced less fruit until, after four or five years, it produced nothing at all. There was no known cure for it. Lo and behold, a miracle happened. They discovered that North American species of grapes were immune to it. So by grafting European vines onto the rootstocks of North American species the problem was solved. The portion of the vine that was susceptible was above the ground, and the immune part, with the roots, was under the soil. Today, most European vines are grafted to prevent phylloxera. The baby vine is usually bench grafted, then dipped in some sort of wax that hardens like a cast to prevent the graft from breaking. It is then put in some loamy soil or potted, and is kept in a nursery until a firm root system develops, about a year later. It's interesting to note that phylloxera never really went away. It's still around to some extent in many vineyards, but the damage is minimal. Keep in mind, too, that interesting mutations of the bug have developed. In California they discovered a resurgence of phylloxera in what they thought were resistant, grafted plants. Apparently it (phylloxera) decided that the once-resistant root stock was now the best place to raise a family. It's not unlike infestations of cockroaches that eventually get used to sprays and are no longer affected by them. California had to tear out many vineyards and replant on new clones of rootstocks to the tune of billions of dollars.

Dear Dr. WineKnow:

How long will a grape vine live?

Diagnosis: This depends on the species, its heartiness, and how resistant to disease it is. Generally, grape vines can live hundreds of years, but do not produce fruit, great fruit, or much fruit all that time.

Dear Dr. WineKnow:

I've purchased wine made from old vines. It even said so on the label. They always seem to be more expensive. Why?

Diagnosis: Have you ever seen a mean-looking vine? Then take a look sometime into a vineyard with older vines – these dudes are gnarly and crooked with hard, hard wood. It's true, there are many wines on the market that actually state on the label "made from old vines." What immediately comes to mind are some from California. "Old Vine" Zins (zinfandels) are very popular these days.

Basically, the reason why wines made from old vines are so expensive is twofold. First of all, the winemaker must get some return on a vine that has been kept healthy and producing for say one hundred years. It's like buying an antique. Secondly, and more importantly, as a vine gets older, after a certain point, it produces less fruit. Mind you, the quality of the fruit will be great; there's just very little of it. So you are paying for the fact that these vines produce very few high-quality grapes. For many producers it simply doesn't pay to keep making wine from old vines. They simply have to charge too much for what fruit and wine comes from them. The market for wines like these may be small, and the vines may require too much work for what it is worth.

Dear Dr. WineKnow:
I've read about "clonal selection" when it comes to grape vines. Could you explain what this is?

Diagnosis: This term conjures up images of Frankenstein, genetic mutation, and weird, scientific experiments, doesn't it? Well, scientific it is, weird it isn't. The truth of the matter is that, for every grape variety, there are a number of different clones. Each clone acts slightly different and produces interesting variations of the grape. More importantly, some clones are more or less susceptible to adverse weather, disease, and so forth.

Prescription: Don't split "heirs." By examining a potential growing site's climate and soil composition, the grower can plant the best possible clone of a specific grape for that area or climate. Often, many producers run into problems in their finished wine because they didn't plant the right clone, that is, say, winter hearty or resistant to diseases. This is very evident with fussy grapes like Pinot Noir.

Grape Families
There are basically three species or families of grapes, sort of like a social class system.

Vitis vinifera

These are the cream of the crop, the upper class, the aristocracy, if you will. Most of these noble grape varieties are European, have a long history, and generally make the best wine. They include such favourites as Chardonnay, Riesling, Sauvignon Blanc, Cabernet Sauvignon, Pinot Noir, Gamay, and Merlot. There are about fifty used in winemaking.

Hybrids

These are middle-class grapes. They are crosses of native North American vines with *vitis vinifera*. The purpose of these vines is to create stock that is hardier, higher yielding, earlier ripening, more disease-resistant, with the benefit of obtaining some of the character of the noble group. They include such varieties as Seyval Blanc, Vidal, Maréchal Foch, and Chancellor. They produce less elegant wines than *vinifera* and usually don't live as long.

Vitis labrusca

These are considered the lower class. They are native North American varieties which were found growing naturally in this part of the world. Usually, they are crossed with *vinifera* to create hybrids. Such varieties as Concord, Delaware, and Niagara produce "foxy"-type wines and have little stature in the wine world. They do, however, make great jams, jellies, and grape juice. Although they are sturdy, quite winter hardy, and fairly disease resistant, most wine-producing regions in North America pull them out to plant more fashionable varietals. Don't get too down on them though. If it were not for these wines and their resistance to a certain little root louse back in the 1860s, the wine world may never have recovered from the scourge of phylloxera.

Common Grape Varieties and Their Origin

PLACE OF ORIGIN	VARIETY	RED	WHITE	SPECIES
FRANCE	Aligoté		X	vinifera
	Auxerrois		X	vinifera
	Baco Noir	X		hybrid
	Cabernet Franc	X		vinifera
	Cabernet Sauvignon	X		vinifera
	Chardonnay		X	vinifera
	Chenin Blanc		X	vinifera
	Cinsault	X		vinifera
	Colombard		X	vinifera
	Gamay	X		vinifera
	Jacquère		X	vinifera
	Malbec	X		vinifera
	Maréchal Foch	X		hybrid
	Marsanne		X	vinifera
	Merlot	X		vinifera
	Muscadelle		X	vinifera
	Muscadet		X	vinifera
	Petite Sirah	X		vinifera
	Pinot Blanc		X	vinifera
	Pinot Meunier	X		vinifera
	Pinot Noir	X		vinifera
	Sacy		X	vinifera
	Savagnin		X	vinifera
	Sauvignon Blanc		X	vinifera
	Sémillon		X	vinifera
	Seyval Blanc		X	hybrid
	Vidal		X	hybrid
	Viognier		X	vinifera
	Welschriesling		X	vinifera
PORTUGAL	Alvarinho		X	vinifera
	Bual (Madeira)		X	vinifera

PLACE OF ORIGIN	VARIETY	RED	WHITE	SPECIES
	Sercial (Madeira)		X	vinifera
	Touriga Naçional	X		vinifera
GERMANY	Bacchus		X	vinifera
	Kerner		X	vinifera
	Morio-Muscat		X	vinifera
	Müller-Thurgau		X	vinifera
	Riesling		X	vinifera
SWITZERLAND	Chasselas		X	vinifera
U.S.A.	Emerald Riesling		X	vinifera
(CALIFORNIA)	Zinfandel	X		vinifera
HUNGARY	Furmint		X	vinifera
	Hárslevelu		X	vinifera
	Kadarka	X		vinifera
ITALY	Barbera	X		vinifera
	Dolcetto	X		vinifera
	Gewürztraminer		X	vinifera
	Grignolino	X		vinifera
	Lambrusco	X		vinifera
	Nebbiolo	X		vinifera
	Picolit		X	vinifera
	Primitivo	X		vinifera
	Sangiovese	X		vinifera
	Vernaccia		X	vinifera
AUSTRIA	Grüner Veltliner		X	vinifera
	Silvaner		X	vinifera
GREECE	Aglianico	X		vinifera
	Malvasia		X	vinifera
	Muscat		X	vinifera

PLACE OF ORIGIN	VARIETY	RED	WHITE	SPECIES
GREECE	Xynomavro	X		vinifera
SPAIN	Carignan	X		vinifera
	Grenache	X		vinifera
	Mourvèdre	X		vinifera
	Palomino		X	vinifera
	Pedro Ximénez		X	vinifera
	Tempranillo	X		vinifera
	Viura		X	vinifera
EASTERN EUROPE	Pinot Gris		X	vinifera
FORMER U.S.S.R.	Rkatsiteli		X	vinifera
SOUTH AFRICA	Pinotage	X		vinifera
MIDDLE EAST	Syrah	X		vinifera

The Royal Treatment

The headline read "Grapevine Runs Rampant, Swallows Up Tractor." Though not quite a man-eater like the voracious plant in *Little Shop of Horrors*, a grapevine can grow into a monster if left unattended or undirected. Its tentacles shoot out in all directions, with leaves that could substitute for bath towels. In my backyard, I have two vines – over fifty years old, with stalks that resemble tree trunks. They form a trellis that stretches some twenty-five feet by twelve feet. It's wonderful to sit under it when the sun beats down on a hot summer day. Although I trim it back several times a season, it still manages to get out of hand. I can't imagine the kind of beast it would become if I didn't control it. It would most likely take over my house. I wonder where my cat went . . .?

Picture the grape grower as the director, producer, and stage manager of his main feature called "The Vineyard." It's up to him or her to set the stage, organize the players (vines) and direct their performance (growth), so that the resulting show (ripe fruit) stands a chance at winning the Oscar (decent wine). He or she alone controls the production. The treatment of the vines is all important.

Dear Dr. WineKnow:
How close are grape vines planted to one another in a vineyard?
Diagnosis: Close only counts with horseshoes, grenades, slow dancing, and perhaps vine planting. Seriously, "close" is a relative term regarding vine planting. There are really two things to consider in this answer: the distance between vines within the row and the distance between rows. Although spacing is a fundamental part of planting a vineyard, there is substantial variation worldwide. This can vary from 1 m both within and between the rows in the "Old World" to 2.5 m between vines and 3.7 m between rows in the "New World." Vineyard density is very important, as it determines grape yield, quality of fruit, and, ultimately, the money that can be made. High-density planting means more plants overall, with less space between the rows. This is great for hand-harvesting but not good for tractors.

As a rule, "Old World" vineyards tend be planted more densely than "New World" vineyards for one basic reason. Most were put in the ground before tractors came on the scene and hand-harvesting was the norm. Today, many "Old World" growers planting new vineyards persist with dense planting and utilize narrow tractors to work them.

Dear Dr. WineKnow:
Will the way grape vines are attached to those wires I see in vineyards affect the quality of the fruit?
Diagnosis: This is one situation where being "wired" is the only way to go. The wires that grape vines are attached to in vineyards are called "trellises," and they are very important to the vine's

growth. They direct which way – east, west, north, south – the vine will grow. They also provide the vine with the best possible growth pattern to expose the fruit to the sun. Furthermore, they provide support to the vines and keep them from growing out between rows, making it impossible to move between them. Trellising is important, as every grape vine's physical growth pattern differs. Trellising is used in order to expose the fruit for ripening and to allow for airflow between vines and clusters, and generally to ensure the vine is prolific. Certain trellising systems would hinder and inhibit the growth of specific vines. Many a grape grower experiments with different trellising systems to see which works best for a particular variety at their locale.

Dear Dr. WineKnow:
I've visited vineyards when they have been pruning the vines. What exactly does pruning accomplish?
Diagnosis: When you visit wineries and their vineyards, you might see people out in the fields actually cutting parts of the vine away. This happens a number of times during the year. They will clip portions of the hard wood, clumps of leaves, and even bunches of grapes.

Pruning is fruit's way of dieting. It is a very slimming procedure and accomplishes a number of things. In the late winter/early spring, trimming some of the hard wood helps the vine direct its juices to new growth. In the middle-to-late growing season, trimming back some of the leaves helps expose the fruit to more sunlight, thus increasing ripening. Actually cutting off bunches of grapes induces the vine to focus on what fruit remains, and thus concentrates sugars and acids.

Dear Dr. WineKnow:
I'm always amazed how straight the rows of grape vines are in vineyards. How do they manage to do it?
Diagnosis: In the old days, lining up a vineyard was done by hand or a wire laid out to keep the planting straight. Straight rows of

vines enable fruit to ripen evenly from vine to vine and allow people and tractors to move freely between them.

Growers with money may plant their vineyards by laser. It's expensive but ideal. This foolproof method renders rows that are perfectly straight, no matter what the lay of the land.

GRAPE FLASH

Did you know that rose bushes are often planted at the ends of rows in vineyards? Why, you ask? Although roses do make the vineyard more beautiful when they are in bloom, this is not their function. They are the barometer of the vineyard. Being very sensitive, they are usually the first plant to show signs of disease or infestation. By monitoring the rose bushes in the vineyard, the grower can stay on top of any potential threat to the vines. A healthy rose bush in the vineyard means a healthy grape vine.

Dear Dr. WineKnow:

What does a grape grower/producer do during the winter months? Does he or she sit around playing cards?

Diagnosis: So you think most growers/producers will skunk you in gin rummy, eh? If they are good at it, it's certainly not from having tons of time in the "off" season. If you think being a wine producer is only a warm-weather job, you had better think again. Just because grape vines are not growing and wine is not being made, doesn't mean there is nothing to be done. It is a full-time job.

The winter months may be the only available time to work indoors upgrading the winery, to bottle or finish off wines that have been ageing in barrel, to sell what stock is available, to prepare marketing strategies for the coming season, and countless other tasks. As far as the vineyard is concerned, much can be done ahead to ready the vines for the growing season. Ploughing, aerating the soil, weeding, spraying, pruning, readying training posts, putting vine cuttings in the greenhouse are but a few of the tasks that need to be done in the "down" time.

Dear Dr. WineKnow:
What happens to a grape vine during the winter months?
Diagnosis: Because they are smart vines, they take a nap. Seriously, during the winter months, the grape vines do go dormant. There is no growth, because the sap is not running. In cooler climates, some less-than-winter-hearty vines are lost for one reason or another.

The magic temperature for a grape vine is 50°F. This is the temperature at which a vine becomes active and the sap starts to flow. Below this, the vine is asleep.

Dear Dr. WineKnow:
There is a lot of talk today about organic fruits and vegetables. Is there such a thing with wine grapes and wine?
Diagnosis: Naturally! Organic grape growing is on the rise today. What "organic" means is that no artificial fungicides or pesticides are used in the growing of these grapes, and no additional sulphur is added to combat bacteria in the fields. The unfortunate part of this is that organic production is restricted to the vineyard and not the winery. So, even though the grapes have been grown organically, the winemaking may not adhere to organic procedures. Machinery may still be sulphured to kill germs. There is also no international standard for organic production. Sure, many wine regions the world over have certain standards, but they differ from region to region. Until some unified, international standards come on the scene, organic production will be somewhat hard to define.
Prescription: Don't get sick over it. If you find that you are affected by artificial fungicides and pesticides or by excessive sulphur, perhaps you should be drinking organic wines. Beware though. The majority of wine retailers don't have sections in their stores saying "organic wines." Many bottles are not even labelled as such. Be sure to ask the retailer for help in locating his or her organic

wines in the store. If sulphur bothers you, then ask to see how many parts per billion a particular wine contains. If you are susceptible, it doesn't take much to give you that splitting headache or upset tummy. If this numerical information cannot be provided, don't buy the wine. There are some wine agents who deal specifically with organic products. Since their reputations are based on what they sell, they are probably the most reliable sources. You might want to inquire at your local wine shop as to the names and contact numbers of agents who handle organic product – or do a search on the Web.

Dear Dr. WineKnow:
Am I having flashbacks to my "hippy" days? I've heard that the moon and stars govern grape growing – like wow, man!
Diagnosis: No, you are not dreaming. Yes, some vineyard – and ultimately winery – operations are governed by the position of the planets and phases of the moon. This interesting, alternative approach to growing grapes for wine does induce images of the 1960s. Indeed, biodynamic farming is now a part of wine growing. Strictly organic in nature, biodynamic grape growing relies heavily on the cosmic background of astronomy and the influence of astrology. This "growing" concept is actually nothing new and has been going on for thousands of years. Many ancient civilizations depended heavily on it to grow crops and guide life. A multitude of modern wine growers, including the French, are utilizing this "age of Aquarius" technique, and they swear it makes a world of difference in better-quality fruit, healthier vines, and less loss to the elements.
Prescription: Modern followers of biodynamics study astrology and astronomy and the life cycle of grape vines and put the two to use with amazing results. Different aspects of the growing patterns of vines are aligned with the changing cycles of the moon, the position of the stars, and so on. Try asking your retailer for any wines that utilize biodynamic grape growing and see if you can tell the difference.

BIODYNAMIC GRAPE GROWING

Specialty Grapes

Like specialty channels on television that offer unusual program-
ming, specialty grapes provide the winemaker with the raw
material to create rare products for the consumer. The majority
of grapes in a vineyard end up as still, dry to medium-dry table
wine. However, some remain on the vine long after the regular
harvest in hopes that they will gain higher sugar levels. Selections
produced from these grapes are sweeter and known as "late-
harvest wines." Although in theory simply waiting to harvest
sounds relatively easy, it is, in fact, a real pain. Grape growers
must combat marauding birds and other beasts looking for food.

The weather is becoming cooler and unpredictable. Overall, it's a lot more work to produce these grapes.

Some grapes are left on the vine deep into winter and are set aside for "icewine." If leaving grapes out after the regular harvest seems like a lot of work, imagine the headaches these icewine grapes can create. You have the deep freeze and chilling winds of winter to contend with.

Finally, there is a phenomenon that sometimes occurs in grapes, creating amazing wines. Some develop a fungus (noble rot) which shrivels them up, resulting in wonderful sweetness and acid in the finished wines.

Dear Dr. WineKnow:

How on earth are grapes grown for icewine in the middle of winter? **Diagnosis:** Icewine, or Eiswein, as the Germans call it, is the ultimate late-harvest wine. The grapes, usually white, are not only left on the vine past the regular harvest time but well into winter, usually until December or January. In order to qualify for icewine, they must be naturally frozen on the vine. Herein lies the key. In fact, there must be several days of sub-zero temperatures in order to freeze the grapes into hard marbles before they can be harvested. Since there is literally no food left anywhere for birds or other animals, the grapes become the main target. Growers do all they can to ward off the beasts – from netting the rows to setting up cannons that go off regularly. The growers must also combat bitter cold and strong winds. When the grapes are ready to be picked, they must be hand-harvested, as a mechanical harvester would only crush the frozen berries. This is usually done in the middle of the night, when it is the coldest. Overnight temperatures are usually lower than daytime, giving a larger window of opportunity to pick and crush before temperatures rise.

Growing and harvesting icewine grapes is very labour-intensive. If you want you can help harvest the grapes; many wineries bring people in to do the job. Just let them know you're interested. There is usually no payment involved, but you will be well fed and lubricated.

For your efforts, you will probably receive a finished bottle of the icewine you helped harvest. Be aware, though, that if you volunteer to do this, the call to harvest could come at midnight. It's also awfully cold work, so bundling up like Nanook is mandatory. However, it really is a wonderful, fascinating experience.

Dear Dr. WineKnow:
Are red grapes ever used for making icewine?
Diagnosis: Up until recently, this nectar of the gods has been reserved for selected white grapes, because they are winter hearty and usually adapt better to late-harvesting. However, with the success of other sweet red wines like port, the door opened for the possibility of red icewine.

Indeed, some people are now making icewine from red grapes. The varietals experimented with include Cabernet Franc, Cabernet Sauvignon, Pinot Noir, Merlot, and even Dornfelder. Some very decent examples are being produced in Canada.

Dear Dr. WineKnow:
How do producers avoid the tannin from the skins in red icewine?
Diagnosis: As with the human body, the skins are a covering that protects the internal part of the fruit. When making other sweet red wines like port, tannin is an integral part of the overall structure and taste. However, it is not desirable to have a tannic icewine, but tannin really isn't an issue for red icewine. Remember that these grapes are frozen. When they are processed, there is no damage to the skins. The juice is pressed off before significant skin contact takes place. This way, the tannin in the skins is avoided.

Dear Dr. WineKnow:
I'm perturbed. If the skins are basically avoided in red icewine, then what colour is it?
Diagnosis: It's true, the skins do provide colour to most red wine. Many red grape varieties don't possess red pulp, so wines made from these without their skin contact will be pink or rosé. Since the

skins are not damaged in the process of making red icewine, and are eliminated along with the ice, most are exactly this colour.

In extremely great years, a little more colour might appear in red icewine made this way. However, some winemakers are experimenting with grape varieties like Dornfelder that actually have red pulp.

Dear Dr. WineKnow:
While recently in California, I noticed they produce icewine too. How can they grow icewine grapes in such a warm climate?
Diagnosis: The short answer: they don't. You will see products called icewine in many parts of the world. However, remember that icewine grapes need very cold weather with consistent sub-zero temperatures. Keep in mind, too, that the key to icewine is that the grapes are naturally frozen on the vine. All this requires a very cold winter, which California does not have.
Prescription: Pour a glass of "vin de glacier." That's the term used for the California version. What you see in California is not icewine but a product that is made from late-harvested grapes artificially frozen in a freezer. Yes, it is sweet and rich but not the real thing. It is an inexpensive, interesting facsimile. Also, since there is little snow in California, no one has to freeze their butts off collecting the grapes in the middle of the night in sub-zero weather.

GRAPE FLASH

Did you know that "icewine" originated by accident? It happened in Germany well over one hundred and some odd years ago. One of the contracted grape growers was overlooked when it came time to harvest his grapes. He notified the producer, who instructed him to harvest the grapes anyway, even though it had snowed and was cold. The wine was made and discovered to be wonderfully special. The rest is, of course, history. Icewine has become world-famous as one of cool-climate viticulture's real prizes.

Dear Dr. WineKnow:
Who produces more icewine, Canada or Germany?
Diagnosis: The more consistently cold winters one has the, more chances of growing grapes to make icewine.

Since Canada has consistently cold winters, we are ensured an icewine crop pretty much every year. Germany doesn't have winters that are consistently cold enough to produce this gem. So Canada is the winner here, producing far more than Germany.

Dear Dr. WineKnow:
I've seen horrible pictures of furry, hairy, shrivelled grapes on the vine. Is this some kind of atmospheric condition that does this to grapes?
Diagnosis: Although it sounds awful, it's actually a good thing. If the truth be known, this fungus, known as "noble rot" or technically "botrytis," is a marvel, producing some of the world's finest wines. It is the basis for such renowned liquid treasures as Sauternes from France and Beerenauslese and Trockenbeerenauslese from Germany. True, it does actually dry out and shrivel the grape, rotting it with fur and hair, but it does other things that are a wonderful secret. It concentrates the sugar and acid like nobody's business. The resulting wine is usually unctuously sweet and rich. One drawback exists, though. There is a very fine line between "noble rot" and just plain, old-fashioned "rot."

Dear Dr. WineKnow:
Can a grower force "noble rot" to form on grapes?
Diagnosis: Actually, no – "noble rot" is a freak of nature. There is no way to force this fungus to grow on grapes. It happens naturally. Sometimes, and for some wine styles or varieties, it appears even if you don't want it. I suppose if someone could simulate the exact conditions for it, forcing it might be possible, but at what cost.

So "noble rot" remains a chance happening. Certain wine regions are notorious for "noble rot," because the conditions are always right. If you examine the regions that are known for it, you can recognize certain climatic and topographical phenomena that seem to nurture its growth. Ideal conditions tend to be hot, hazy, almost-misty mornings, in which the haze lifts by midday and the intense sunlight persists. In other regions, some growing seasons yield similar conditions, causing it to appear.

Dear Dr. WineKnow:
Are certain grape varieties more likely to be affected by "noble rot" than others?
Diagnosis: As a rule, grape varieties possessing more natural sugar are susceptible to it. In a very hot year, grapes that normally don't have gobs of natural sugar may find themselves in possession of some.

Designer wines, take note: fungus is all the rage. A simple examination of the wines that usually possess this fungus will give us information on what varieties are prone to it. In Sauternes, France, it is the Sémillon grape that is the source. In Germany and Canada, Riesling and Vidal seem to take to it well. Even Gewürztraminer is occasionally prone. In the Loire Valley, France, the grape of choice is Chenin Blanc. Aside from known regions, wherever these grapes are grown, they seem most likely to develop "noble rot" if the conditions are right.

Dear Dr. WineKnow:
Is "noble rot" a beneficial thing on grapes intended for dry wine?
Diagnosis: Since this fungus generally concentrates the sugar and acid in grapes, it's not usually desirable in those intended for dry wines. Perhaps a little is okay in varieties on which it works well to add some slight botrytis character to its dry version. But with Chardonnay and Cabernet Sauvignon you would not want this complexity.

Next time you drink brandy, think "maybe noble rot was here." A winemaker might downgrade certain grapes possessing "noble rot" to blended wines or low-end products or sell them off for brandy production.

Dear Dr. WineKnow:
Is "noble rot" ever found on icewine grapes?
Diagnosis: Since the main grapes used to make icewine are those susceptible to it, "noble rot" is occasionally found on them. But if you recall what is involved in making this incredible, sweet number, you can see it's not desirable. When making icewine, there must be sufficient water in the frozen grapes to be able to separate the ice from the juice. "Noble rot" dries out the grape, pretty much eliminating the water.
Prescription: Fungus should not climb into bed with an icewine. Although a bit of botrytis character in an icewine might be nice, a lot really is not possible. Frozen grapes with a lot of the fungus are not usually used to make icewine.

Harvesting

During the growing season, the grape grower monitors the vineyard's progress very carefully. Once the grapes are ready to be picked, no time must be wasted. It's imperative to get the berries off the vines as quickly as possible and into the winery for processing. If there is too much time between the point the grapes are off the vine and the time they are actually crushed, pressed, and fermented, oxidation will occur, possibly ruining the wine. Speed here is of the essence.

There are a couple of methods of harvesting grapes, one faster than the other. Both have their pros and cons.

Dear Dr. WineKnow:
How are grapes harvested by machine?
Diagnosis: This method of gathering grapes, "mechanical harvesting," is fast, relatively efficient, and economical. The machine, which resembles a "U-shaped" tractor, goes up and down the rows, shaking the dickens out of the vines. The grapes fall on trays at the bottom of the tractor and are transferred to the winery.

Over the "long haul," a machine will keep costs down, although the initial layout is high. If the winemaker wants to make a reasonably-priced commercial wine, then mechanical harvesting is the way to go.

Dear Dr. WineKnow:
Are wines harvested by people better than machines?
Diagnosis: Because people have eyes and brains, they don't pick grapes that are rotten, unripe, mouldy, broken, or covered with animal droppings. A machine can't reason and will pick all grapes regardless of their condition. There is less separation of waste material at the winery with this type of grape gathering.

Generally, wines produced from hand-harvested fruit are better, because the quality of the grapes is better. This method is often reserved for higher-end wines.

Dear Dr. WineKnow:
Why are wines made from hand-harvested grapes more expensive?
Diagnosis: Hand-harvesting means better-quality fruit and less separation of waste at the winery. However, it's very time-consuming and expensive to have people walk through a vineyard and pick grapes. It's also very hard, backbreaking work. Mechanical harvesters are quick and effortless.

The extra cost is passed on to the consumer in the retail price. If you consume enough wine, you begin to see the benefits of this extra charge and overlook it.

CHAPTER 2

NECTAR OF THE GODS

Making It

*T*urning grapes into wine is a most amazing, magical procedure. How winemaking actually came about is not known. Perhaps it started with prehistoric people, who gathered wild grapes in order to use their sweet juice as a thirst-quencher. Having left some in a vessel of sorts, they discovered it had evolved into a different drink, one that made them happy and elated. The grape juice had fermented and turned into wine. Maybe this started the ball rolling and launched mankind's fascination with turning the simple fruit into this wonderful nectar.

As time passed, winemaking became more and more complex and sophisticated. Innovative technology helped overcome basic obstacles in the process, allowing the grapes' individual characters to come through. Now the winemaker was free to create, mold, and sculpt these liquid delights into personal expressions of art. Although computers are a large part of modern winemaking today, it is still the winemaker's input and direction that determines what goes into the bottle. This is the part of wine where the makers have the most say.

Aside from the details, the general process of winemaking is relatively simple. When the grapes arrive at the winery, they are initially separated from the stuff that is not needed via a crusher/destemmer machine. This unit lightly crushes the fruit and eliminates the stems and pips (seeds). Then the remaining mash is pressed to produce juice. The juice is then fermented in some format, cleaned up, aged for some time (possibly in wood), and bottled.

WINE PRODUCTION
Wine Making Process

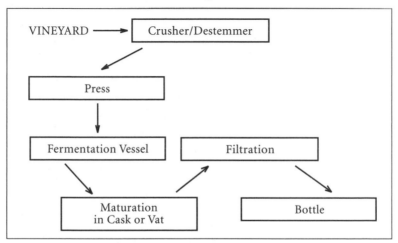

Three main categories of wine result. Still wine, including reds, whites, and rosés, is the most common. Reds utilize the skins for colour and tannin. Most whites do not utilize the skins, so there is no colour to be had. Even white-skinned grapes possess tannins, bitter oils, and phenols which could affect the finished wine, making it bitter. Rosé uses the skins, but carefully.

Sparkling wines are those into which bubbles have been introduced through some process.

Finally, fortified wines are made by adding pure grape spirits or brandy to wines during some point of their production.

The art of winemaking is a process of creation, not unlike raising children, then sending them off. It's not uncommon to hear winemakers refer to their wines as their children. Think about it. They give them life, mold, direct, and shape them. Finally they send them out into the world or down someone's hatch, as it were (that last part of the process is *not* like raising children).

The Simple Facts

Although the winemaking process is generally quite simple, the knowledge required to make wine successfully is very complex. The winemaker needs to have more than a basic understanding of biology and chemistry. Since much equipment is utilized in its creation, technological expertise is also required. And since wine is something that is appreciated orally, he or she should possess a reasonably decent palate, as well. After all, what good is producing a biologically and chemically sound wine using modern equipment if it tastes like shoe polish? Take the amateur or home winemaker. Like the "bathtub gin" produced during Prohibition, without scientific knowledge about blending et al., the amateur's end product can often be unsophisticated and harsh. Bathtub gin, in some cases, actually caused blindness.

THE GRAPE

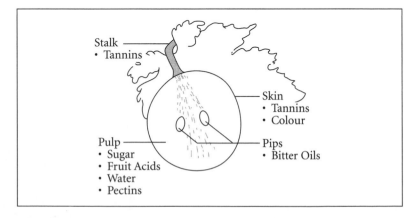

Dear Dr. WineKnow:
I'm having an argument with a friend. He says the skin of the grape is the most important part of winemaking. I say it's the pulp. Who's right?

Diagnosis: Since there aren't too many red grapes in which the pulp is red, the skins must be included in the making of red wine to give colour. If we examine what is required for wine from the grape we can easily resolve this disagreement. The grape contains pectins, fruit acids, sugar, and water. Yeast feeds on the sugars in the grapes, producing carbon dioxide and alcohol. Fruit acids within help balance out the sweetness of wine in the flavour. Pectins, or the jelly-like interior of grapes, act as the vehicle to carry both of the aforementioned sugar and fruit acids.

In essence you are both correct. Without the pulp there would really be no wine. If it were not available, we would need a knife and fork instead of a glass to enjoy it. Certainly the pips or seeds and the stems can be removed, as they contain bitter oils and phenols that would make wine taste weird. Without skins, however, very few wines would be red in colour.

Dear Dr. WineKnow:
When professional tasters describe wine, they talk about all kinds of fruits, vegetables, flowers, and so forth that they smell and taste. Are these things actually used in the winemaking?

Diagnosis: If I had a dime for every time this question comes up I'd be a rich "wineknow." Many things in everyday life are used to describe the smell and taste of wine. Every possible food, flower, spice, and chemical seems to come into play at some point.

These descriptors simply help communicate the language of wine (I heard it through the grapevine). The only product used in making grape wine are grapes. All the other descriptors are a product of its production. Wine is one of the few products on earth that contains so many smells and flavours.

Dear Dr. WineKnow:
Is there anywhere in the world where grapes are still crushed by foot?
Diagnosis: Check out Dr. WineKnow's house on Saturday night, and experience his own version of "bathtub claret." Or you could look back to the Greek and Roman times, when it was the only way to lure the juice from the grape. Since the advent of modern technology, grapes around the world are crushed mechanically in most commercial winemaking. It's certainly much faster, especially with the volume some producers are processing.

Stomping the grapes by foot is still popular among some home winemakers in certain parts of the world. To see it used commercially, however, you'll probably have to look to Portugal and the production of port. It would seem that many producers are going back to this traditional method of crushing grapes, because they claim it yields better-quality wines. Here grapes are placed in shallow stone tanks called "lagares" and trodden by barefoot men and women for up to six hours. The slow crushing of the grapes extracts maximum colour without breaking pips and stalks, thus reducing tannins and acids. Would you believe the natural warmth from human legs slowly raises the temperature of the must (fermenting juice) enough, allowing the yeast to go to work on the sugars? From personal experience, I can tell you it is very hard, foot-staining work (as a side note, it took two weeks for the dye to wear off my legs and feet).

GRAPE FLASH

Did you know that all parts of the wine grape are utilized for something? Obviously, the most important parts are used for the wine. However, the pips (seeds), stalks, and skins of white grapes are sometimes watered down, refermented, and distilled into a brandy of sorts (marc in France, grappa in Italy). If this is not done, the residue is reintroduced to the vineyard as compost. Nothing goes to waste.

Dear Dr. WineKnow:
Why are some red wines soft and round, while others are hard and aggressive?
Diagnosis: There could be many reasons for this, including the grape(s) used, oak contact, and fermentation temperatures. The most common reason, however, is the type of press used to extract the juice. Grapes that are hard-pressed are usually crushed in a press where metal works against metal, literally squeezing the life out of the grapes. When this happens, many bitter, harder components from the skins remain in the juice – and ultimately in the finished wine. Wines that are soft-pressed utilize a press where an inflatable rubber bag fills with air and delicately seduces the juice out of the grape without many of the harder components from the skins.
Prescription: Read the back label of your wine carefully. Occasionally, it will mention how the wine was made. Otherwise, pick better-quality wines. These will often be more expensive, but most of the better wines are made through a soft press.

Dear Dr. WineKnow:
When touring wineries I've noticed that most use stainless-steel equipment. What's the benefit of this?
Diagnosis: Stainless steel provides the most neutral of environments to ferment wine. There's absolutely no personality about it; no extraneous aromatics or flavours will be imparted to any wine produced in it. The containers also come in jacketed formats that make it easy to run hot or cold water over them, thus controlling fermentation.
Prescription: Have you got a lot of money? If so, buy stainless steel. Winemaking equipment is very expensive. Unless you are an extremely serious amateur winemaker or are planning to go professional, it's probably best to make do otherwise.

Dear Dr. WineKnow:
Is there a difference in how "Old World" and "New World" wines are made?

Diagnosis: More than a geographical description of where the grapes are grown, these terms refer to a philosophy about wine-making. "Old World" winemaking seems to highlight "terroir" (the soil and climate that the grapes are grown in) in their wine, with the fruit (sweetness) in the background. The use of oak is also much subtler. "New World" winemaking tends to produce wines that are fruit-driven, with more aggressive use of oak. Terroir is understated.

It's a toss-up really. It is extremely interesting to taste wine with people who grew up with both influences. The difference in likes and dislikes as far as their palates go is fascinating. It's really a matter of what you are used to.

Fermentations

Fermentation is the process by which grape juice becomes wine. It's a rather simple equation. The sugar in grape juice is converted into alcohol and carbon dioxide via the action of yeast. The wine-maker has at his or her disposal several techniques by which to do this: natural fermentation, malolactic fermentation, barrel fermentation, and carbonic maceration. The resulting wine's character can be somewhat altered, providing varying characteristics in the finished wine.

Dear Dr. WineKnow:
I've tried making wine at home but find it very hard to control fermentation. Sometimes it just stops. What am I doing wrong?
Diagnosis: Fret not, my friend, your problem is simply explained. It's not so much what you are doing but what you are not. Fermentation generates heat. If the temperature cannot be controlled, decent wine, if any, cannot be made. This was the problem with many a winemaker years ago. The yeasts that are used to ferment wine are very sensitive to heat and cold. They operate best between 5°C (40°F) and 30°C (90°F). If the temperature goes

outside this range, then fermentation will stop, as you've experienced. This is known as "sticking," and sometimes it can't get unstuck to start again. Even if it restarts, changes may have taken place in the sugars to spoil the wine. In one case in point, my father-in-law decided to make his own wine, using the crab apples in his backyard. Since he had no previous experience and had never read anything about winemaking, his end product was high in alcohol and the fermentation process resulted in undue pressure in the bottles. In the middle of the night, you could hear the sound of corks exploding off the tops of the bottles. Interesting wine, though! Put hair on your chest.

Prescription: You "must" follow this advice. To avoid this danger, the must (fermenting juice) may have to be cooled in warm weather and heated in cool weather. If you are using tanks, this can be achieved by pumping cold or hot water over them. Unless you are relatively serious about home winemaking, you may want to rely on one of those "ferment-your-own" wine facilities that are springing up all over the place. They have temperature control.

Dear Dr. WineKnow:
I often buy grapes to make my own wine. What's that grey, waxy stuff on the skins of all grapes that doesn't wash off?

Diagnosis: This fascinating haze or bloom on each grape is a blend of wild yeasts, wine yeasts, and bacteria by the millions. They are carried on the wind and by insects. The wine yeasts, in particular, were important to early winemakers, since they were necessary for "natural fermentation." Once the skin of the grape is broken, these wine yeasts feed on the sugars within, producing alcohol and carbon dioxide and making wine.

Wines today can still be produced through "natural fermentation," but much attention should be paid to the following: fermentation must take place in an airtight container to ensure killing the wild yeasts and bacteria present on the grape skins. Furthermore, be prepared for a long wait, as this process is very slow. That's why most winemakers today don't rely on it. (If wine is inoculated with artificial yeast, such as most winemakers use, it overrides any natural grape yeast that exists.)

GRAPE FLASH

Did you know that winemakers of today inoculate the must (grape juice) to initiate fermentation? They actually throw some specially designed, fast-acting yeast into the fermentation vessel to start things going. Occasionally, they will add some already-fermenting wine to get the ball rolling. Exactly what yeast is used by each winemaker seems to be a big secret. They don't often like to divulge the specific strain they use for particular wines.

Dear Dr. WineKnow:
How do they get that buttery character in wines like Chardonnay? I really love that creamy complexity.
Diagnosis: Actually, that buttery character is the result of "malolactic fermentation." This secondary fermentation, stimulated by a bacteria (leuconostic oenos), takes place naturally, reducing harsher malic acid (the kind found in green apples) into softer lactic acid (the kind present in milk). Overall, it tends to make the wine more stable. It can be controlled by winemakers (they can inhibit it if desired).
Prescription: It's better with butter! Malolactic is more beneficial to some grape varieties than to others. As a general rule, wines produced in cool climates possess higher acid levels and benefit from "malolactic fermentation." Warm-climate wines are often lower in acidity and may need to be prevented from going through MF so as to retain whatever is available. That is done by keeping wine at cool temperatures or not inoculating with lactic bacteria. (Sometimes the addition of sulphur dioxide also prevents MF.)

Dear Dr. WineKnow:
On the back label of some wine bottles, the term "barrel-fermented" is used with reference to the wine. Could you explain this method?
Diagnosis: Some winemakers choose to ferment certain wines "in barrel." This technique is used principally for white wines, as it is too hard to remove the skins in red wine through the small bung hole of a barrel. Chardonnay and some fine sweet wines are made this way, and there are certain benefits to the method. The barrel protects the wine from oxygen during fermentation. It allows for the controlled extraction of wood flavours into the wine. Because barrels have a large surface-to-volume ratio, artificial temperature control is seldom needed. It also makes it a lot easier for barrel ageing and lees (dead yeast) contact, as the wine is already in the same container.

Although "barrel fermentation" does a great job of adding richness and length on the palate, it does have a few disadvantages. Barrels are much more labour intensive to clean, fill, and empty than are tanks. Overall, producing wine in barrel is more costly. This is why this method is usually reserved for higher-priced wines. The extra degree of complexity gained often outweighs the extra costs.

Dear Dr. WineKnow:
Beaujolais is my favourite red wine. It's always so deeply coloured yet soft and round without any of the hard tannins of other red wines. How so?
Diagnosis: Carbonic maceration. Sounds yummy, doesn't it, kind of like chewing bubbles. Beaujolais utilizes this technique for making wines soft and consumable earlier – which has been around for ages. With carbonic maceration, the grapes are generally not crushed but thrown into an airtight fermentation vessel, whole or in bunches. A blanket of carbon dioxide covers the intact berries and actually suffocates them. Fermentation takes place within the cell walls of each grape, causing colour to leach

out of the skins into the pulp and juice. Because the skins are not crushed, very little tannin and, ultimately, bitterness is extracted from them.

Caution should be taken with this technique. The concept of 100 per cent carbonically macerated wines is really elusive. The mere pressure of some grapes on top of others breaks skins, allowing natural fermentation to take place as well. Thus the term "carbonic maceration" is applied to any situation where there is a proportion of wine being fermented this way. Winemakers will often carbonically macerate some grapes and back-blend them in to his/her satisfaction.

Dear Dr. WineKnow:
What do we get by blending red and white grapes together?
Diagnosis: Why, rosy cheeks, of course. You might think this is how rosé is created, but it isn't as a rule. Almost everywhere in the world rosé wine is made by leaving red grape skins in contact with the fermenting juice just long enough to obtain the desired colour, then removing them. Blending red and white wines together is usually frowned upon, except in Champagne, where they actually blend some still, red wine into the mix before the second fermentation to make the wine rosy.
Prescription: Rosés come in different formats, too. Sometimes they are called "white Zinfandel" (made from Zinfandel grapes), "blush," or "Blanc de Noirs." All of these will ensure a pretty-coloured wine, meant to be consumed young – for the most part – probably within the first three years of the vintage on the bottle.

Dear Dr. WineKnow:
What happens if a wine doesn't produce enough alcohol? Do they just pitch it?
Diagnosis: If you are looking for the "best buzz for your buck," alcohol is one of the key ingredients in wine. For most consumers, though, it also provides structure and longevity to a wine. Alcohol is a direct result of the amount of sugar in the grapes at the time of

harvest. During fermentation, the yeast feeds on the available sugar, producing alcohol and carbon dioxide. The more sugar available, the more alcohol can be produced. Occasionally, sugar levels in grapes are low in cool viticultural areas, especially in poor growing seasons. Thus, fermentation may be fighting to produce reasonable alcohol in a wine.

Prescription: When this happens "chaptalization" may be used. This is the addition of sugar to the fermenting must to increase the alcohol (not the sweetness). This procedure is not allowed in certain wine regions around the world, such as Italy and other warm viticultural areas.

GRAPE FLASH

Did you know that sometimes certain finished wines do not contain enough acid (the sour component) to balance them? Acid levels in wine are extremely important to their structure. Without enough, the wine comes across as "flabby" or "cloying" in the mouth. The process of adding more acid to a wine is known as "acidification." It is not allowed by the regulatory bodies in some wine regions. This lack of acidity can be a major problem in warm viticultural areas, so in this case some acid adjustment is allowed.

Dear Dr. WineKnow:

What do winemakers do with wine produced in a poorer year, especially if it is an expensive one?

Diagnosis: I dunno, throw it out? Hey, not every year is great for growing grapes. There are a number things a grower can do in the vineyard to reduce the yield and concentrate the fruit in a poorer year. Even the winemaker can do just so many things in the winery to increase the quality of poorer fruit. But often, even after utilizing all vineyard and winemaking techniques, the finished wine for an upscale product is still mediocre.

Prescription: The producer would either use it in a blend, download it to a more commercial wine, or create a rosé – if it's red. If it is really inadequate, they may just use it for brandy production. Occasionally, they will create the original wine, but charge less for it. Truthfully, it's not to the producer's advantage to market an upscale wine that is simply not up to snuff. There is a reputation involved here.

Dear Dr. WineKnow:
How do I know if a winemaker is good at what he or she does in a great vintage? Everybody out there is making decent wine.
Diagnosis: The bottom line is one can only make as good a wine as the raw material that is started with. You're right that, in great years, everybody should be making great wines.
Prescription: Pay attention during poor vintage years and take the time to judge a winemaker's ability. Someone who can take less than adequate or mediocre fruit and create a decent wine has what it takes. Take not this time to "whine" over wine, but to build up knowledge about makers for the future.

Sparkling Moments

Nothing quite tickles the nose and excites the palate like a glass of bubbly. No other wine in history has become as synonymous with celebration. This launcher of ships, symbol of the high life, and official wine of the "occasion" has earned its world-famous reputation mainly because of the "fizz." The fizz, of course is what sparkle is all about. Getting it into the wine is the art.

Dear Dr. WineKnow:
Why is Champagne so expensive? Is it just because it comes from France?
Diagnosis: Mais non, mon ami! The reality is that the method of production and quality of the wine produced drives up the cost. The

"champagne method" produces the best bubbly with the smallest, bubbles that last the longest in the glass. But it is also extremely labour-intensive, involving two fermentations: the first to make the wine and the second to create the bubbles. Furthermore, it blends many wines together to come up with a specific taste. Most importantly, the second fermentation takes place in the same bottle. The whole process is very specifically spelled out in Champagne, France. **Prescription:** If bubbles tickle your fancy, but you don't want to pay the Champagne price tag, there are alternatives. Look for wines from other countries that are made this way. Somewhere on the bottle they will say "champagne method," "traditional method," "second fermentation in the bottle," or, in Spain, "cava." These might cost a bit more than other bubblies that are made differently, but the cost is nowhere near that of Champagne.

GRAPE FLASH

Did you know that "riddling" was not the sole domain of Batman's arch-enemy, the Riddler, but a major part of the champagne method, as well? After the second fermentation, the dead yeast must be removed from the wine. Traditionally, the bottles were gradually tilted from a horizontal to a vertical position and shaken, all by hand, to get this deposit to settle at the neck, so it could easily be removed. This slow process, taking six or more weeks, was done in a "riddling rack," or *pupitre*, a sandwich-board type of wooden unit with holes. However, this tedious manual method takes a long time. It was the Spanish back in the 1970s who came up with an automated version to speed up the process. Enter the gyropalette, or "pupimatic," as I like to call it. This computerized machine, capable of holding hundreds of bottles, mechanically tilts and shakes the entire mass at specified, programmed times, reducing "riddling" to three or four days. However, some producers still prefer to hand-riddle their bubbly today.

Dear Dr. WineKnow:
I like bubbly but I can't afford even "champagne-method" wines. As a student, I have a Mercedes taste on a Volkswagen budget. Is there anything out there for me?
Diagnosis: There sure is. Bubbles can be put into a wine three other ways. Mind you, the quality overall may not be as good. The next best method, after the "champagne method," is the "tank method" – often called "Charmat," after the chap who invented it, or "cuvée close." There are two fermentations here, but the second takes place in a large tank. The wine is then bottled under pressure to preserve the fizz. Then there is the "transfer method," which is rather interesting. The wine in this case is second fermented in the bottle, but then dumped into a large tank to clean it up and rebottled under pressure. Finally, the method of least quality is "carbonation," or "injection." A single fermented wine simply has carbon dioxide pumped into it. The resulting wine possesses large bubbles that disappear very quickly.
Prescription: You don't have to sacrifice good taste. Some bubblies will mention the method of production on the bottle. California, by law, is obliged to put it on wine labels. If the bottle says nothing about the method of production, it is probably safe to assume, in most cases, that it utilizes something other than the "champagne method." German sparkling wine generally uses the "tank method." If in doubt, ask your retailer. Price is also generally a good indication of method of production. "Champagne-method" wines are the most expensive and "carbonation/injection" wines, the least.

Fortifiably Good

Fortified wines are the big guns of the still wine set. These powerful numbers are not for the weak of heart. They contain anywhere from 15 to 24 per cent alcohol by volume. They can pack quite a punch, so they should be consumed moderately. When fortified

PORTO
LBV 1994
LATE BOTTLED VINTAGE

Vinho do Porto do Produtor
da Região Demarcada do Douro

Produzido, envelhecido e engarrafado na

QUINTA DO
INFANTADO®
VINHOS DO PRODUTOR, L.DA

0,75 l.   JOÃO LOPES ROSEIRA, Herd.[os]
Gontelho · Covas · Alto Douro   19,5% vol.
Produce of Portugal

wine happens to be sweet as well, its stability and staying power are incredible, more so than any other wine.

Dear Dr. WineKnow:
What exactly does fortification do for a wine?
Diagnosis: Fortification is the process of adding brandy or pure grape spirits to a wine. It originated many years ago, when the addition of brandy helped preserve a wine on long ocean voyages. World-famous port and sherry are made this way. However, the point at which the brandy is added differs with both wines. Port has the brandy added during fermentation. When 40 per cent

alcohol is added to a fermenting wine, the yeast is killed on contact. Since the yeast has not yet consumed all the sugar, much of it remains in the wine. That's why most port is sweet. Sherry, on the other hand, has the brandy added after fermentation. All sherry is fermented to a bone-dry state, then fortified. Sweet sherry is produced by adding back some sweet wine.

Fortification helps wines live long, since alcohol is a great preservative. Most ports and sherries will live comfortably for decades.

Dear Dr. WineKnow:
I'm into aroma therapy, but what on earth is "aromatized wine"?
Diagnosis: An aromatized wine is a fortified wine (grape brandy added) that has had other flavouring agents macerated into it. Herbs, roots, flowers, plants, seeds, barks, peels, and nuts give this fortified wine unusual aromatics and flavours. One of the classic examples is vermouth that is flavoured with such things as nutmeg, coriander seeds, cloves, cinnamon, rose leaves, quinine bark, hyssop, angelica root, wormwood, chamomile, orange peel, and elder flower, to name a few. It's a regular smorgasbord of earthly delights.

You may not want to dab a little behind your ears, but if your taste leans to the exotic, perhaps this type of wine is for you. Just keep in mind that, being fortified, they contain more alcohol and can do a number on you. Drink sparingly, or you may find yourself doing a horizontal tasting.

Dear Dr. WineKnow:
I was in a French restaurant the other day and noticed the term "vin doux naturel" (naturally sweet wine) on their wine list. Is this like late-harvest wine?
Diagnosis: Contrary to the English translation, these wines could actually be considered "unnaturally sweet." Normally, sweet wines contain so much natural sugar that yeasts cannot convert it all to alcohol and die off leaving much behind. VDN, as it is called for short, has pure grape spirits or brandy added to it halfway through

to stop fermentation (fortification). This kills the yeast on contact, preventing it from converting the rest of the sugar. The resulting wine is sweet, with dominant grape flavours, and strong, with more than 14 per cent alcohol.

If you have a hankering for this type of wine, some delicious offerings are available from the south of France and usually represent great value. You had better like the muscat or grenache grape, though, as most are normally made from these.

Stylistically Speaking

Over the years, certain general expressions and terms describing wines have evolved. They have almost taken on stylistic cult status. Some of them are not even formally acknowledged but are used more colloquially. It's amazing just how powerful many of these are in conjuring up and denoting a particular image of a wine.

Dear Dr. WineKnow:
I'm hot on the trail of "table wine." I'm discovering that it seems to mean different things to different people.
Diagnosis: Elementary, my dear Watson. There is an interesting dual meaning to this term. For most wine lovers, the generic term "table wine" refers to everyday wines that we drink with meals or on their own. These can be red, white, rosé, sparkling, or fortified. In wine areas, it's a different story. The term here usually means simple wines with the lowest-quality production standards. In fact, in many countries, table wines actually contain wine from other countries. As long as the minimal required percentage comes from the country stated on the label, the rest can come from anywhere. The grapes from the stated country also usually come from all over the country, not from any specific region. Although cheap and cheerful, these wines don't usually provide great gastronomic pleasure.

If you want reasonable quality, stick to wines that come, at least, from a particular region. Better still are those from individual villages. The best come from single vineyards and are labelled Château or Domain something or other. (Outside France, they're Estate or Vineyard.) If you must consume table wine, try to choose those that have a grape variety on the label.

Dear Dr. WineKnow:
On a vacation in California, I noticed a fair amount of "jug wine" being sold. Is this a particular style of wine?
Diagnosis: "Jug wine" is the American equivalent of "vin ordinaire" or "plonk," usually sold in larger sizes. After Prohibition ended in 1933, most inexpensive California table wine was bottled in half-gallon and gallon jugs or flagons to cater to thirsty immigrant labourers from the Mediterranean and eastern Europe. Gallo was one of the pioneers of this practice. However, as this generation aged or passed on, newer generations with more sophisticated palates turned to such things as "fighting varietals."

After all, how serious can a wine be that conjures up images of a "jug band"? There are still a number of jug wines available today. Their modest price and large size make them ideal for parties or large gatherings where the key is quantity rather than quality.

Dear Dr. WineKnow:
What on earth is "plonk"?
Diagnosis: This rather vague term does not refer to a style of wine. It's an English expression used commonly to describe a wine of undistinguished quality. Word has it that it originated in Australia as an Anglicized form of the word "blanc," French for white wine.

Dear Dr. WineKnow:
Are "blush" wines and "white Zinfandel" the same thing?
Diagnosis: Most are sweetish, lightly fragrant, and faintly spritzy. Would you believe these lightly coloured wines made from dark-skinned grapes, emanating from California in the late 1980s, were a marketing triumph? Surplus Zinfandel grapes, turned into rosé and called "blush" or "white Zinfandel," were and remain the dominant

type, and are still very popular today. In fact, they spawned many other pink wines, such as white Grenache, Cabernet Blanc, Merlot Blanc, and Blanc de Pinot Noir.

Dear Dr. WineKnow:
I'm into Italian wines and those from Tuscany are my favourite. I see some wine shops advertising that they sell "Super-Tuscan" wines. Are these made a special way or something?
Diagnosis: Yes, it's Super-Tuscan – a mild-mannered wine by day, a veritable gem by night. These wines acquired their names as products that were produced outside of DOC (Denominazione di Origine Controllata) and DOCG (Denominazione di Origine Controllata e Garantita) laws. In other words, the producers didn't follow the production standards of a specific appellation in Tuscany, and so could not put that indication on their label. They may have been created from lower yields, contain grape varieties or percentages that were not allowed, and so on. Because of this, they can only be labelled as "vino da tavola" (table wine).

Many of these wonderfully-made, age-worthy numbers are on every collector's list and have garnered worldwide acclaim. However, they're "super" not only in quality but also in price. Most are expensive, in limited supply, and usually sell out very quickly after release. Incidentally, this concept has spread to other Italian wine regions, and "Super-Italian" wines are popping up all over the country.

Dear Dr. WineKnow:
What's all the hype about "nouveau" wines? It seems most countries are now producing them.
Diagnosis: As you probably know, the word "nouveau" is French for new, and that's exactly what it's all about. Although it was the French that started it, this phenomenon has now spread to other wine-producing countries, and most make this style of wine. The concept is to create a red wine from the new harvest, as quickly as possible, to help celebrate it. In doing so the wine is usually

carbonically macerated like Beaujolais, fermented for only about four days, and aggressively stabilized. As a result, a fruity, soft, aromatic, easy-drinking, youthful red is produced. Beyond what the wine stands for is the incredible marketing savvy involved. Marketing 101 teachers around the globe would be delighted. Through the hype created before its release (the third Thursday in November annually for the French, though dates vary for others), enticing people to be the first to taste the new wine of the vintage, it creates a buying frenzy that is astonishing. In fact, in this period most producers cover the cost for the production of their entire vintage, making any other revenue from their remaining wines total profit.

Prescription: *Do* use this refreshing, uncomplicated little number as a great excuse to get down and par-tay! *Don't* buy this style of wine expecting great complexity and ageing ability. It's just not that kind of creation. Served cool, "nouveau" wines are best consumed within weeks rather than months or years after the harvest. Although it's not unheard of for a well-made nouveau from a good vintage to be fine even after two to three years, drink it young.

GRAPE FLASH

Did you know that the excitement and sales of "nouveau" wines are on the decline? With most countries around the world producing "nouveau" of sorts, it's not surprising to see sales fall somewhat. Overall, there's simply more of it out there. I'm sure some of the pricing has not helped either. Since it's usually bottled with artistic, avant-garde labels, and depends on expensive marketing, it's hard to keep the cost down.

However, I believe there is a way to breathe new life into the "nouveau" phenomenon. Sell it in bulk. Set up large tanks in malls, shopping centres, and wine shops and have people bring empty containers or bottles that can be filled for so much a litre. Do away with the packaging altogether. Although the presentation may suffer, think of all the savings on bottling and labelling on the producer's side. The great bottom line is the cost to the consumer, at a fraction of the price of the bottled version. This tactic, I believe, would ignite interest and sales again. If "nouveau" really is a celebratory wine that should flow freely, this is probably an ideal venue for it.

Dear Dr. WineKnow:
What's the story with "de-alcoholized" wine?
Diagnosis: It's the never-ending story of truth, justice, and, recently, the Canadian way. These styles of wine are becoming more popular as consumers combat the problem of drinking and driving, as well as health issues. They also contain fewer calories, so folks on calorie-restricted diets can imbibe. Wine can be de-alcoholized in several ways: vacuum distillation; evaporation under vacuum and inert gas at low temperatures; reverse osmosis; and pervaporation. The resulting alcohol usually ranges from less than 1 per cent to around 2 per cent.

All processes of removing alcohol are expensive and the cost may be passed on to the consumer. Aww, no fun. Once the alcohol is removed, wine loses its stability, so it is even more important to practise sterile, hygienic bottling to avoid bacterial infection. These wines don't have great staying power either, so immediate consumption after purchase is best.

To Oak or Not to Oak — That Is the Question

The use of oak treatment in wines is an interesting topic. Much of the expense of making wine comes from the use of oak barrels, and their expense is inevitably passed on to the consumer. However, for many wines on the market today, oak is an integral part of their production and flavour profile.

Dear Dr. WineKnow:

Why is oak the wood of choice for treating wine?

Diagnosis: Believe me, producers over the years have experimented with many different kinds of wood. In California they even played around with redwood, but it didn't work. Some places in Europe still use chestnut and cherry wood, but these don't really add anything to the wine. Some wood is too soft and transfers odd flavours to wine. Others are too porous. Oak was finally decided on for some very good reasons. It is hard, supple, and watertight. It displays a natural affinity to wine, imparts qualities and flavours that are complementary and enhancing, and is relatively easy to work with.

The grain in oak is very important to wine. Wide-grained oak tends to be more tannic than tight-grained. From wide-grained oak, more wood character comes through into the wine. Tight-grained oak supplies subtler influences. Not just any species of oak will do, either. There are two main categories, red and white. Red is porous and not reliably watertight, so white is most commonly used. All oak is either air- or kiln-dried. The air-dried process is slower, and usually provides better oak for barrels.

Dear Dr. WineKnow:

Why are wines oak-treated?

Diagnosis: Wine is wood-treated by a winemaker for several reasons: to harmonize and marry flavours, soften and round out the palate, add wood complexity, and reduce tannins in red wine.

Ultimately, it's the winemaker's decision to oak-treat a wine or not, depending on the style he or she desires.

Dear Dr. WineKnow:

Not all grape varieties seem to come in contact with oak. Why do some get it and others don't?

Diagnosis: Certain styles and grape varieties don't have a natural affinity to the character that oak adds. In these cases it just doesn't mesh and harmonize, or totally overpowers the wine. If the wine is delicate, light, or fruit-driven, oak is generally not used, and the wine does better without it. Wines that are meant to be consumed over the short haul, say within a few years of the vintage, don't usually see it either.

Some wines that would fall into this category are Beaujolais and its nouveau versions, Grignolino, Dolcetto, Frascati, Pinot Bianco, and Soave. Some grape varieties that don't usually utilize oak are Riesling, Gewürztraminer, Muscat, Vidal, Pinot Grigio, and Gamay.

GRAPE FLASH

Did you know that there is such a thing as too much oak influence? This is a major ongoing concern among both winemakers and consumers the world over. Oak usage should compliment and enhance a wine, not overwhelm and dominate it. There are many wines on the market today that are over-oaked. Sometimes certain wines are not structured for the amount of oak utilized. When there is too much oak in a wine, it's hard to experience the fruit and other complexity. It may even be difficult to decipher the grape variety. It also makes it hard to drink and increasingly difficult to match to food. However, not all of this can be blamed on the winemaker. The world's love affair with massive oak in wines helps stoke the fire. The winemaker is only catering to consumer tastes. The next time you smell and taste a wine that offers up aggressive oak overtones, above all else, consider this: If the only thing I'm experiencing is wood, then maybe "Château 2 x 4" is not a great drinking experience. If a winemaker has to oak a wine to this point, one has to wonder if he or she is trying to cover something up — such as poor winemaking.

Dear Dr. WineKnow:

I've noticed that wine that has been aged in oak longer displays more wood character than those aged for a shorter time. Is it as simple as prolonged exposure?

Diagnosis: Wood character is quite important in wine. It adds aromatics and mouth feel and softens and rounds out flavours. The simple answer to this question is, yes, it is a matter of prolonged exposure. The more time the wine spends in oak, the more influence the oak has on it.

Dear Dr. WineKnow:
Does the age of oak make a difference?
Diagnosis: You bet your cask it does! The newer the oak, the more interplay between wine and wood, and, ultimately, the more oak complexity that transfers into the wine. In fact, after three or four years, an oak barrel imparts little wood flavours to a wine. It merely acts as a receptacle.

Chances are, when you smell and taste a wine that displays a lot of vanilla, new oak has been used. Older oak will give less vanilla notes and subtler characteristics to a wine. Given the price tag of new barrels, you now know why certain wines that are always aged in new oak are so expensive. Every year, the winemaker must invest in new barrels for that particular wine. Ladies, out of perfume? Dab a bit of this wine behind your ears; it will drive the men simply wild.

Dear Dr. WineKnow:
In France, I tasted the same wine out of different-sized barrels. Boy, what a difference in aromatics and flavours!
Diagnosis: The size of a barrel makes a huge difference in imparted flavours. The smaller the barrel, the more interplay between wine and wood. Again, more oak complexity is transmitted. The larger the barrel, the less influence.

I hate to re-state the obvious, but size counts. If the wine exudes lots of vanilla notes, more than likely, it was aged in smaller, new oak barrels.

Dear Dr. WineKnow:
Certain wines I taste seem to have a toasty character. Sometimes it's stronger than in others. Why?

Diagnosis: You've heard the expression, warm as toast? Wine-makers can, and often do, order barrels charred or toasted on the inside to their specifications. Of course, they can purchase them straight up (untreated), if desired. Yes indeed, the barrels are actually turned upside down over an open flame and charred to the winemaker's request, usually light, medium, or full toast. The wine that ages in these charred barrels takes on the flavour and degree of the toast.

If you taste a wine that delivers real smoky aromatics and flavour, a full toast was probably used in the preparation of the barrel the wine was aged in. More delicate toasty, biscuity, nuances might indicate a light to medium toast. Most winemakers favour a medium toast in their barrels, as full might be too much and light, not enough. The amount of toast passed into the wine from a barrel can also be controlled by the length of time it is kept in it.

Dear Dr. WineKnow:
What do winemakers do with older barrels that no longer add wood complexity to wine?
Diagnosis: Often, these barrels are sold. Whisky distillers might buy some to age their spirits. Amateur winemakers may utilize them for home winemaking. Many become flower planters for homeowners. However, some winemakers hold on to them. As mentioned earlier, they can be used to store wine, like a tank. Others will have the inside shaved to expose new wood, thus making them virtually new again. This practice can only be done a few times, since, each time, the barrel's thickness decreases, reducing its stability. It's like a shave and a haircut.

It's next to impossible to tell whether a wine has been kept in old barrels, because if they are used no apparent wood complexity exists. It's also difficult to figure out whether a wine has been aged in a shaved barrel or not. One thing is certain. There is probably not a winemaker on the planet who will admit to ageing wine in shaved barrels.

GRAPE FLASH

Did you know that wine aged in barrel loses up to 10 per cent of its volume due to evaporation? Oak is an interesting material. Because of its grain, it tends to be porous, allowing some small amounts of air in and out. Winemakers usually fill barrels to the brim to start. Sometimes they top them up and sometimes they don't.

BARREL AND PARTS

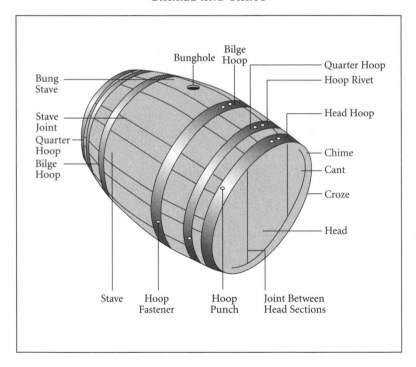

Dear Dr. WineKnow:

At a wine tasting, the winemaker said he used oak chips in the wine. I was too embarrassed to ask what he meant.

Diagnosis: With a little onion dip, they're delicious. Otherwise, this winemaking tool is an extremely inexpensive alternative to using barrels. Like barrels, oak chips can come from Europe or America, and the size, age, and degree of toast play a part in the wood complexity they add. They are most effective when used like a tea bag during fermentation, as the heat that is produced extracts maximum flavour. Occasionally, the wine can become so oaky that it may have to be back-blended with some unoaked wine to soften the blow. This method of adding wood complexity to a wine is not overly popular.

Using oak chips really does detract from the whole "mystique" of barrel-ageing. I'm actually surprised this winemaker admitted using them. Since it is not considered "chi chi," most are not likely to confess to it, and you'll never see it mentioned on the label. Besides, oak chips produce volatile acids in wine, reducing its ageing ability. How can you tell if they have been used? A wine description that mentions "oak influence" or "oak maturation" on the label, without actually stating any form of barrel, is usually a good clue to their use.

Dear Dr. WineKnow:
Can oak from anywhere in the world be used for wine?
Diagnosis: Oak trees are indigenous to the temperate northern hemisphere. It would seem to make sense to use whatever is convenient. However, this isn't the case.

The best oak for wine tends to come from America and Europe.

Dear Dr. WineKnow:
What's the main difference in flavours that American and European oak add to wine?
Diagnosis: European oak can be tight and wide-grained, and adds smoother, subtler flavours to wine. American oak, on the other hand, is more aggressive, adding many upfront flavours like vanilla and spice and textures like astringency. It tends to be looser grained, as a rule. American oak seems to be used more for red wines than white.

Dear Dr. WineKnow:
Where in Europe and America does most oak used for wine originate?
Diagnosis: The European oak most favoured by winemakers, worldwide, comes from France and is usually air-dried. The interesting thing about French oak is that the many forests throughout the country provide oak that adds slightly different flavours to the finished wine. Some oak is also used from the Balkan area, such as what used to be Yugoslavia. Often used for large casks and vats, this oak tends to be more tannic or sappy, and sometimes just plain neutral. Portugal does provide a small amount of oak. It's subtler than locally used chestnut and cheaper than French oak. The best American oak hails from Minnesota, Iowa, Missouri, Wisconsin, and Arkansas.

Oak barrels are not cheap. If French oak is your thing, be prepared to dish out anywhere from $700 to $900 apiece for a new 225-litre barrel. The American counterpart costs less, at approximately $300 to $500 apiece. It's no wonder wine aged in oak, especially French oak, is expensive. If you are thinking about getting into the forestry business, grow oak trees.

Common Barrel Names, Sizes, and Where Used

NAME	SIZE	WINES/REGIONS/COUNTRIES
Foudre	Varies	Alsace, France
Pièce	216 litres	Beaujolais, France
	228 litres	Burgundy, France
	205 litres	Champagne, France
	220 litres	Anjou/Layon/Saumur, France
	225 litres	Vouvray, France
	215 litres	Mâconnais, France
Barrique	225 litres	Bordeaux, France
		Rhône, France
Fuder	1,000 litres	Mosel, Germany

NAME	SIZE	WINES/REGIONS/COUNTRIES
Stück	1,200 litres	Rhine, Germany
Pipe	560 to 630 litres (534.2 for shipping)	Port, Portugal
	418 litres	Madeira, Portugal
Butt	490.7 litres	Sherry, Spain
Gönci	136 litres	Tokay, Hungary

Dear Dr. WineKnow:
How many different types of oak come out of France?
Diagnosis: French oak is usually designated by the forest it was grown in, and there are a number of them. The western Loire and Sarthe produce tight-grained, excellent-quality oak. The Limousin forest delivers wide-grained oak. The forests of Never, Allier, Tronçais, Vosges, Jura, Bourgogne, and Argonne all supply tight-grained oak.

It is through trial and error that most winemakers come to a decision as to which forest provides the best French oak for their particular product. This is definitely a case of your not seeing the forest for the trees. For instance, Limousin oak is used exclusively for brandy, especially cognac. Never, Allier, and Tronçais are used for wine and brandy. Vosges is used for wine, while Jura and Bourgogne are used for Burgundy. Argonne is widely used in Champagne.

Dear Dr. WineKnow:
What countries utilize American oak barrels?
Diagnosis: Spain is a large advocate of American oak. Although they have laid back a bit with overall oak usage, American still remains the oak of choice. It's no surprise that the United States uses a lot of it. Canada uses a fair bit, especially for red wine. South America seems to like it, too, as does Australia.

Perhaps it has something to do with the heat factor. An overview would suggest that warm viticultural areas in the world like Spain, California, Chile, Argentina, and Australia favour or use a lot of

American oak. Riper, more powerful wines are produced there, which can handle the attack of this oak better than cool-climate wines. If you are not a big fan of these regions' wines, it could be because of the choice of oak treatment. You may want to seek out wines from these areas that utilize French oak.

CHAPTER 3

OH BROTHER, WHERE ART THOU?

Accessing It

*B*efore you can store, age, serve, and finally enjoy wine, you must obtain it. If you can't get hold of it, all those other points are irrelevant. In today's world we are very fortunate to have a wealth of selection when it comes to wine choices. Product from literally every part of the globe is available to us. Most wine shops have an enormous array of wines to choose from. There are, however, several additional places and ways to purchase wine, some easier to deal with than others.

Once you've finally found and obtained a wine you want, understanding the label, and its relation to the contents, can sometimes be challenging. There are certain terms and words that provide insight into the wine within. You need to know what they are.

The Search

Where do I buy my wine? This is the big question on most wine lovers' lips. For the consumer today, there are many ways of purchasing wine. Everything exists, from government-run monopolies (Ontario, British Columbia, Nova Scotia, Newfoundland, New Brunswick, Quebec, and Manitoba in Canada; Hungary; and Sweden) and private retailers to auction houses and wineries themselves. Picking and choosing the right venue, depending on where you live and how much travelling you do, may sometimes be a little difficult.

Dear Dr. WineKnow:
Is price an indication of quality when it comes to buying wine?
Diagnosis: Getting what you pay for applies to most things in life. However, when it comes to wine, the answer is not as simple. What one person views as a quality wine could be drastically different than another. Certainly limited-production, rare, single-vineyard, classified growths and older product will cost more, sometimes regardless of quality. You pay for a wine's reputation, age, and availability.
Prescription: Get the best bang for your buck. To obtain the best possible quality for your dollar, look on the labels for grape varieties, vintage dates, village names, and châteaux or domain bottling.

Dear Dr. WineKnow:
I usually buy my wine in regular wine shops owned by a monopoly. Are there any other outlets available to me?
Diagnosis: Unfortunately, for those living in an area where alcohol sales are controlled by a monopoly, your choices are few. Since most monopolies are government controlled, selection is usually dictated by popularity and politics to a certain degree. There are, however, some other options available to you through a monopoly.
Prescription: Most government-run retailers offer specialty listings that bring in small allotments of rare, one-of-a-kind, high-end, small-production product. These are sometimes located in separate stores.

Dear Dr. WineKnow:
If I purchase a wine at a store and it turns out to be defective, will they take it back for a refund or replacement?
Diagnosis: Defective wine, in one form or another, is a fact of life today. Corky wines, especially, are a major headache. It would be unethical and bad business practice for a retailer not to replace such a product or give a refund.
Prescription: Do not return an empty bottle or one with only a drop left in it for replacement. When returning a defective wine to a retailer, ensure that at least half of the wine is still in the bottle. Even if you have served it out to guests before you realize it is problematic, pour it back in the bottle to return it to the store. I don't know any retailer who would argue if you brought this much back. Show some consideration and faith. After all, the retailer may want to take it up with his distributor if enough of the same stock is returned as defective.

GRAPE FLASH
Did you know that the only place you're likely to get a deal buying volume of any one wine is through private retailers? You can totally forget about this concept if purchasing from a monopoly. However, private retailers might swing a deal with you, if you agree to buy volume of a specific wine.

Dear Dr. WineKnow:
Will I get a better deal if I purchase wine directly from a winery when I visit it?
Diagnosis: There's nothing quite like buying wine from the place of production. It makes the experience that much more personal and magical. You may have the opportunity to chat with the winemaker or owner and get insight that makes the enjoyment of the wine, when consumed, special. You may even have a larger selection

of product to choose from and may find wines not available in other outlets.

Prescription: If you are seeking charm and ambiance, go directly to the source, but if it's bargains you're looking for, you'll probably have to look elsewhere. The occasional winery might reduce prices slightly if you buy volume, but not on individual bottles.

Dear Dr. WineKnow:

What do wineries do to prevent wine from freezing when shipping in the winter?

Diagnosis: The business of wine rarely takes a holiday, so wines must be transported all year round. Air freight is used a lot. One of the key problems in winter, as you suggest, is ice-cold temperature and its effect on wine. Whether the wine is in truck transport to a port or airport or is sitting on tarmac or a dock, waiting for other wine to join it to fill a container, the temperature can ruin it.

Prescription: There is a solution to this problem. For an additional charge, heated containers can be used to ensure that the wine stays at a reasonable temperature. The consumer gets stung with the extra charge at the retail end – as per usual – but at least the wine is intact.

Dear Dr. WineKnow:

What do wineries do to prevent wine from "cooking" when shipped in the summer?

Diagnosis: Again, in very warm weather wine might sit around in transit somewhere for days, maybe even weeks, in super high temperatures. This is probably worse for the wine than freezing. It just cooks.

Prescription: The alternative solution here is air-conditioned containers which keep the wine nicely cooled. Of course, the consumer would pick up the extra charge for this on the bottle, but it's well worth it.

GRAPE FLASH

Did you know you can buy a specific wine long before the grapes that are going to be used for it are even off the vine? This is called buying "futures." It's a program involving buying young, red wines early in their life – at more reasonable prices. If a producer holds back wine for ageing and releases it later when it's ready to drink, the cost is significantly higher to the consumer. But the wine can be purchased on paper, before the grapes are mature and harvested, and you get a better deal and are expected to age the wine to maturity yourself when finally bottled. This is most notably applied to red Bordeaux.

Contact your local wine merchant, agent, or liquor board for details. Since a substantial deposit is always required, make sure to choose a reputable company that won't be out of business and can deliver the goods when the time comes. Carefully examine the contract so that no hidden costs appear after the fact.

Dear Dr. WineKnow:

What about buying wine at auction? Are prices more expensive or less?

Diagnosis: Buying wine at auction is certainly a viable alternative for some people, but they must know their wine. Generally, wines are sold in lots, and each lot could be anything from one bottle to a case or two of mixed or similar wines. Although charity auctions donate the money to a good cause, they are not the best place to purchase wine. Selling prices tend to be high, because of the charity factor. Better prices are available at regular auctions through well-established auction houses like Sotheby's or Christie's.

Prescription: Going once, going twice, sold! If you intend to buy wine at auction, obtain the catalogue well in advance and study it carefully. Do some homework and know what wines are worth. On average, regular retail prices are approximately two and a half times more expensive than auction prices. So there are good deals to be had, provided the product has been handled and stored properly. That's why it is imperative to buy only through a reputable auction house. Keep in mind too that, if you buy out of country, there may be shipping charges and taxes to deal with, making the purchase less of a good deal.

Dear Dr. WineKnow:
What about selling wine at auction?
Diagnosis: Although charity auctions provide money to a good cause and usually issue an income-tax receipt to the donor, they don't put money in your pocket for the wine sold. If making money from the wine is the point, deal with reputable, established auction houses.
Prescription: This will probably cause you more headaches than the wine is worth. You need to know that, just because you approach an auction house to sell your wine for you, it doesn't necessarily mean they will do so. The wine will have to be unusual, rare, limited in availability, or high end. The bottles, of course, would have to have been stored properly and be in reasonably good shape. They won't take just any wine. Even if they agree to try and sell it at auction for you, they may not get the base price for which you agree to let it go. Finally, they take a percentage of what the wine sells for as their fee.

Dear Dr. WineKnow:
Will wine agents obtain wine for me that isn't usually available?
Diagnosis: Most wine agents handle a reasonable selection of product, either dealing through a monopoly or directly to private retailers. I doubt very much if they will try and obtain a small amount of something different. Only if they see potential for a unique product that they can add to their portfolio in substantial volume, might they give it a go.

Prescription: Looking for the unusual? In some monopolies, there is something called an agent's, or consignment, warehouse. Here, very small amounts of unusual product are brought in and kept in warehouses, for a limited time period, and sold directly to the consumer, without the benefit of a retail outlet. Although the only way of knowing what's there is to contact each agent and inquire, it is another venue for accessing wine.

GRAPE FLASH

Did you know that there is a way of obtaining a wine you tasted somewhere in the world but is not available where you live? This happens all the time. With world travel so accessible these days, experiencing new and exciting wines is common. Unfortunately, there is so much product out there that it is virtually impossible for any retailer – whether government-owned or private – to carry it all. If you had the forethought and had actually visited the producer, you could have ordered some right there. However, people usually taste a wine in a restaurant or hotel in their travels. Most monopolies, through their private stock system, will access any product in the world for you, provided you do the following: you must order at least a case of twelve, you must provide all the pertinent information, such as address and contact numbers of the producer; and you have to pay all the shipping/delivery charges and taxes. It could take a long time, maybe up to a year, to take delivery, but it can be done. Private retailers might do the same for you but, more than likely, the volume of purchase would have to be much more substantial to make it worth their while.

Dear Dr. WineKnow:

I don't drive. Is there some way of buying wine without my going out to purchase it?

Prescription: You simply call up your local wine store and they'll come right over with it. Of course, I jest, but don't be surprised to find something like this down the road.

Certain private retailers will take orders over the phone or on-line and deliver wine to you, for a nominal charge. Monopolies will deliver wine for an extra charge, but I believe the order must be placed and paid for from one of their retail outlets. There also is a delivery service, similar to a taxi, that will pick up wine from a store and bring it to you for a cost. You may have to pay for the product, and even the service, up front. Ask your retailer.

Dear Dr. WineKnow:
What about those "make-your-own" wine places? Is the wine any good?
Diagnosis: One would have to be living in a cave not to notice all the "make-your-own-wine-on-premises" stores that have been popping up lately. Using their equipment, space, and guidance, you actually make wine of your choice for what amounts to maybe a buck or two a bottle. Generally, grape-juice concentrates are used to make the wines, and you either purchase their bottles or provide your own for filling.
Prescription: As for the quality, it's not bad. For everyday drinking and a feeling of creativity, it's worth the time, effort, and cost. From what I've tasted, though, you may not want to hang on to wines made this way for too long. Most are best consumed over the short haul.

The Label Says It All

You've heard the expression "the eyes are the windows to the soul," haven't you? When it comes to wine, the labels are the "keys to the kingdom." They supposedly open the doors of enlightenment about what's in the bottle. The label should give the potential consumer a good picture of what to expect from a wine. Unfortunately, some countries' wines are hard to understand, and their labels simply don't give much information about the content. They seem to expect you to know all about them. This really adds to the intimidation factor of wine and its "snob appeal." Most people simply won't buy a bottle if they don't know what is in it. Expecting people to know exactly where in a country a wine is from, the grape varieties and so forth, is rather ludicrous. No one wants to walk around with an encyclopedia when shopping for wine. The label should say it all. Wine education is a great beginning to deciphering labels. In addition, spending time browsing in a wine shop to familiarize yourself with labels and their origins is extremely helpful. Although lots of practice will be required before you feel totally comfortable with choosing wine, every bit of experience should take the edge off your uncertainty and fill in many of the blanks. After that, it's practice, practice, practice.

Certain information on wine labels is mandatory and gives the basics about a wine. This information is usually required by law, and applies to most wines. Other statistics provided on labels refer to the production of specific vinos. They often help explain why one wine is more expensive than another (for instance, because more work is involved in making it). But although some information is required, most tends to be optional. Sparkling wine seems to have its own set of descriptors on the label that are both production- and style-oriented. Other information that appears on labels is there more to market and help sell the wine than it is to describe its production technique or style.

Understanding what a label says is imperative. After all, if the label is all you have to go by when purchasing a wine, it's best you know what it means.

Required Data
Okay, here are the goods. This is the really important information, the stuff that almost every wine label has on it. It's pretty hard to

produce wine without having most of this information appear. However, some of it varies in required extent, depending on where it is made.

Dear Dr. WineKnow:
Exactly what information, by law, must appear on wine labels?
Diagnosis: Certain main categories of information are required on most wine labels, but only a guideline can be stated here. For detailed information, you must contact the individual countries, wine regions, or legislating bodies. Furthermore, international, national, regional, and local criteria may also vary.

Here's what is usually required:
- Wine style or designation: Words like table wine, quality wine, vin de pays, etc. (a quality indication or style).
- Geographical Reference: Usually a country descriptor like French or Italian, a region's name like Burgundy, Bordeaux, or Appellation Something, or designated viticultural area like Napa or Sonoma.
- Volume: Amount of wine stated in oz., cl., or ml.
- Alcohol: Alcoholic strength usually expressed in "%."
- Vintage: (If applicable) The year the grapes were grown, harvested, and made into wine.
- Name/Address of Producer/Bottler: Usually on the bottom of most labels.
- Varietal Information: (If applicable) Only on bottles that are varietally labelled.
- Government Warnings: (If applicable) In some countries, due to health and safety concerns, labels carry warnings about sulphites, danger to pregnant women, cautions about operating machinery, etc.

Dear Dr. WineKnow:
If a wine label specifies a region or country, does all the fruit that goes into making that wine come from that region or country?

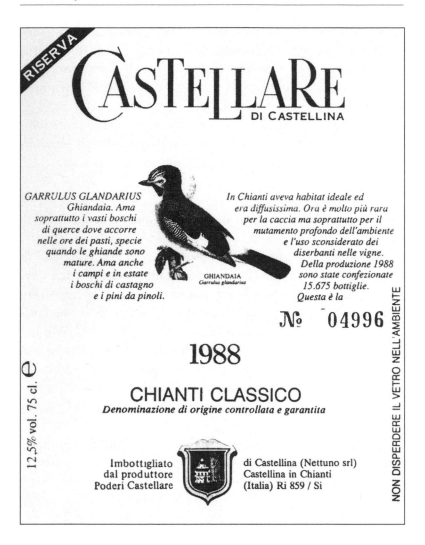

Diagnosis: A formidable question, indeed! Generally, regional designation means 100 per cent from the stated region. However, country definition can vary depending on where in the world the wine is produced. In the "Old World," countries are not utilized as much as sub-regions or villages. Usually, a wine labelled according to a sub-region or village comes from that area alone. In the "New

World," however, it's all over the map. In some countries or sub-regions, as long as the required minimum percentage is filled, the rest can come from elsewhere and still wear the country or sub-region designation on the label. The percentage that is required can vary from 75 per cent and up.

Prescription: If this is a real concern, you may want to check individual wine regions' production and labelling laws before purchasing. "New World" wines are especially notorious in this area.

Dear Dr. WineKnow:

How does a wine get to wear its country's quality designation on the label?

Diagnosis: Quality designations like "AOC" in France, "DOC" in Italy, and "VQA" in Canada, are important guides in wine purchasing. They are the consumers' assurance that a wine came from the place of origin, was made according to production standards of a particular area, and actually tastes the way it should. Without this designation on the label, anything in the bottle is possible. Although these designations don't necessarily imply greatness, they do guarantee a certain quality level and type of taste. Chances are, a wine wearing a quality designation of this kind will be better than a plain "table wine."

Quality designations are not mandatory. It's up to producers to apply for them or not. However, it is in the producer's interest to have something like this on his label.

GRAPE FLASH

Did you know that the term "estate-bottled" on wine labels is a "New World" expression implying that the wine comes from grapes grown on vineyards that belong to the winery? It can be from one or several properties, as long as it is theirs. You might say it is equivalent to the terms "château" or "domain-bottled" in Europe. This term can be somewhat confusing

> though. It may very well include vineyards that the winery
> doesn't actually own but with which it has long-standing con-
> tracts or leases. In any case, the wine carrying this designation
> is usually pretty good.

Dear Dr. WineKnow:
Certain wines specify a particular vineyard on the label. What exactly does this mean?
Diagnosis: Single-vineyard bottlings of wine are very popular today. If a wine label states, for example, "Smith Vineyard," under the name of the wine, it means all the grapes that went into making that wine came from the Smith Vineyard (a single property).
Prescription: Single-vineyard bottlings of wine generally have more character, as they reflect a single piece of land's ability to produce fruit and, ultimately, wine. They tend to cost a little more, as well. These types of wine are considered quite chic or "in."

Dear Dr. WineKnow:
If a wine label specifies a year, does all the fruit come from that year?
Diagnosis: Vintage dates on wine bottles indicate the year the grapes were grown, harvested, and made into wine. As previously discussed, fruit from better years usually yields better-quality wines. In better years producers would probably want to utilize that year's fruit. It would serve no purpose to include a lesser year's grapes. In poorer or low-yielding vintages, fruit from other years might be included. Like varietal labelling, winemaking by-laws usually allow for a minimum percentage of the stated vintage's fruit to be used. The rest can come from other years. This amount varies from country to country and region to region.

Regardless, one thing is certain: the large majority of grapes come from the stated vintage on the bottle. Most reputable producers use 100 per cent fruit from the stated vintage.

GRAPE FLASH

Did you know that, on French wine labels, certain words that appear after the grower's name specify exactly what he or she does? Not all producers or growers work the same way. Some actually own vineyards, others merely buy product and sell it under their own name. The descriptors can be confusing to the purchaser. They include "propriétaire," "propriétaire-recoltant," "négociant," and "vigneron." "Propriétaire" means the person owns the vineyard, but doesn't necessarily work it. If "recoltant" is attached to it, then he or she owns and works the vineyard but may not make the wine. "Négociant" is someone who buys the grapes, makes the wine, and sells it under his or her own name. Finally, the "vigneron" designation implies the person grows the grapes and makes the wine.

Dear Dr. WineKnow:

Even though many wines are labelled with a specific grape variety on the front of the bottle, the back label mentions others that are in the wine. How is this possible?

Diagnosis: If the truth be known, many wines labelled a specific grape variety are not 100 per cent produced from the stated grape. Sometimes the back label tells you and sometimes it doesn't. The reason for blending is that certain varietals have hard edges or are extremely tannic and would not be very "drinkable" straight up. By adding something else to the blend, the winemaker can round out the palate and add further complexity.

This is all part of varietal labelling regulations. Most wine regions state that, in order to label a wine with a specific grape variety, there must be a minimum percentage of that grape in the wine. The "New World" is notorious for this. For instance, in California, the percentage is seventy-five. As long as at least that amount of the stated grape is included, the rest can be topped up with whatever is desired. The "Old World" seems to do this a lot less. One thing you can be sure of is that, if a grape variety is stated on the label, that variety makes up the majority of the fruit in the wine.

Prescription: Unfortunately, if the label doesn't state something, front or back, the only way to find out is to contact the agent, distributor, or producer.

Dear Dr. WineKnow:
Certain wines state two or three grape varieties on the front label. Does this mean the wine is made from equal amounts of each?

Diagnosis: Common sense would dictate that this should be the case, however, this generally is not so.

Most regional wine laws regulate this sort of thing. If more than one grape variety is stated on the label, they must be listed in order of volume used, largest to smallest. Therefore, a label reading "Chardonnay-Sémillon," for instance, would contain more Chardonnay than Sémillon in it. The back label might give the percentage breakdown.

Dear Dr. WineKnow:
Sometimes I see only the word "Cabernet" on the label of a wine.
Which Cabernet are they referring to, Sauvignon or Franc?
Diagnosis: "Life is a Cabernet, my friend." This is a short form to
denote either or both Cabernet Sauvignon or Cabernet Franc. This
occurs only occasionally. Sometimes, it's a way of economizing on
space on the label.
Prescription: Usually the back label fills you in on exactly what it
means. If only one grape is used to make the wine, then the term
usually implies Cabernet Sauvignon.

Common Production Terms
These are common terms that indicate a specific style of wine,
depending mainly on a special way that it has been produced. In
some cases it's mandatory information on a label, in others it's up
to the producer as to whether it appears or not. In certain situations it is the sole reason that the cost of the wine might be more.

Dear Dr. WineKnow:
Why are wines that are labelled "reserve" always more expensive?
Diagnosis: The extra six letters cost more when the labels are
printed, and that cost is passed on to the consumer. All kidding
aside, the term "reserve" implies that the wine is somehow different and usually better than a regular bottling. No matter where in
the world this term is used, it always means the same thing. In
general, the term means the wine in question has been kept longer
at the winery. You can count on it being aged longer in either barrel
or bottle, or a combination of both, before it's released for sale.
Sometimes, it is produced from older vines/better-quality fruit, or
aged in new oak, or has been made with more care. These wines
usually live longer, too.
Prescription: The bottom line is this. If you want to spend less on
wine, don't purchase "reserve" wines. All of these things increase
the overall production cost. Someone has to cover the cost of wine
taking up space at the winery, either in barrel or bottle. Think of it

as rent. New barrels are very expensive. This cost has to be considered in the overall picture. Older vines produce less fruit and better vineyards are harder to maintain, thus requiring more man hours and, ultimately, money.

Dear Dr. WineKnow:
Certain wine labels say "unfiltered" on them. What's the point here?
Diagnosis: Wines are usually filtered before bottling to remove any excess residue from fermentation and ageing. As a rule, we like our wine to look clean, clear of suspended particles and the such. That's just the way we are. Filtration also removes microscopic yeast particles that could remain dormant in a bottled wine and start refermenting again when in contact with heat in a shop. So why wouldn't a producer filter wine?

Many a winemaker, however, believes that filtration actually removes some of the wine's character, along with the residue and any microscopic yeast. Theoretically, if one racks (pouring the wine from one tank or barrel to another, leaving behind the residue) the wine carefully several times, filtration is not necessary. Although the chances of retaining some yeast that might come back to haunt you are higher, it doesn't seem to bother the producer. Furthermore, these unfiltered numbers may not look perfectly clear and almost certainly will throw a deposit in the bottle. Surprisingly, unfiltered wine tends to be more expensive. Go figure why one less thing done to the wine, by very expensive equipment, would jack up the price.

Dear Dr. WineKnow:
I sometimes see "supérieur" on French wine bottles and "superiore" on Italian bottles. I'm not sure as to what they mean and if they are the same thing.
Diagnosis: These terms on both French and Italian wines do basically mean the same thing. They both imply that the wine in question contains slightly more alcohol than the basic requirements, usually one-half to one per cent. In the Italian version, some additional ageing is generally involved as well.

Prescription: In either case, wines bearing "supérieur" or "superiore" on the label will cost slightly more.

GRAPE FLASH

Did you know that the word "cru" on some French wine labels means the wines are the cream of the crop, the highest-quality and most expensive wines? The term means vineyard and translates as "growth" in English. They are usually officially classified thus by a governing body. The designation is based on the vineyard's location, its soil, the quality of the fruit it produces and ultimately the finished wine, its consistency over years, and the price it fetches at auction. The "cru" system is divided into different tiers or levels, depending on the region. In Bordeaux there are five classified crus or growths with a lower category called "cru bourgeois." In Burgundy and Champagne there are two levels, grand cru and premier cru. Alsace possesses one level, grand cru. Even Beaujolais has a cru system, with ten villages wearing the designation.

Dear Dr. WineKnow:

Does the term "sur lie" mean anything on wine labels? How does this relate to wine?

Diagnosis: This term often appears on labels of wines from the Loire Valley in France. More specifically, you'll likely see it on Muscadet produced between the Sèvre and Maine rivers. Sometimes, it appears in the winemaker's notes on the back label. It translates to "on the lees" – the bed of spent yeast (lees), that is. After the yeast ferments all the sugar out and dies, wine is usually racked (poured) off it. Some winemakers decide to leave the wine sitting on the dead yeast to impart a little more character to the wine.

Prescription: If you like a slight spritz, try Muscadet. This additional time on the dead yeast cells imparts a slight, carbonic spritz to the palate, often experienced on the tip of the tongue. In other wines, it sometimes provides a creamy texture or mouth feel not dissimilar to what slight oak ageing might add to a wine.

Dear Dr. WineKnow:
When I see sherry bottles in the store, they sometimes have the word "solera," followed by a year on the label. Sometimes the year is very old. Is this the year the wine was made?
Diagnosis: The term "solera," with respect to sherry, refers to a method of production. It involves blending wines together to smooth out differences between vintages. All sherry is made this way. A minimum of three rows of oak casks, each row containing sherry of a single type or vintage, are stacked one upon another. The bottom row, called the "solera," contains wine of an exceptional vintage, often the oldest. Every subsequent row (*criadera*) contains wine of each previous vintage. The top row is always filled with the newest, freshest wine. After the required ageing period, sherry that is to be bottled is drawn from the "solera," the bottom row or oldest cask. These casks are then topped up with wine from the row above, and so on. In other words, the younger wines refresh the older ones. As this system blends wines of different harvests, sherries can't be vintage-dated, and are thus recognized by the "solera" they were created in.
Prescription: A wine labelled "Solera 1895," for instance, is not a wine from that year but a wine drawn from a "solera" started in 1895. If you think there is a lot of that 1895 wine in the bottle, think again. Depending on the number of oak casks in the "solera," the amount could be extremely minuscule.

Dear Dr. WineKnow:
I'm a huge Italian wine fan and notice the term "ripasso" on some bottles. What's this all about?
Diagnosis: This interesting Italian term, literally meaning "repassed," is mostly seen on Valpolicella of the Veneto in the north of the country. It's a technique of adding extra flavour and alcohol to this

normally lighter red wine by placing it on the lees (dead yeast) of Amarone and letting it sit there for a while.

Prescription: The resulting wine has more character, body, tannin, and alcohol and also possesses some of the oxidized and botrytis ("noble rot") flavours of Amarone. I call it Valpolicella with attitude.

GRAPE FLASH

Did you know that the multi-digit number on quality German wines provides more information about its production than any other country's wine? Talk about details! This ten-to-twelve-digit number must be shown on all labels of quality German wine (QbA and QmP). It's known as the "AP" number, short for Amtliche Prufungsnummer. Easy for me to say! It proves the wine has passed Germany's official testing procedure through lab analysis and a blind taste test by a panel of experts. All but the last two digits are numerical codes for different things. The first, from left to right, signifies which of the country's testing stations or control authorities awarded the AP number. The next three indicate the town or village where the wine was made. The following three refer to the wine estate or bottler. The next two relate to the current number of bottling (all bottles are numbered like lithographs). The final two are a short form for the testing and bottling year.

Dear Dr. WineKnow:

I acquired some older tawny ports from a friend, and some say "colheita tawny" on the label. Is this a special kind?

Diagnosis: Boy, are you lucky! This is absolutely one of my favourite styles of wood-aged port. "Colheita tawny" is another name for "date of harvest" port. The Portuguese word "colheita" means crop, harvest, or, ultimately, vintage. This single-vintage tawny port is aged at least seven years in wood before bottling.

You'll notice that, besides the vintage or harvest date on the label, it also states the year of bottling. Gotta love these supple, elegant wines reminiscent of dates and toffee! They're heaven in a glass.

Dear Dr. WineKnow:

Why do old tawny ports, especially colheitas, have the name and information stencilled with paint directly onto the bottle? Considering the cost of these, you would think a label could be provided.

Diagnosis: Colheita tawny port is one of the rarest styles and more favoured by the Portuguese-owned houses. Being from a single harvest, they are very individual and very indicative of the vintage.

There is usually not much of this style made and it will be bottled at different times. Since the date of bottling must appear on the label, it doesn't make sense to print one set of labels, since the next batch bottled from that vintage will carry a different one. They merely stencil the information onto the bottle. I think it adds a bit of rustic flare to the packaging.

Dear Dr. WineKnow:

My father has a number of bottles of Hungarian Tokaji Aszú in his collection. The word "puttonyos" preceded by a number appears on the label of almost every one. Can you tell me about it?

Diagnosis: The term, synonymous with this Hungarian dessert wine, is an interesting one. Botrytized berries (grapes affected by "noble rot," which concentrates the sugar and acid) from the northeast of the country are made into a paste and blended with a base wine. This paste is generally measured in "puttonyos" or containers, each holding forty-four to fifty-five pounds.

The more "puttonyos" are added back to the base wine, the sweeter, richer, and more expensive it is. By Hungarian law, the number of containers or "puttonyos" must appear on the label. So Tokaji Aszu may be sold as three, four, five, or six "puttonyos." Incredibly yummy flavours of honey, dried apricots, sultana raisins, nuts, and orange peel abound, all framed by beautiful, bracing acidity.

Fizz Facts

Sparkling wine is an animal unto itself when it comes to labelling practices. Although all the same required information appears, there are expressions and terminology that are particular to it. Most of it originated in Champagne but now carries over to pretty much all sparkling wine the world over. In fact, some terms have crossed over to still wine and are regularly utilized on their labels.

Dear Dr. WineKnow:

All quality French wine says "Appellation" this or that on the label. Why doesn't Champagne?

Diagnosis: Very observant of you! All quality French wine, if it is AOC (Appellation Origin Controlled), wears the individual AOC of its production area on the label, usually under the name. Champagne is the only French AOC wine that doesn't have to. The word "Champagne" is enough.

Because it is so unique, world-famous, and the ultimate "king of bubbly," it possesses a status all its own.

Dear Dr. WineKnow:

I don't understand Champagne labelling. Are those that have no year on the bottle inferior?

Diagnosis: When it comes to Champagne, the word "inferior" does not apply. What the lack of year means is that the wine is "non-vintaged." More specifically, it is made up of many different wines, from different vintages. Because it utilized so many years, it can't put a single year on the label.

The blending of many different years allows the winemaker to come up with a consistent taste, so that the wine is always the same. This way the house style stays intact and offers a guarantee. No matter where in the world you purchase this "non-vintage," and no matter when it was produced, it will deliver the flavour and quality you are used to.

GRAPE FLASH

Did you know that a Champagne with a single year on the label is still a blended wine? It is a blend of many wines, all from the same vintage. So 1990 Dom Perignon is a Champagne made up of many wines, all from the 1990 vintage. Vintage Champagne usually has more ageing potential than non-vintage. Because it uses wine from the same year, it varies in character and quality from vintage to vintage.

Dear Dr. WineKnow:
Some bottles of Champagne and still white wine occasionally have the words "blanc de blancs" on the label. What does this mean?

Diagnosis: This interesting phrase actually started out in Champagne but has now carried over to still wines as well. It is a very popular expression on bottles of table wine.

Literally translated, it means "white from white." More specifically, it denotes a white wine that is made from white grapes only. Since the only allowable white grape in Champagne is Chardonnay, all "blanc de blancs" Champagnes are made exclusively from Chardonnay. In other wines, it merely denotes the use of white grapes, in general.

Dear Dr. WineKnow:
I've seen bottles of Champagne and rosés that are labelled with "blanc de noirs." Please explain.

Diagnosis: This is another Champenois term that has extended its usage beyond sparkling wine and into rosés.

This literally means "white from dark." In English, it represents a white wine made from dark or red grapes. If the skins aren't used, the resulting wine is usually white or rosé in colour. When it comes to Champagne, specifically, the only red grapes allowed are Pinot

Noir and Pinot Meunier. Therefore, a "blanc de noirs" Champagne is made from either of these two red grapes or a blend of both (usually if one grape is utilized, it's Pinot Noir). In other wines, it merely denotes the use of red grapes, in general.

Dear Dr. WineKnow:
Certain bottles of French bubbly use the term "crémant" on the label. I've no idea what this stands for.
Diagnosis: This is yet another expression that originated in Champagne, but is not longer used for it. The term is now used on other French, champagne-method wines such as Crémant d'Alsace, Crémant de Bourgogne, etc.

It's a champagne-method wine with less fizz. The term crémant applies to a part of the champagne method of putting bubbles into a wine. To induce the second fermentation that creates the bubbles, a blend of wine, yeast, and sugar is added to the primarily fermented wine. The yeast feeds on the sugar, producing alcohol and carbon dioxide (the bubbles). Normally, enough of this blend is added to create five to six atmospheres of pressure (basically units of pressure) in the bottle. "Crémant" means that less is added, creating only about two to three atmospheres.

GRAPE FLASH

Did you know that the sweetness designation on Champagne bottles is very confusing to most people? Someone wrote to me saying they had bought a Champagne that said "extra-dry" on the label, yet it was more like medium-dry when tasted. They actually wondered if it was labelled wrong. Well, it wasn't. She got what she bought. "Extra-dry" in Champagne terms actually means medium-dry, about a 2 to 3 in sweetness. Bone-dry bubbly is usually labelled "brut zero." Dry sparkles carries the word "brut" (0 to 2) on the label. You already know what "extra-dry" translates to. The term "sec" on the bottle really means medium, about 4 to 5. If "demi-sec" appears, the Champagne is medium-sweet, approximately 6 to 9. And if "rich" or "doux" appears, the bubbly is very sweet. If you're confused, believe me, you're not the first person to be baffled by this labelling.

Dear Dr. WineKnow:
I recently purchased a Champagne in a specialty wine shop that said "R.D." on the label. Nobody could tell me what it means. Can you?

Diagnosis: This acronym stands for "Recently Disgorged." No, it's not some form of torture the wine went through, but a very important part of the champagne method of production. In this method, once the yeast finishes doing its thing, it dies and remains in the bottle until extracted. The extraction process is called "dégorgement," or disgorgement. This is usually done directly after the second fermentation has completed creating the bubbles, right before corking. However, some Champagne houses, for certain wines, like to leave the wine sitting on this dead yeast for quite a while in their cellars, until just before it is ready for sale. They then disgorge the sediment, cork the wine, and distribute it. If this is done, they may put the letters "R.D." on the label, indicating that the Champagne was "recently disgorged." Usually they indicate when this was done as well.

As this procedure adds more character to the wine, it is a great selling point. Word of note: disgorgement is usually done only for upscale wines, and bottles are generally more expensive.

Dear Dr. WineKnow:
What does "Cava" mean on Spanish sparkling wine?

Diagnosis: The term "Cava" was established in 1970 in Spain to describe traditional champagne-method wines.

Cava wines represent great value for the dollar. This is a very popular style of sparkling wine, mostly from the Penedes region of northeast Spain.

Dear Dr. WineKnow:
I've seen the word "crackling" on some bottles of bubbly. Is this the same thing as "sparkling"?
Diagnosis: The good doctor has not heard the term "crackling" used for wine in a vine's age. Crackling wine is one which has a natural fizz or effervescence from some residual carbon dioxide. It is not like sparkling, which has had the bubbles deliberately created through some additional method (i.e., champagne method).

Most wines that use the term "crackling" on the label tend to be inexpensive and often sweeter.

Marketing Expressions
No matter how great a wine is, if someone doesn't buy it, nothing is gained. The bottom line for most producers is realized at the cash register. To this end wine is presented in attractive bottles with aesthetically pleasing labels. Further to this cause, certain phrases, terms, and expressions are used on labels to help promote the wine. In some cases, they may actually refer to some part of the production or imply a style of wine. In others, they will describe the wine's taste and suggest possible food matches. You'll even see well-known, common terminology from other very famous wine regions used to help promote a similar, but not exact, style of wine. The display of medals and awards received in competition is a widely used tool to help showcase a wine. All of these serve one purpose . . . to sell the wine.

Dear Dr. WineKnow:
I see a lot of wines, especially Australian, labelled with the word "bin" and "vat," followed by a number. What's this all about?
Diagnosis: Are bin or vat numbers real or simply a marketing ploy to get the consumer to think the wine is something different or special? Perhaps both.

Individual tanks, barrels, vats, or casks of the same wine might be more interesting, better, or different enough to bottle separately and to designate as such on the label. Maybe a certain bin (stockpile of wine) shows some extraordinary characteristics that the winemaker wants to bottle and market alone. Thus these terms usually imply something different.

However, sometimes this is not true. Occasionally, some of these terms become branded names for individual products or varietals within a winery's portfolio. This is the case with the Australian wine, Lindeman's Bin 65 Chardonnay.

Dear Dr. WineKnow:
I see many French wines that say "cuvée" this and that on the label. Is this important?
Diagnosis: This French wine term tends to have different meanings, depending where it appears.

The term "tête de cuvée," for instance, refers to the best wine a producer creates. This is most commonly used in Sauternes. For sparkling wine, it usually means the initial – and often, best – juice that the press produces. However, more often than not, it's a general term, meaning blend or container of wine.

GRAPE FLASH

Did you know that the term "meritage" (pronounced like "heritage") on some bottles of U.S. wine means the wine is blended from more than one grape? This is an interesting trademarked name for American wines, mostly Californian, that are made from a blend of grapes similar in style to red and white Bordeaux. There is, in fact, an association that dictates the requirements. The reds are made exclusively from the two Cabernets – Sauvignon and Franc – Merlot, Malbec, and Petit Verdot. The whites can use Sauvignon Blanc, Sémillon, and Muscadelle. Overall production must not exceed 25,000 cases per year. Some of these wines are outstanding and can easily rival Bordeaux for quality. The term has almost become synonymous for any blended wine produced in the "New World." They can be a "meritage" made in heaven.

Dear Dr. WineKnow:

What does "trocken" and "halbtrocken" mean on the labels of some German wines?

Diagnosis: Like so many other people, my introduction to wine was through sweeter styles such as those from Germany. I remember fondly my days of sipping Liebfraumilch. However, for food-matching, the Germans created two new styles in a drier vein. One ferments all the sugar out so it tastes dry (trocken). The other leaves some in so it tastes semi-dry (halbtrocken).

Prescription: Keep on "trocken." Both terms, trocken and halb-trocken, imply the wine will work well with food. However, take note. Because of German wine's high acidity, the best examples of these food-friendlier styles result from using grapes that are at least *spätlese* (late-harvest)-quality level or higher at the time of harvest. Only these provide the richness to properly balance the acid when the sugar is gone, and if rich enough grapes are not used, the wine will be sharp.

Dear Dr. WineKnow:

I've seen the letters "BA" and "TBA" on some bottles of sweet Canadian wine. I'm confused. Is this the same as "Beerenauslese" (BA) and "Trockenbeerenauslese" (TBA) in Germany?

Diagnosis: Like their German counterparts, these acronyms refer to the state of the grapes at the time of harvest, and are governed by stringent wine laws. Germany prohibits the identical labelling on non-German wines. Therefore, German "BA" (Beerenauslese), made from late-harvested berries affected by "noble rot" (botrytis), becomes "Botrytis Affected" on Canadian wines. "TBA" (in Germany, Trockenbeerenauslese), made from late-harvested grapes dried out like raisins from noble rot, in Canada stands for "Totally Botrytis Affected."

Whatever the "BA" and "TBA" stand for, you can be sure the wine wearing this lettering will be sweet and rich. The use of the same lettering works in favour of the Canadian wines, as most people are familiar with the world-famous German bottlings.

Dear Dr. WineKnow:

Who comes up with the tasting notes on the back labels of wine bottles? They rarely match what I'm tasting in the wine.

Diagnosis: Tasting notes on back labels of wine are meant to give the consumer some idea of what the wine will taste like. They are not the gospel. Beyond the identification of certain wine styles or varietal characteristics, the rest is purely subjective. Sometimes the notes are brief: "clean, fresh and crisp." Other times, too much is said.

In my experience, the best tasting notes come from the wine-maker. He or she created the wine and understands it like nobody else. Usually they also have the best palates to do the job.

GRAPE FLASH

Did you know that some avant-garde producers are trying to totally demystify some wine by reducing its name to something basic on the label? Wines simply titled "Red Pop" or "Rotting Grape" add a little humour to the sophistication of other wine labels. However, in almost every case, these wines are very simple and not high-end product. Nonetheless, people do purchase them as conversation pieces. Now, if someone were to come up with a high-end wine aptly titled "Good Stuff," it might make a difference.

Dear Dr. WineKnow:

I've tried some of the suggested food matches on the back labels of wine. Sometimes they don't work because they are too vague.

Diagnosis: If the label simply says a wine goes with chicken and fish, this is not definitive enough. Besides, seasonings, spices, sauces, and cooking procedures alter the flavour and, intrinsically, the wine match.

Prescription: Some well-chosen descriptors like "simply prepared," "pan-fried," "herb-encrusted," and so forth might be very useful. Try a little something that takes the dish in a certain direction.

Although it's usually the marketing people who prepare the label, a chef would be a great choice to provide these notes – or alternatively, the winemaker.

Dear Dr. WineKnow:
The other day I purchased a North American wine labelled Burgundy. Funny, but it tasted nothing like the Burgundy I'm used to from France. What do you suppose the problem was?
Diagnosis: There was probably no problem with it at all, except the dreaded "generic labelling" phenomenon. This idiosyncrasy is very common in the "New World." Many producers in North and South America, South Africa, Australia, and New Zealand label their wines with "Old World" terminology to help better market and sell the product. In the "Old World," such terms as Burgundy, claret, Champagne, port, and sherry imply a very specific wine or style, made a special way, from certain grapes. This is not always the case in the "New World." Occasionally, the same grapes are not utilized and/or the method of production differs.
Prescription: When purchasing a wine like this from any "New World" country, be aware. Read the front and back labels very carefully to see if it is indeed a reasonable facsimile of the original. This will certainly help avoid disappointment.

Dear Dr. WineKnow:
So many wines nowadays advertise on the label that they have won a truckload of medals in wine competitions. How important are these awards?
Diagnosis: Medals won in wine competitions are great marketing tools. They generally guarantee quality and represent the cream of the crop, often from around the world. However, too many awards on a label can be overwhelming and defeat the purpose.

Be assured that these awards are not obtained easily. Usually, a broad, objective group of professionally skilled tasters diligently judge them in blind tastings to be of superior quality.
Prescription: Simply consider them a stamp of approval, if you will.

CHAPTER 4

TO HAVE AND TO HOLD

Storing and Ageing It

A fter a wine is made, it needs to be stored and possibly aged to perfection. Although some wineries do retain wine in tank until needed, most package their wines in some way, and the almighty bottle is usually the thing that captures and holds the wine. Originally, bottles were made from hand-blown glass and were indeed works of art. No two were exactly the same. In fact, many people today collect these, and they are probably worth a good few dollars. Nowadays, of course, bottles are mass produced by machine. Although a few people may keep the unusually shaped and coloured ones around for display, after they are emptied, most end up being recycled, melted down, and made into yet another bottle.

The bottle is the container that will carry the liquid to its ultimate end – consumption. As it is the final venue for wine, its colour, shape, size, and structure have important influences on the stability and evolution of what rests within. Variations in bottles have the power to affect a wine's ageing and taste.

One of the most important components of the bottle's structure is its enclosure, the cork. There is much controversy about this today.

Furthermore, the care and maintenance of the bottles are perhaps the most vital factors affecting wine's drinkability. Even if the bottle plays some part in affecting taste, it is storage conditions that really can make or break a wine. No other aspect of wine, before it is opened, carries as much clout. Storage conditions can affect stability, health, ageing, and taste, long before you even have the opportunity to get a wine to your mouth. Since most wine leaves the winery healthy, this is perhaps the single most common reason why good wine goes bad.

All Bottled Up

As the bottle is a wine's world until that moment when we uncork it and take appreciation to the ultimate step, many things about this wonderful container provide interesting insights into wine's vulnerability.

Dear Dr. WineKnow:
Why are most wine bottles green and brown, while others are just clear glass?
Diagnosis: Break out your shades, girlfriend, because wine is light sensitive. That's why it's stored in the dark. Exposure to light in the bottle can harm or ruin the contents. Dark-coloured glass helps keep light at bay. Traditionally, in countries such as Germany, certain coloured bottles were used for a specific area's wines (green for the Mosel, brown for the Rhine). The introduction of wine bottled in clear glass is an interesting practice. For rosé and dessert wines, clear glass helps show off the pretty colour. Although a great marketing tool, it can be detrimental to the wine.
Prescription: Keep your wine in the dark. For any wine, other than rosé or dessert wine, the only conclusion to be drawn from it being

THE PARTS OF A BOTTLE

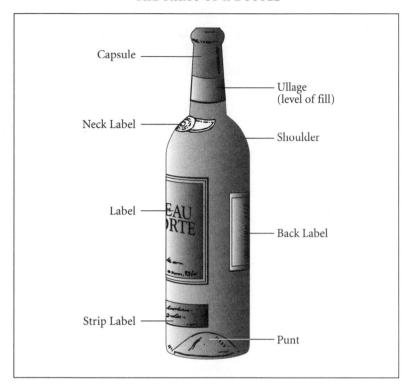

Capsule

Ullage
(level of fill)

Neck Label

Shoulder

Label

Back Label

Strip Label

Punt

bottled in clear glass is this: it is not meant for long ageing and should be consumed over the short haul.

Dear Dr. WineKnow:

I have in my collection different sized bottles of the same wine. When I recently opened two different sizes of a specific wine, I noticed they didn't taste the same. Has one or the other gone bad? **Diagnosis:** What you are experiencing is the effect of bottle size on maturation. Wine in smaller bottles evolves or matures quicker than wine in larger bottles. The larger the volume, the slower the maturation.

Prescription: Size matters. Go through your wine collection, noting when the same wine is bottled in different sizes. Whatever date on which you have decided that specific wine will be ready to drink should be moved up drastically for 375 ml. bottles and moved back slightly for anything larger than the standard 750 ml. size.

COMMON BOTTLE SIZES

NAME	SIZE
Nip	187 ml.
Half-Bottle or Split	375 ml.
Bottle	750 ml.
Magnum	1.5 litres (2 bottles)
Jeroboam	3.0 litres (4 bottles)
Rehoboam	4.5 litres (6 bottles)
Methusalam	6.0 litres (8 bottles)
Salmanazar	9.0 litres (12 bottles)
Balthazar	12.0 litres (16 bottles)
Nebuchadnezzar	15.0 litres (20 bottles)

Dear Dr. WineKnow:
Do bottle shapes make any difference to the way the wine inside behaves?
Diagnosis: Certain countries and wine regions have developed specifically shaped bottles so their wines will stand out in the marketplace.

Although bottle shapes with more surface area might allow the product within to age slower, there is no evidence that suggests that differently shaped bottles, containing the same volume, affect wine in any way.

COMMON BOTTLE SHAPES

Some wine regions the world over have created a traditional bottle shape for their wines. Many other countries now utilize these shapes.

NAME	SHAPE/STYLE	COUNTRIES/WINES/ VARIETALS USING THEM
Bordeaux	Round-shouldered with punt, green or brown	Bordeaux (France), Italian wines (Tuscany), Cabernet Sauvignon, Sauvignon Blanc
Burgundy	Slope shoulder with fatter body, green or brown	Burgundy (France), Italian Barolo and Amarone, Chardonnay, Pinot Noir
Flute	Tall, goosenecked, green or brown	Alsace (France), Germany (green-Mosel, brown-Rhine), Vinho Verde (Portugal), Riesling, Gewürztraminer
Boxbeutal	Flat, flask-like flagon	Germany (Franconia and Baden), Some South African and Chilean, Mateus Rosé (Portugal)
Champagne	Thicker and heavier with deeper punt	Champagne (France), all other sparkling wines

Dear Dr. WineKnow:
In a wine shop recently, I noticed a wine bottle shaped like an animal. Is this a trend we'll be seeing more of?
Diagnosis: To make their products stand out on store shelves, some producers today are opting for unusual packaging for their wines. Totally different from traditional bottles, they could very well take

BOTTLE SHAPES

| Burgundy | Champagne | Burgundy | Alsace | Boxbeutel |

the form of animals, toys, or anything that would better market and distinguish the product. When empty, these bottles are toys.

Prescription: Look to tradition. As to whether this is a trend, it's hard to say. I certainly hope not. Consider this though. Most of these avant-garde bottles are usually used in the "New World." Somehow, I just can't see "Old World" producers doing this. Generally, products that utilize this type of packaging are not high end. As a rule, it's probably safe to say that most good producers will continue to package their wines in traditional bottles and perhaps put their marketing artistry to work on labels instead.

Dear Dr. WineKnow:

I do a lot of entertaining and usually purchase wine by the case. The bottles in the case rarely taste exactly the same. Some are great, others are acceptable, and the odd one just isn't up to snuff. What could cause this?

Diagnosis: This is an age-old problem known as "bottle variation." It is the hope of all wine producers that every bottle of a specific wine be exactly the same. However, due to many extraneous factors, this isn't always the case. Everything from the internal environment of individual bottles to differing bottling dates can make a difference, leading to a somewhat altered taste experience.

Prescription: Buy from a known producer. Countries with advanced wine technology and high production standards tend to have fewer problems with bottle variation than do those from the Eastern bloc. Although it is impossible to avoid to some extent, you'll find it to a lesser degree in wines from reputable producers and countries.

Dear Dr. WineKnow:

Why are sparkling-wine bottles so much heavier than regular wine bottles?

Diagnosis: This wine, due to the bubbles it contains, is under a lot of pressure (usually three to six atmospheres of pressure). That's about the pressure in your car tires. Thicker, heavier glass is required to sustain it. In fact, years before this type of bottle was revolutionized and thickened, the men and women who worked in sparkling wine cellars used to receive danger pay. Bottles would be exploding left and right.

You'll notice that thicker bottles are also less susceptible to temperature change. Chill that bottle slightly longer than you would a still white wine.

Dear Dr. WineKnow:

What's the purpose of the little piece of material covering the cork on wine bottles?

Diagnosis: This is called the "capsule." Its purpose is really aesthetic: to hide the cork and streamline the overall look. I suppose the capsule protects the cork to a certain extent, as well. Often it is stamped or embossed with the winery's name.

Traditionally, the capsule was made from lead. However, certain countries have banned the use of this material for fear of lead poisoning and now force producers to use plastic for sale in their market. The capsule can also be one of the first signs that the wine is problematic. A cork pushing the capsule out, or wetness around it, indicates that something is not quite right with the wine.

Dear Dr. WineKnow:

Does the indentation in the bottom of wine bottles mean anything?

Diagnosis: It could be football thing, but it's not. This indentation is called a "punt" and its concave character provides structural strength to the bottle. This is especially important when bottles are lying on their sides ageing or in storage. Without it, a slight tap on the bottom edge could easily break the bottle. The punt also helps decrease the pressure inside the bottle by providing more surface.

Generally, wine bottles that have punts are more expensive. For many servers, it's also a great spot to rest the thumb while holding the bottle at the bottom while pouring.

GRAPE FLASH

Did you know that all bottles are not filled to the same level? Just walk through a wine shop and examine the fill levels of different wines. On the bottling line of a winery, the fill might vary ever so slightly from bottle to bottle. We're not talking much here, perhaps a quarter-inch at most. More than an inch difference could indicate a potential problem. Too much air in the bottle could oxidize the wine. The air pocket between the cork and the surface of the wine is called the "ullage." If you come across a wine where the fill is substantially low, choose another. This might save you a return trip to the store to replace a bad wine.

Dear Dr. WineKnow:

Sometimes the fill level of bottles of older wine is really low. How do you know if the wine inside is any good?

Diagnosis: It's quite common for older wine in bottles to have lower fill levels. As wine ages, some evaporates through the cork. Only approximations of what is considered acceptable fill can be made, depending on the age of the wine.

Prescription: Normal fill, especially for new or young wines, is roughly a quarter- to half-inch from the cork. A fill level that is at the top of the shoulder or bottom of the neck is acceptable for wines over fifteen years of age. Mid-shoulder fill is acceptable for wine that is over twenty-five years of age, although it may be questionable. Beware of younger wines with this fill level. The cork may be shot. I would be extremely wary of any bottle with low-shoulder fill, regardless of age. A bottle with below low-shoulder fill will almost certainly be undrinkable.

FILL LEVELS OF BOTTLES

- Cork
- Normal Fill
- Low Neck/Top of Shoulder
- Mid-Shoulder
- Low-Shoulder
- Low

Dear Dr. WineKnow:
I'm not familiar with those boxed wines I see in wine shops. They always seem to come in large sizes.

Diagnosis: These are better known as "bag-in-box" wines. This packaging evolved in the 1970s to provide the consumer with a volume purchase (usually three to four litres) that was lighter and sturdier than bottles. It is made up of a collapsible plastic bag inside a box with a handle. The wine is accessed via a tap. The packaging was created for large gatherings and parties or for people who wanted a single glass of wine over a long period of time.

Prescription: Beware of bagged wine. Several drawbacks exist. The container is hard to make airtight, and thus the wine deteriorates rather quickly. That is probably why most have a date stamped on them somewhere. However, most people who purchase this product would probably not notice or object to its tiredness near the end of the carton anyway. The other issue is that only inexpensive wine seems to be put in it. It was and, to a certain extent, still is popular in North America, Australia, New Zealand, Great Britain, and northern Europe.

Discreet Enclosures

Ah corks, the nemesis of the wine industry! It's hard to believe that this little piece of material holds so much power and causes so many problems. Other than glass, the cork is the only part of the bottle separating the wine from the world. Its role is simple: to keep the wine from spilling out and to assist maturation and evolution by allowing minuscule amounts of air in. Even though it represents an integral part of the bottle, it also offers a bit of allure. There's nothing quite like the sound of a cork popping as it is extracted from a bottle.

Dear Dr. WineKnow:
Why is cork used as the major enclosure of wine?
Diagnosis: Hail, oh great *Quercus suber* (see Grape Flash below).

Cork is used as the major enclosure of wine because it's porous, flexible, and reasonably soft. Even while in the bottle, cork allows controlled small amounts of air into the wine to help it evolve. Its flexibility allows it to be squeezed into the opening of a bottle, where it adheres to any size or shape. Its softness enables a corkscrew of some sort to be inserted, so the whole thing can be withdrawn. Perhaps, most of all, the cork reinforces that "celebration" of wine. True wine lovers would agree that the popping sound of a cork extracted from a bottle is truly music to their ears.

GRAPE FLASH

Did you know that cork comes from the cork tree, a species of oak whose Latin name is *Quercus suber*? It's actually the bark that is used, because it's so thick and resistant and can be removed without harming the tree. Cork grows most effectively along the western coast of the Mediterranean, especially in Spain and much of Portugal. Although cork forests grow in North Africa, on the west coast of Italy, in Sicily, Sardinia, and Corsica, and in French Provence, it seems to favour the Iberian peninsula. Because cork trees require a certain amount of rainfall, a relatively warm climate and specific elevations, the best – and most – hails from Portugal, followed by Spain. In fact, the largest producer of cork in the world is the Amorin group, located in Portugal's best cork region, Evora.

Dear Dr. WineKnow:
Are all corks the same?
Diagnosis: Corks have individual personalities. Although they all serve the same purpose, not all corks are created equal. They come in different sizes. Corks can vary in length from 25 mm to 60 mm (1 to 2.3 in.). The normal diameter for a cork is approximately

24 mm, but smaller and larger corks are not unheard of. The size depends on the opening of the wine bottle. Some corks are smoother and some rougher. The quality of the cork can vary, as well. They are usually graded into eight different quality levels. The least expensive is an agglomerate, which is made up of cork particles stuck together. Some are made from cork dust. Others have a natural cork disk at both ends. The best-quality cork is in one piece and is made from natural cork.

Prescription: Examine your cork closely. As part of the packaging of a specific bottle, the cork is generally an indication of the overall quality of the wine and even the producer. Reputable producers usually use better-quality corks, especially for their higher-end wines. As might be expected, they can range drastically in price. The longest, natural cork can cost five to six times more than the shortest, agglomerate one.

Dear Dr. WineKnow:
Are there any benefits to longer corks?

Diagnosis: Since the cork is what separates the wine from the world, the more of it in the bottle, the better. A shorter cork may wear out faster. Even if the wine is stored improperly and the cork dries out somewhat, the chances of a longer cork drying out completely from end to end are less than with a shorter one. Ultimately, it will probably stay intact longer and do the best job of enclosing the wine.

Press your advantage. You will find that, if you are buying a higher-end wine from most producers, the cork will be longer. A shorter cork indicates that the wine below it may not be capable of ageing. Perhaps the only argument against the use of longer corks has to do with the fill level. A longer cork means lower fill level, as it takes up more space in the bottle. However, I'm sure the majority of wine buyers can live with this, as the amount we're talking about here is minimal. The advantages to a longer cork, especially for ageing, far outweigh the amount of wine lost due to fill.

Dear Dr. WineKnow:
I understand that most problems with wine are caused by bad corks. How so?
Diagnosis: "Corky," or "corked," is a term used to describe wine that has been spoiled by a contaminated cork enclosure. This is one of the most common wine defects and gives the wine such an "off" smell, similar to mouldiness, that it really can't be consumed – or at least, not with any pleasure. Sometimes the contamination is slight, causing a delicate "corkiness." Other times it is so intense that one sniff of the wine curls your hair. Either way, corked wine is no fun.

Part of the problem of corkiness in wine has had to do with the processing of the corks in manufacture. Corks were generally bleached in strong chlorine solutions before washing and drying. This treatment produced a chemical called "trichloranisole," or TCA, which reacted with other compounds in the cork, assisted by ever-present moulds. However, the cork industry has banned the use of chlorine since 1997 and has replaced chlorine bleaching with other chemical washes. Since corks are porous they can also pick up and absorb mouldy spores during other times of their preparation. Improper storage or shipping might infect them. They could easily pick up problems from other surfaces, such as damp cellars at the winery or the lining of shipping containers.

Dear Dr. WineKnow:
The corks in sparkling wine are very different. Why do they mushroom out when extracted from the bottle?
Diagnosis: These are more commonly known as "Champagne corks" and have to be made to very specific standards. Generally, they are much wider than conventional corks, approximately 30 mm. Usually cylindrical, they are driven halfway into the bottle neck, forcing them to mushroom inside the bottle. When they are extracted, the mushroom shape opens out.

Considering what these corks have to hold back as far as pressure goes, it's not surprising that they are bigger and really stuffed into the bottle.

GRAPE FLASH

Did you know that sparkling-wine corks are made up of several different pieces glued together? Usually natural corks are punched whole from the bark. However, because these corks are wider, that doesn't work. So they are created by sticking two to three pieces of agglomerate together with natural cork touching the wine itself. As might be expected, sparkling wine corks are generally more expensive (although using agglomerates and just a little cork helps keep the cost down), and they do not require a corkscrew to extract them.

Dear Dr. WineKnow:

Why do sparkling wines have those wire muzzles over the cork?

Diagnosis: It's definitely not because they bite. Sparkling wines are all under pressure, some more than others. They contain carbon dioxide that's just dying to escape. That's what the bubbles are all about. Champagne-method bubbly is under the most pressure, five to six atmospheres' worth. The cork pounded into the bottle would simply not be enough. The pressure inside would eventually spit the cork out, if there weren't something holding it back. This is where the wire muzzle comes into play.

Prescription: Muzzle your wine. Be aware that the wire muzzle is rarely defective. Do not tamper with it or remove it until you are ready to open the bottle. This could be the only thing keeping the cork in place.

Dear Dr. WineKnow:

When I recently opened a wine, I was shocked to find a plastic cork in the bottle. Is this the way of the future?

Diagnosis: Because of all the problems associated with "corky" wines resulting from the use of real cork, many producers world-wide are starting to use synthetic variations. This material totally eliminates the problem. Whether corks will all be synthetic down the road is questionable. Better producers and high-end wines will probably never use them. Purists among producers will stick to the real thing. Somehow synthetic corks are viewed as detracting from the quality. Meanwhile, the cork industry is busy experimenting with the real thing, trying to overcome this problem.

Prescription: Don't be taken aback the next time you uncork a wine to find a plastic cork, as many more wineries start using them. Hey, they come in designer, rainbow colours of red, blue, lime green, and pink, and look and act like the real thing. They even maintain the "ritual" of wine by requiring a corkscrew to withdraw them. Just rejoice that they give your corkscrew something to do.

Dear Dr. WineKnow:
How does wine age under these plastic corks?

Diagnosis: Aye, there's the rub. This is a question of great concern to most wine collectors. We know what natural cork enclosures do and how they assist wine in ageing. Unfortunately, in my opinion, there really has not been enough experience with plastic corks to allow us to draw conclusions about their effect. Certain wineries claim they have been researching and experimenting with ageability of wines under them for a while. Considering that plastic corks haven't been around that long, I don't see how that's possible. Perhaps some producers jumped on this bandwagon a little too early.

Prescription: Drink 'em young. Until enough time has passed to definitively prove that wine does indeed age respectably under plastic corks, they should be viewed with scepticism. For the time being, wine meant to be consumed over the short haul (within one to two years from the vintage) are probably fine under plastic corks.

Dear Dr. WineKnow:
What about those funny corks with the plastic caps on top? You see them on many fortified wines like sherry and port and some sweet selections.

Diagnosis: The types of wines that use this style of cork are generally those that are consumed over a longer period of time. The plastic cap on top enables the cork to be pulled out easily and replaced regularly. It's no different than a decanter plug, except it is much snugger to keep air out.

Although they are not as airtight as conventional corks, they tend to make the job of opening and closing bottles much easier. These types of wines are usually packaged with a foil or plastic seal over the cork to keep air at bay. Unfortunately, once opened, they don't provide the best deterrent against air and spoilage, even after recorking, and are strictly for convenience.

GRAPE FLASH

Did you know that screw caps are one of the best enclosures for wine? They form an airtight seal and rarely leak. Unfortunately, their association with inexpensive wine is legendary, and it is a next-to-impossible task to rise above this image, since better wines simply don't use them. Until producers start using them for better-quality wine, they will continue to get a bad rap. Some producers, however, are experimenting with them on better vino. One of their main drawbacks is their total lack of "romance." There's just something inordinately bourgeois and pedestrian about unscrewing a wine bottle as opposed to uncorking it.

The Age of Reason

A question I always get asked is whether wine is a living thing. I'm afraid the jury is still out on that. However, wine does have a life cycle. It starts out young, reaches a peak, and then declines. This cycle is different for each and every wine. The idea, of course, is to drink all wine when it is at its peak, or best drinking

WINE'S LIFE CYCLE

stage. This involves ageing it. In order to do so, meticulous care must be taken to ensure that the wine arrives at maturity in a healthy, sound state.

Dear Dr. WineKnow:
Are all wines age worthy?
Diagnosis: Wines with a lot of "stuffing" between the front and back end will generally age better. The reason for ageing certain wines is to soften tannins where applicable, marry flavours, and harmonize character. As a rule, red wines age better than whites. Exceptions include sweet wines, fortified wines, and some sparkling wines. What a wine requires to age is reasonable fruit, alcohol, balance, and, in the case of red, some firm tannins. It's also a matter of structure.
Prescription: Learn to love older wines. The more you get involved with wine the better you'll be equipped to handle this aspect. You'll come to realize that certain grape varieties (such as Cabernet Sauvignon and Nebbiolo) and wine styles (Bordeaux and Amarone) generally age better than others. Some vintage years produce wines with better fruit and structure than others, making them more age worthy. The more experienced you become at tasting, the better you'll be able to determine, by taste, which wines can age.

Dear Dr. WineKnow:
Even if a wine is age worthy, will it improve with age?

Diagnosis: Not necessarily! Some wines will keep for a while, but not get any better. In other words, they have what it takes to exist for some time but don't need that time to evolve into the perfect wine. Many wines are merely cellared to provide a stash on hand for consumption over a certain time period.

Prescription: Again, the best barometer for this kind of knowledge is experience and wine education. The more you learn about and taste wine, the better your ability to judge these things.

Dear Dr. WineKnow:
Which type of wine will age the longest?

Diagnosis: Try a little Madeira, m'dear! This Portuguese wine from the island of the same name, off the coast of North Africa in the Atlantic, is renowned for its longevity. Fortified with brandy, heated for months, and aged up to fifty years in barrels before bottling, some can live as long as a couple of hundred years in ideal cellars. Its amazing acidity, higher alcohol content (18 to 21 per cent), and often its residual sugar render it one of the most resilient wines made.

Prescription: When looking for Madeira, you'll usually find it labelled by grape variety, ranging from drier to sweet. Sercial is the driest. Verdelho is medium-dry. Bual is medium-sweet, and Malmsey is very sweet and rich. It used to have the image of being the "tipple" of the over-sixty crowd, but lately it's become highly popular with Gen Xer's and is back in vogue. Now, if there was only more of it available to the consumer!

Wine in Shops

Before wine actually reaches your home and storage space, it spends time in a shop waiting to be purchased. The way it's handled and stored there is of utmost importance. What's the point of having ideal storage conditions at home if the wine was improperly stored at the shop? The damage may already have been done. For instance, if you see a wine that is not stored horizontally, chances are, the cork is dried out.

Dear Dr. WineKnow:
In a wine shop, how do I know if a particular wine is ready to drink or needs more ageing?
Diagnosis: If you've got a corkscrew, any wine is ready to drink. However, whether the wine in question will show its best is another story. Sometimes, there are what are called "shelf-talkers" (stickers or cards attached to wine bins in the store) that give this kind of information.
Prescription: Wine education is probably the most important attribute in knowing which grape varieties and wine styles need ageing or not. Vintage charts (available through trade commissions) are helpful to determine good years of production. Furthermore, reading regular wine columns and publications for advice on what to buy, drink, and cellar make a big difference. If all else fails, ask for help in the store. Most major stores have knowledgeable staff or a consultant on hand who can give you some advice in that area.

Dear Dr. WineKnow:
I know that wines with a cork enclosure should be stored on their sides to keep the cork moist. However, when in wine shops, I often see wine displayed standing up. When I inquire about it, shop owners tell me the product moves so fast that the corks don't have time to dry out.
Diagnosis: I have the same concerns. I suppose a standing bottle helps the label show better and makes a better display, but it doesn't do much for the wine. Since we are not in the store constantly, it's really hard to say whether there is a large turnover of that particular product. We have to take the shop-owner's word for it. Furthermore, it also makes you wonder whether they are actually storing the wines cork-side-down in their warehouse.

Prescription: All I can suggest is to request a bottle from the back and hope that it, at least, has been stored properly in the warehouse.

Dear Dr. WineKnow:
I worry about wines in stores that are sitting in sunlight near windows. They are often warm to the touch. What do you think?
Diagnosis: Yes, there's nothing quite like a wine that's been cooking in the sun. Since wine is light-sensitive, this is not a good practice. Even the dark-coloured glass most wine is bottled in won't help in this case.
Prescription: Keep your wines in the dark. As you probably know, ideal storage conditions for wine include darkness. Perhaps a discreet word to the retailer regarding this practice is in order. If you plan to purchase one of these wines, simply ask for one from the back.

GRAPE FLASH

Did you know that wine already bottled and sitting in a shop can start to ferment again? You've probably seen evidence of this, but not known what it was. The corks in certain bottles seem not quite flush with the lip and actually appear to be pushing against the capsule. What's happening here is that the store is too hot or the wine is hot from sitting in the sun. Any microscopic particles of yeast that weren't removed through filtration may come out of dormancy in the heat and start fermenting again. Because fermentation creates carbon dioxide, it starts pushing the cork out of the bottle, trying to escape. Avoid purchasing wines with this problem. More than likely they are "off" and will not taste good.

Dear Dr. WineKnow:
Sometimes bottles of wine in the shop are wet at the top, around the capsule. What's the problem here?

Diagnosis: This is definitely not a good sign. If the cork or capsule is wet, chances are that wine is leaking out. If wine is leaking out, you can bet your swizzle stick, air is getting in and oxidizing the wine.
Prescription: Avoid leaky wines like the plague. You will only be sadly disappointed and have to return the bottle.

Dear Dr. WineKnow:
I've been in a few wine shops where many of the bottles have dirty, soiled labels.
Diagnosis: It's not normal for wines to leave the producer with soiled labels; it obviously doesn't make for a great presentation. Probably something has happened to the wine, either in transit or at the shop. What's more, it may be an indication of how the shop has handled the wine.
Prescription: If you notice much of this, shop elsewhere.

Cellaring at Home

There's something quite wonderful about being able to run down to your cellar in your home to retrieve a bottle of wine rather than having to go out to a store to get it. It just makes life so much easier. Keeping wine at home requires certain care, especially if you want to maintain its health and control its destiny. It's even more important if you are planning on ageing some to perfection. Proper storage conditions are absolutely essential to keeping and ageing wine. Without it, wine may be a bad investment. It is therefore imperative to monitor conditions regularly, keeping tabs on its development. As certain wines have only limited lifespans and others require so long to reach drinkability, you don't want to lose track of their progress.

I recall an unfortunate tale of a client of mine whose very expensive wine collection I helped put together. One day he went down to his cellar to retrieve a bottle of decent red Bordeaux for dinner. Upon opening it, he discovered it was tired and over the hill.

Assuming it was just an isolated, bad bottle, he returned to the cellar to get another from the three cases he had originally purchased. Again the wine was gone when opened. What are the odds of pulling two bottles of the exact same wine and finding them no longer good? Pretty slim, I would guess. Now panicking, he started uncorking bottle after bottle from the three cases, only to find all of them were toast. He had obviously lost track of this particular wine and all three cases of it went to that great vinegar plant in the sky.

Believe you me, there's nothing sadder than investing money, time, and space in wine only to have it go down the tubes before you've had a chance to enjoy it, simply because you forgot it. My suggestion: label either the box or the section, indicating when the wine was purchased and even a "guesstimate" of when the wine might expire.

Dear Dr. WineKnow:
Is wine collecting a good investment?
Diagnosis: Unfortunately, wine is not quite like stocks, bonds, mutual funds, or real estate. It doesn't intrinsically increase in value as time goes on. There are simply too many variables involved, such as handling, storage conditions, a wine's reputation, and so forth. However, there is a certain amount of money to be saved by buying young wines cheaper to cellar today than when they are mature and more expensive down the road. Furthermore, the limited availability of certain products that you have stashed in your cellar, will more than likely make them escalate in value. However one of the real, and perhaps most important, complications to potential profit margin, is the fact that it's illegal to sell wine without a licence. Even so, not a lot of people are getting rich from the resale of wine.
Prescription: An investment adviser I'm not, but I can tell you this. The real investment here is good taste and knowing that many wonderful moments lie corked up in bottles, practically under your nose, waiting to be set free. It's the sheer joy of being able to

run down to your cellar any old time, night or day, and pick out
something delightfully interesting to swill.

Dear Dr. WineKnow:
I store my wines in a small cubbyhole next to my workshop in the
basement. However, when I opened the last few bottles, the wine
smelled a little like paint. What on earth is wrong?
Diagnosis: The smell of paint or chemicals from your workshop
has penetrated the corks of the wines. Wine corks are very porous,
allowing small, measured amounts of air into the wine. In this
case, the smell of paint has settled in.
Prescription: Never store wine near strong smells. Relocate your
wines immediately and hope and pray that all are not affected.
Chemicals, the odour of cooking or food, and cleaning solutions
can permeate your goods. Find a neutral place in your home to
keep the wines.

Dear Dr. WineKnow:
I live in an apartment and store my wines in a small wine rack in the
living room. I bought a few wines that I was told needed three more
years of ageing before drinking. Out of curiosity, I decided to open
one for a special occasion recently and found it already mature.
Diagnosis: Sounds to me like a temperature problem. Many apart-
ments are very warm to the point where windows have to be
opened in the winter. Although the wine in question needed three
more years of ageing, the fact is that the heat in your living room
was just too much for the wine, and it aged faster.
Prescription: Provide ideal cellaring or storage temperature for
wine. This is approximately 55°F (12°C). Anything above or below
this temperature will either speed up or slow down its maturation.
In your case it speeded it up. Although it's difficult in an apartment,
move your wine to a rarely used closet and store it directly on the
floor, not on a carpet. Alternately, you might invest in one of those
electric, fridge-like units that simulates an ideal cellar.

> ### GRAPE FLASH
> Did you know it's not a good idea to store your wines in the refrigerator? You were obviously a Boy Scout or Girl Guide when growing up since your motto is "be prepared." I understand that you want it chilled when somebody drops by, but extended time in that cold environment could alter the wine's flavour. Unless you are expecting company or are planning on serving wine soon, the fridge is not the place to keep it for long periods of time. It's simply too cold. Utilize the fridge only for chilling before serving. I don't know anyone who couldn't wait a short while for a wine to chill down.

Dear Dr. WineKnow:

My wines are kept in boxes under the basement stairs. However, my son loves to play down there and is up and down constantly. Should I be worried about the state of my wines?

Diagnosis: You should be, my friend! If little Jimmy is running up and down the stairs forty times a day, right over your wine, this is not a good thing. The constant disturbance and shaking is not ideal for your wine's stability. In older wines, the sediment is forever being churned up.

Prescription: Try shifting your wines to a quieter, vibration-free part of the basement. Avoid placing them near the furnace, as well. The kicking on and off of air-conditioning in the summer and heating in the winter is also bad.

Dear Dr. WineKnow:

My wine cellar feels very damp. So much so that some bottles develop mould on the corks under the capsule. Is there a solution to this problem?

Diagnosis: Obviously, your cellar is too humid and causing bacterial mould to form on wet corks. More than likely, it smells dank and mouldy in the space, as well. This can be a real problem if it seeps into the wine. It could cause the liquid to become mouldy and undrinkable. Although a certain amount of humidity is required to prevent the outer portion of the corks from drying out, too much is dangerous.

Prescription: Invest in a dehumidifier and let it run constantly. Monitor the humidity and, when it reaches approximately 70 to 75 per cent (ideal wine-cellar humidity), turn the unit off. Start it up again when necessary.

GRAPE FLASH

Did you know that there are now computer wine programs on the market that can help document and monitor your wines' progress at home? These fascinating programs contain maps, wine-region information, vintage charts, places for tasting notes, and much more. What you have to do is keep them updated. Every time you obtain new wine or drink some, it must be recorded, along with the pertinent information. This is extremely helpful, especially when your collection starts to grow to hundreds of bottles or more.

Dear Dr. WineKnow:

What do you think about those wine-storage units that look like refrigerators? Are they any good?

Diagnosis: As far as the romantic side of wine goes, there's nothing quite like a wine cellar in your basement. It's probably the closest thing to what you find at a winery. However, not everyone has space for something like this, even if they live in a house. Apartment dwellers have even less space, and can forget about this concept entirely. Just keeping your wine somewhere in your living space can be detrimental unless storage conditions are right. These units simulate perfect conditions by controlling temperature, humidity, and vibration electronically. That's right, they plug into an A/C outlet. In other words, they are portable wine cellars that can be taken with you should you move. They work very well and, for the most part, are quite handsome.

These units come in different sizes, based on bottle capacity, and are priced accordingly. You can pay for extra options like glass doors and such. Make sure you choose a size wisely for your space and potential needs. Many people find that they end up having more wine than the units can hold and outgrow them. Should there be a power failure, the unit should maintain the correct temperature for some time as long as the door is not opened too often. The amount of wine in the unit will also determine how long the temperature remains correct. If it's full, the time will be shorter. When purchasing one of these units, pick a reliable retailer, so you have someone to go back to if there are any problems.

Dear Dr. WineKnow:
I like Franconian and Baden wine from Germany. However, I find those flat, flask-like bottles they come in impossible to store properly in my cellar. Any ideas?
Diagnosis: Such are the dilemmas of life in a wine world. In order to quench your vinous thirst, sometimes a sacrifice or two in the cellar must be made. These bottles, better known as "boxbeutals" aren't really shaped for conventional storage systems, which cater to Bordeaux- or Burgundy-type bottles.
Prescription: Dr. WineKnow, at great personal expense, will come out to your place and help consume all the wine in those inconvenient bottles. Short of designing and building some special shelving for this shape bottle, here's a suggestion. Line up several of them neck to neck, flat, so that they fit together like a jigsaw puzzle. Then place a piece of cardboard or wood on top and make another row. Repeat the process until you've filled the space. This is the method used in many parts of Germany.

Dear Dr. WineKnow:
I have outgrown my wine cellar and have friends who would love to collect wine but don't have the room. Short of renting someone's

basement, is there any place out there where we could keep our wines?

Diagnosis: This is a very common dilemma. Many people would love to collect wine but simply do not have the space, because they live in an apartment. Others, once they start to collect, find that they outgrow their cellar and have far more wines than they can properly store.

Prescription: Call Rent-a-Wine. There are some public wine-storage facilities out there to make your life easier. These professional wine-cellaring services offer climate-controlled warehouses with individual locker or walk-in cellars complete with racking/ shelving. With constant monitoring, security, back-up equipment systems, and access twenty-four-hours-a-day, seven-days-a-week, these state-of-the-art facilities are the perfect alternative for your wine storage needs. Some even have a members' lounge, complete with tasting rooms. They usually charge per case per month. These are popular in the United States and Quebec, and I'm sure you'll be seeing more of them popping up. Look under "Wine Storage" in your Yellow Pages, or ask retailers who sell wine paraphernalia.

GRAPE FLASH

Did you know you don't have to have hundreds or thousands of bottles of wine to have a decent collection? Several bottles of the best wines from each region or country can make a nice cellar. You may want to include all styles, as well. Here's a sample of a well-rounded, international, sixty-five-bottle collection.

France: 6 Bordeaux (3 red, 2 white, 1 Sauterne),
         8 Burgundy (3 red, 3 white, 2 Beaujolais),
         2 red Rhône, 2 rosés, 2 white Loire,
         2 white Alsace, 1 champagne.
Italy: 15 red (5 Tuscany, 4 Piedmont, 4 Veneto), 2 white

Spain:	2 red, 1 Cava, 1 sherry
Germany:	4 white (1 dry, 1 medium-dry, 1 medium-sweet, 1 sweet)
Portugal:	2 red, 1 port
California:	2 red, 2 white
Oregon:	2 red
Australia:	2 red, 2 white
Chile:	2 red
Canada:	1 red, 1 white

CHAPTER 5

DELIVERANCE

Serving It

G etting the wine from the bottle to your mouth is one of the most important parts of appreciation. The first order of business is opening the bottle. Without this, all other aspects of deliverance are pointless. There is a correct way of uncorking wine and many tools to help the job go smoothly.

Next, preparing the wine for appreciation is a fundamental part of the process, and it can affect what is tasted. Such elements as serving temperatures and breathing time are absolutely essential to a wine's ability to properly show its stuff. Occasionally, a wine must be treated a certain way, even before it is actually opened. Needless to say, many a wine has not shown well because of poor or improper preparation.

Finally, it is the glass that brings the wine to the senses, and it too can give or defer pleasure. Size, shape, design, and temperature can all affect what is perceived in wine. Like wine itself, glassware also requires certain maintenance to do its job properly.

In fact, the serving of wine is so important that a certain amount of ritual and ceremony have evolved around it. Of course, you could merely swig directly out of the bottle. However, making sure the brown paper bag doesn't touch your lips is not the most important thing about appreciation. For civilized folks in social settings, it has become as vital to look good serving and drinking wine, as it is to perform the ritual correctly.

The Opening Ceremony

Getting to the wine is critical to enjoyment. For most wines with a cork enclosure, a corkscrew handles the job most effectively. Real men, of course, don't use a corkscrew. They simply bite the top of the bottle off. For the rest of us, many screws exist on the market, some simple, others complex. Some are easier to use than others. In my experience, the simpler the tool, the better.

Opening bubbly is a whole different ball game, and requires extra care and technique. A corkscrew is not required to get at this fizzy liquid.

Dear Dr. WineKnow:
I sometimes cut my fingers trying to remove the capsule from around the neck of a wine bottle. Any ideas of a better, safer way of removing it?
Diagnosis: This can be something of a problem, especially if the capsule is made of lead. As discussed above, certain parts of the world have banned this material for use in capsules, but many are still being used in various markets. The sharpness of lead is very much like a knife and can do substantial damage to the hands. I know from first-hand experience. Even if you use the knife portion of a "waiter's helper" on your lever corkscrew, it's not hard to wound yourself if you don't do it properly or your hand slips. If you use the knife portion of a waiter's-helper corkscrew or a regular knife, carefully rotate the blade around the neck of the bottle above or below the lip and lift off the cut portion of the capsule.
Prescription: Stock up on Band-Aids or get something on the

market called a "capsule cutter," or "foil cutter." It removes the capsule easily and painlessly, regardless of what material it is made of. It's a small, U-shaped object with two little sharp metal wheels at both ends. You simply grip the neck of the bottle just below the lip with the unit, squeeze, and rotate the cutter around the bottle once or twice. Off comes the capsule with a clean cut. No fuss, no muss! You'll save a lot of money on Band-Aids with this little gizmo.

CAPSULE CUTTER

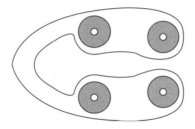

Dear Dr. WineKnow:
There are so many corkscrews on the market. Is one superior to others?

Diagnosis: The best corkscrew is one which extracts the cork easily and doesn't destroy it in the process. If brute strength is your thing, try the simple "T-bar." However, the helix (curly screw portion) of this style is often too short for longer corks. Most of the better screws on the market rely on the principle of leverage. Enter the "waiters' helper," or the lever corkscrew. This most practical, inexpensive, mobile, universal utensil contains a short knife for cutting the foil away. And who can forget the "butterfly," with its two wings that rise up as the screw is inserted into the cork? A certain amount of strength is required to push down on the wings to extract the cork. Companies like Screwpull have a whole line of state-of-the-art cork removers that make the job a snap.

Prescription: Consider toning your pecs. Choose a corkscrew that works the best for you and one that fits your budget. Generally, screws that apply leverage are easier. Whatever screw you decide on, ensure that the only sharp part of it is the point of the helix. Helixes with sharp sides will shred the cork.

CORKSCREWS

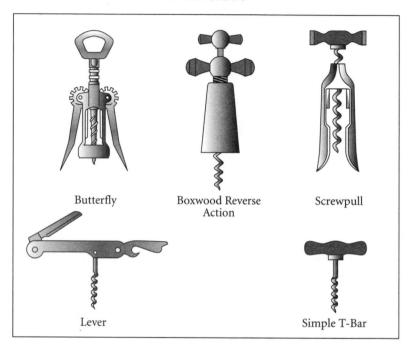

Butterfly   Boxwood Reverse   Screwpull
             Action

Lever   Simple T-Bar

Dear Dr. WineKnow:
How do you uncork an older wine, where the cork might crumble?
Diagnosis: Extracting an older cork from an older bottle of wine with a conventional corkscrew can be very tricky. You're quite right. They often crumble and disintegrate because of their age and make a holy mess.
Prescription: Use an "ah-so," honourable wino. An "ah-so" consists of two steel blades, one longer than the other, that, when inserted down the sides of the cork, removes it with a twisting pull. Since the cork is not penetrated but gripped, it usually comes out intact. Although this tool requires some degree of expertise, it

actually works equally well for any cork, young or old. It's also great for stubborn corks that simply will not come out with traditional types of screws. The neat thing is that, by reversing the process, you can replace the cork in the bottle, as well.

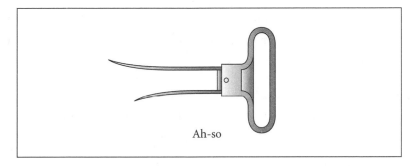

Ah-so

Dear Dr. WineKnow:

I have a problem serving old red wines because of the sediment. Kindly direct me on how to deal with these.

Diagnosis: Since old red wines throw a deposit in the bottle, they need to be decanted off their residue to make them clean and drinkable. The sediment won't hurt you, but it is gritty and not pleasant in the mouth.

Prescription: Don't be so "sedimental." Here's what you should do. Bring the chosen bottle up from your storage space and let it stand four to five hours, unopened, on a counter to let the sediment settle to the bottom. When you're ready to drink it, open it very carefully, so as not to disturb the sediment, and decant it against a source of light. When the sediment reaches the lip of the bottle, stop pouring. Be prepared to forfeit whatever is left in the bottle, as it contains too much sediment to save.

Dear Dr. WineKnow:

When choosing a red wine to serve from my cellar, what is considered "old"?

Diagnosis: For all intents and purposes, the term "old" doesn't necessarily refer to the year on the bottle. What's old for one wine may not be for another. Certain wines mature faster than others. Even the same wine might age differently, depending on the storage conditions.

Prescription: Old, in this case, is strictly a state of being. For serving purposes, let's consider a wine old if it displays any of the following characteristics. It is cloudy, sedimented, hazy, or has chunks of stuff floating in it when examined against a light source in your storage space. Don't get too hung up on vintage years on the bottle.

Dear Dr. WineKnow:

I'm sure most wine drinkers have experienced the problem of a cork being pushed totally into the bottle when they're trying to extract it. What do you do?

Diagnosis: There's probably not a wine lover alive who has not experienced this frustrating little phenomenon at some point. It usually happens with shorter corks. You can see it coming, too. As the corkscrew is inserted into the cork, the little sucker starts to get away from you. The more you struggle to solve the problem, the further the cork goes into the bottle – until it's gone.

Prescription: I used to have a buddy who could rig up a string with a paperclip. He'd fish for the cork in the bottle and usually snag and reel it in. I told him he should have patented it. Unfortunately, there is no tool I know of on the market that can deal with this. Use a straw, pour the wine carefully, or decant it. Don't filter it.

Dear Dr. WineKnow:

I really like Champagne, but am scared silly about opening it. What's the correct way?

Diagnosis: Champagne, unlike still wine, presents a problem for many people. Great care should be taken when opening it because of the pressure within. The bottle should be kept still and motionless at all costs, until opening time. If the bottle is retrieved from the cellar or its storage space, ensure that it rests for a while before you attempt to open it. The mere transfer of the bottle from cellar to table shakes up the contents, increasing the gas's

desire to escape. Don't *ever* shake up the bottle before opening it.
Prescription: Don't hold in your gas. To open, follow this procedure. Remove enough of the tin foil wrap to expose the cork, capped with the wire muzzle. Undo the muzzle. It is most important to keep your hand, palm down, on the cork once the muzzle is gone. Many a bubbly cork has come shooting out of the bottle after the muzzle has been removed. Hold the bottle on a forty-five-degree angle, cork in one hand, bottle in the other. Rotate the bottle around the cork. There is no need to yank on the cork. The pressure inside will spit the cork out. You'll feel it start to give way as the bottle is turned. Be very careful.

GRAPE FLASH

Did you know that a bubbly cork, especially one from Champagne, can be a deadly weapon? There's a lot of pressure bound up in a bottle of bubbly. Science has proven that a champagne-method bubbly cork leaving a bottle, unobstructed, can reach speeds of up to sixty miles an hour. That's like a bullet. I've seen these things shatter chandeliers, break windows, and even make holes in ceilings. Treat them very carefully. Never put your face right over the bottle. Never point a Champagne bottle at anyone when opening it. Try to steer clear of any windows, light fixtures, pictures, and knick-knacks. Using the fridge, which is metal, as a target, in case the cork gets away from you is a good idea. To be safe, you might place a towel over the cork to provide some cushioning as it comes away. If still wary, get someone else to open the bottle.

Dear Dr. WineKnow:
Someone once told me they opened a bottle of Champagne by putting their thumbs under the cork and flicking it. Is this possible?
Diagnosis: Considering the size of the cork and how tightly it is jammed into the bottle, this method of extraction is highly

unlikely. Unless the bottle and/or the cork is defective, this is next to impossible to do. The pressure inside the bottle may force the cork out, but not necessarily assisted by the thumbs.

Prescription: Don't try this at home, boys and girls, as it can be very dangerous and probably futile.

Dear Dr. WineKnow:

Know anything about sabring Champagne? There was a reference to it in an old movie I saw.

Diagnosis: Unsheathe thy sword, varlet, we have a bottle to open. This rather unique, yet perhaps unethical, method of opening a bottle of bubbly originated back in Napoleon's time. Victorious officers returning home from battle would summon for Champagne to quench their thirst. Too tired and impatient to open the bottle correctly, they simply knocked the top off with their sabres.

Prescription: When was the last time you noticed a sword in your cutlery tray? If you strike the neck of the bottle with an upward shot just below the cork, a clean ring of glass should come away. But, again, don't try this at home. This procedure is dangerous and extremely unreliable!

Dear Dr. WineKnow:

I know Champagne comes in some very large bottles. How in the world do you serve and pour them?

Prescription: You obviously hire some weight lifter who is used to benching heavy poundage for the really large bottles. The average person would not purchase these. Larger bottles of Champagne do not roll off the assembly line like regular-size bottles. Usually, they are custom-ordered before they are produced. There is also a charge for the bottle itself, especially for the very large ones. These monster bottles come in a swinging cradle, so the bottle itself doesn't have to be lifted. It merely swings out, enabling it to be poured. Restaurants, bars, and hotels would order these for display purposes.

Dear Dr. WineKnow:
When I open a bottle of bubbly but don't want to drink it all, I'm at odds end figuring out how to keep the bubbles in. With still wine, I normally just push the cork back in, but I suppose that's impossible with bubbly.

Diagnosis: It's impossible to use a regular, still wine cork to preserve it. The bubbly just spits it out after a short period. The pressured bubbles inside are just dying to escape, forcing out anything that's not literally tied down. So the bubbles disappear very quickly and the wine goes flat before you've had a chance to enjoy it again.

Prescription: A "pressure cap" is required. The best are made of metal. A steel-capped, rubber, or plastic plug is hinged with a metal clamp on both sides. When the plug is pushed down firmly into the mouth of the bottle, the two hinged clamps grip the neck of the bottle just below the lip. This prevents the plug from being spit out by the force of the pressure within. To remove the cap, simply push down on the plug and release the two clamps. You'll no doubt hear a pop as if you've just opened a new bottle. This should keep the bubbly fresh.

Any wine paraphernalia store will carry pressure caps.

Dear Dr. WineKnow:
Sometimes, when I uncork a wine, the lip of the bottle at the opening looks a little dirty. Does this mean there's a problem with the wine?

Diagnosis: A little debris on the bottle opening from a cork that is spongy, crumbly, or wet is not uncommon when uncorking a wine. It doesn't necessarily indicate a wine defect.

Prescription: Keep a hanky handy. As a precaution, whether it is dirty or not, it's probably always a good idea to give the mouth and lip of the freshly opened bottle a quick wipe with a damp cloth.

Dear Dr. WineKnow:
I must be a real "klutz." I can't seem to pour wine without it dripping or running down the side of the bottle.

Diagnosis: Don't be so hard on yourself. Pouring wine from a bottle can be messy. There is no spout at the opening of wine bottles to direct the liquid. Even if you rotate the bottle slightly at the end of the pour, there is still no assurance that some will not drip. Why do you think many waiters carry a small towel around with them? In fact, at some events, they actually wrap a towel around the neck of the bottle to catch drips.

Prescription: Purchase a dripless device. You can buy pourers at most wine shops that sell paraphernalia. They come in a flat package and are circular, flimsy little silver things made of a plastic-like material. Just fold one up and insert it into the mouth of the bottle, forming a spout. This directs the wine, reducing, if not eliminating, drips altogether.

There are also drip-catchers, often in silver, that you can slip over the neck of your bottle.

The Temperate Zone

Wine is very susceptible to temperature. If some wines are served too warm the alcohol will stick out. Others presented too cold will be shy and unyielding. The correct serving temperature for different styles of wine is an important issue if you want them to bare their souls in the glass. This aspect of tasting can really affect your appreciation.

Dear Dr. WineKnow:
How do you know when a wine has reached its ideal serving temperature?

Diagnosis: Serving temperatures of wine are important for them to best show their stuff. Usually, approximations of time are utilized in determining how long a wine should chill or remain out at room temperature.

Prescription: Feeling the bottle often is a good indication. Most people get by with this method, content that it doesn't have to be an exact science. Trial and error are the easiest. If the wine is not cool or warm enough, simply chill or let stand longer.

You can also get a wine thermometer. There are wine thermometers out there that can give you accuracy beyond a doubt. They work the same way a meat thermometer measures the interior temperature of a roast, for instance. You place it in the wine bottle, and simply wait until the temperature reaches its ideal. Some thermometers actually have different indications on them for different styles of wine. Nothing is left to chance. Going to this extreme, however, might take away from the hedonistic aspect, and seem a little pedantic.

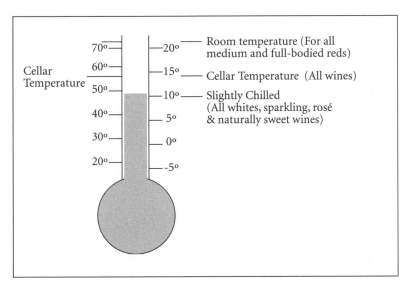

Dear Dr. WineKnow:
I usually chill white wine in the freezer or add ice cubes to a glass of warm wine. For some reason it never has much of a smell or taste. What gives?
Diagnosis: Ice cubes! Dionysus would have your hide. I refer to it as the "chill factor." For some reason, many folks, especially North Americans, love to chill the living dickens out of white wine. They chuck the bottle in the freezer until it is literally frosty. It comes out

of the freezer looking like one of those schnapps bottles with a block of ice around it. When any wine is too cold, the nose is "dumb" (unyielding) and all that can be tasted are minerals and acid (the sour component). Forget about aromatics, fruit, and flavours. Freezer chilling can actually rearrange the molecules in the wine, causing flavours to be altered.

Prescription: Take the chill off. The perfect temperature at which to serve whites, rosés, bubblies, and naturally sweet wines is the one that highlights their positive points. This means SLIGHTLY CHILLED. I'm talking about approximately 5°C to 10°C, no more. This can be ideally and romantically achieved by placing the bottle in an ice bucket, filled with a blend of ice and water, for around fifteen minutes. Alternately, place the bottle down below in the refrigerator for thirty minutes or so. Never, ever, use the freezer to chill wine. For the nonbelievers among you, try this. Chill two bottles of the same wine, one in an ice bucket as suggested and the other in the freezer. Time it so they are both removed simultaneously. Pour yourself a glass of each and taste them. First of all, tell me which one you can actually taste and, secondly, which one tastes better. There will be no doubt after this little experiment.

Dear Dr. WineKnow:
I really like light, fruity, red wines like Beaujolais. Should I serve these at the same temperature as big reds?

Diagnosis: I, too, enjoy those fruity, light reds that wash down food so nicely. As much as I love the big, rich, chewy numbers, there's always a place on my roster for easier-drinking reds. These styles of wines are "fruit-driven." In other words, the fruit seems to be the focus of the wine. They are rarely tannic and hard but softer and rounder. Wines that fall into this category include Gamay, Merlot, Grignolino, and Dolcetto.

Prescription: Consider the type of wine. Although they could easily be served at room temperature (20°C/70°F), cellar temperature (55°F) is better. In fact, consider chilling them ever so slightly (five minutes in an ice bucket, ten to fifteen minutes in the bottom of the fridge). What this does is bring out the freshness of the berry fruit and make them infinitely more quaffable. On a picnic, chill one of these guys down in a babbling brook. The BBQ'd turkey legs, cold cuts, and sandwiches won't mind a bit.

Dear Dr. WineKnow:
The temperature of my wine-storage space in the basement is around 50°F. When I bring a big red wine up and serve it immediately, it doesn't have much smell.
Diagnosis: It sounds like your storage space is pretty close to ideal cellar temperature (55°F). Either way, this is a bit too cool for a big red to show its stuff. It's no wonder the wine doesn't have much of a nose. I'll bet after a while in the glass, it comes to life.
Prescription: Serve big or full red wines at around room temperature (20°C/70°F). What you need to do is bring the wine up from the cellar and let it stand unopened on the counter until it reaches room temperature. This should help.

GRAPE FLASH
Did you know that you should serve all wine, including reds, cooler than normal when dining "al fresco" in the summer? Heat causes alcohol in wine to evaporate more quickly, making it more aggressive and less fruity. Keep whites and bubbly on ice and try using an ice bucket filled with only cold water to refresh reds. There's nothing worse than a lukewarm, "soupy" red wine, when you are dining outside.

Dear Dr. WineKnow:
Whenever I open a red wine at home it seems too warm. What can I do?
Diagnosis: I know the kind of heat you are talking about. I once lived in a place that was so hot, the windows had to be opened in the winter just to make it bearable. This is not the ideal temperature for

red wine. Although it needs to be served at room temperature (20°C/70°F), too warm and it will suffer. The alcohol will stick out like a sore thumb. It sounds like your place is much warmer than what is considered room temperature.

Prescription: Chill out. This may sound weird, but what you need to do under these circumstances is to chill the wine down to around 20°C. Five to ten minutes in the bottom of the fridge should do the job. It may be helpful to purchase a wine thermometer, which measures its temperature.

Deep Breathing

"Stand back and give it some air," demanded the sommelier. "Let it breathe. Otherwise the wine will not open up." I love it when the wine person is right. Breathing time allows a wine to come around and acclimatize to the open air. It brings the bouquet out. Not enough time or too much and it may not show up to its potential.

Dear Dr. WineKnow:

Why is it necessary to open wines to let them "breathe" before drinking?

Diagnosis: Wine immediately opened and poured is in a state of shock. It requires air to bring it to life. It is dumb or unyielding. How long you let it breathe depends on the style and structure of the wine. They can require anywhere from five minutes to three or four hours. That time basically allows the wine to oxidize to a point at which it is most revealing. It's a strange way of putting it, but true.

Prescription: This very important process is called "aeration." Do not underestimate its power. Try opening a bottle of wine, pouring a glass, and immediately tasting it. Let the bottle sit open for a while, pour another glass, and taste it. No doubt you'll get a lot more off the nose and flavour of the second glass than the first, because it's had more air.

Dear Dr. WineKnow:

Is it necessary to let white wine breathe before drinking it?

Diagnosis: Since white wine doesn't contain as many components as red, because of lack of contact with the grape skins, it doesn't generally require a lot of air to do its thing. The same can be said of rosés.

Prescription: For the most part, open and pour. The mere act of pouring whites from bottle to glass is enough to oxygenate them so they deliver nose and flavour. You may want to give fatter, oakier whites a little more air before serving, to let the wood attack subside.

Dear Dr. WineKnow:

Does "bubbly" require breathing time?

Diagnosis: The key to sparkling wine is the bubbles. If they disappear, the wine becomes flat and the whole point is lost. Also, the nature of this style of wine sees streams of bubbles coming to the surface as soon as it is poured. In essence, it is self-aerating.

Prescription: Do not aerate bubbly. Open and pour immediately. As mentioned above, it's a good idea to invest in a pressure cap for bubbly. Replace the pressure cap on the bottle after each pour to retain the fizz, otherwise the wine will go flat pretty quickly.

Dear Dr. WineKnow:

Even if I open a young or big red wine and let it breathe for an hour or two, it still seems closed. Any advice on how to solve this problem?

Diagnosis: When one considers that the opening in a wine bottle is about the size of a dime, the amount of air that can enter it is limited. There really isn't enough surface area to provide air quickly. Young or big reds require a lot of air to bring out their soul. If you leave it uncorked for many hours the wine may receive enough air to open up the wine, but the risk of oxidation becomes a real danger.

Prescription: Decant this style of wine. A large carafe or pitcher, where the mouth of the container is larger to allow more air to come and go will do a better job. Depending on how big the wine is, one to two hours in a decanter should provide better, more open, aromatics.

DECANTER SHAPES

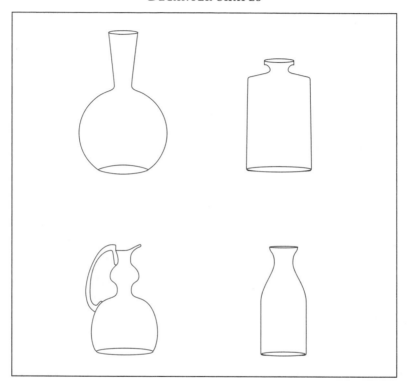

Dear Dr. WineKnow:
My husband called at the last minute and told me he was bringing the boss home for dinner in forty minutes. Fortunately, I had made enough for dinner to accommodate a guest. However, the only wine I had on hand to serve was a big red that needed lots of breathing time. Even decanting it would not be long enough.
Diagnosis: It's really difficult to bring a big red around quickly. There's just too much stuffing and density to aerate it fast.
Prescription: Decanting into a very large container or pitcher

might speed up the process. How about juggling the wine. Get two decanters and pour the wine back and forth six to eight times. This should speed up the aeration substantially.

Dear Dr. WineKnow:
How much aeration time should I allow for an old red wine?
Diagnosis: Since old reds are usually mature, and many of the components are ripe, ready, and fine, they don't require much breathing time. Often the mere act of pouring them into a decanter and then into the glass is more than enough.
Prescription: Consider the alternative. If you wait too long to allow breathing time, the wine may die in the glass before your very nose. Only open old reds exactly when you are ready to drink them. Decant quickly, and immediately pour yourself a glass. This way they will come to life fast and you won't miss any part of their rise and fall.

GRAPE FLASH

Did you know that aeration, or breathing time, is not a substitute for bottle age? A case in point is the story of a former student of mine who had in his possession a wine that theoretically needed approximately three more years of ageing to drink well. In his wisdom, he decided to open it on a Friday, for dinner on Saturday, with hopes that the excess air would bring it around. On paper, this theory doesn't sound bad. In reality, though, it was a very bad idea. Wine needs air to open up and bring out the aromatics and flavours. However, if it is not yet ready to drink or at its peak because it is tannic or hard, aeration will not help. In this case, only three more years in the bottle would help it develop to a drinkable state and nothing in this world could change that. Needless to say, my young student ended up with a closed, oxidized wine for Saturday's dinner.

Dear Dr. WineKnow:

Sometimes when I decant an old red, I use a coffee filter or strainer to get the last bit of wine from the bottle.

Diagnosis: This is a real "no-no." When I previously said to forfeit whatever wine remains after the sediment reaches the lip of the bottle when decanting, I meant it. The use of a paper coffee filter or metal strainer might render that little extra remaining wine but it will be tarnished with a papery or metallic smell/taste and infect the whole decanter. Is this really worth it?

Prescription: Never, ever filter any wine through any material to save the dredges of a bottle. Give it up!!!

Dear Dr. WineKnow:

I recently opened a bottle of wine that smelled kind of funky. I wasn't quite sure if it was defective or not. Anyway, I got busy and forgot about it. When I finally came back to it, I was surprised to find it smelling fine. Can you explain what happened?

Diagnosis: This phenomenon is known as "bottle stink." Imagine this. You're locked in an airtight closet for two years. The door is finally opened. Do you not think some musky, old dull air might emerge? Well, the same sometimes applies to wine. Also, "off" smells can result from moulds and bacteria in corks or capsules and from seeping wine. Even the bottling process might pass on an unpleasant aroma. Sulphur dioxide, added to combat this, also sometimes remains in a wine for a while after uncorking.

Prescription: Open the bottle and hold your nose. If your next bottle of wine smells a bit funny but not "off," it could be "bottle stink." Either decant it, regardless what colour it is, or wait a while to see if the smell goes away.

A Glass Act

The wine glass is the final outpost. It's what carries the wine to its ultimate end, your mouth. Interestingly enough, the glass can

WINE TASTING GLASS

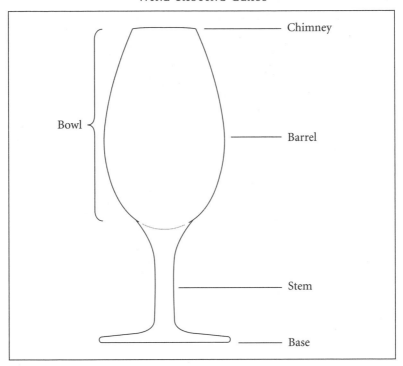

make or break what is perceived in a wine, even if the wine is prepared properly beforehand. It can be the bearer of sad tidings or the herald of ecstasy. It possesses that power. Sad indeed is the occasion when a great wine is foiled by the messenger.

Dear Dr. WineKnow:
What is the best type of glass from which to taste wine?
Diagnosis: The best type of glass is one that highlights a wine's positive points and minimizes its negative ones.
Prescription: Generally speaking, the glass should be large enough to be held comfortably. It should possess a reasonably sized barrel to provide maximum surface area to allow you to swirl the wine, without slopping it on yourself or others. The chimney or lip of the glass should taper inward to prevent spillage and direct aromas and

GLASS SHAPES

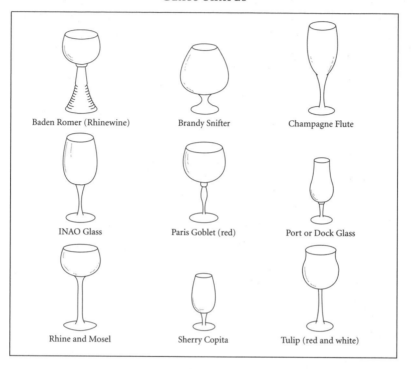

bouquet up to the olfactory senses (nose). It should possess a reasonably long stem for holding, and a good solid base for balance. It's not necessary to spend a fortune on glassware. Get yourself some INAO tasting glasses (developed by the French Institut National des Appellations d'Origin). These good, all-purpose tasting glasses, considered the industry standard, are available through most stores that sell wine-related items and paraphernalia. Glasses like these or something similar should do a nice job in giving you the best chance to appreciate the wine.

Dear Dr. WineKnow:
I find when I taste wine out of larger glasses or those with bulbous bowls, it tastes different than out of smaller, narrower ones. Does size and shape make a difference?

Diagnosis: Yes indeed, size does matter, and so does shape. The size of the tasting glass plays an integral part in your appreciation. Very generally, larger-bowled glasses are preferable to smaller ones, since they provide more surface area for the wine to breathe and release aromatics. This is especially beneficial with red wines. Larger glasses also feel better in the hand. Shape also plays a role. Certain glasses, because of their shape, trap aromatics and don't allow alcohol to evaporate. This can make a wine seem dumb with little bouquet or smell extremely alcoholic.

Prescription: Do not dumb down your wines. As a general rule use larger glasses with bigger bowls for red wines and smaller glasses with narrower bowls for whites.

GRAPE FLASH

Did you know that there is now on the market state-of-the-art stemware that takes wine appreciation to a supreme level? These glasses are specifically designed to enhance the qualities of each wine style and grape variety. Since each wine style or grape variety has a different predominant factor, these glasses are aerodynamically shaped to bring out a specific flavour and emphasize the character. Determination of the shape is based on analysis of how different taste characteristics are optimized on the nose and palate by small variations in glass design.

Certain shapes direct the aromatics and smells to the nose differently than others. How the wine hits the palate when tasted is extremely important. Some focus the wine so that it hits the tip of the tongue first and then allows the flavour to spread out over the palate. Others work differently. It's all a matter of physics.

I have had the pleasure, a number of times, of taking part in various glass seminars conducted by famed glass-maker, George Riedel. We tasted specific wines/grape varieties out of his glasses made for the specific wines. Then we repoured the wines into the glasses that were not designed for the specific style/grape variety. What an astonishing difference in perception it was! Sometimes the alcohol stuck out like rocket fuel. In other cases the wines appeared unbalanced. In still others, they appeared "dumb" (total lack of aromatics or nose). We tried pouring all the wines into one of those "industrial-type" thick glasses and tasting them. They were terrible. You would get more appreciation out of swigging any of the wines directly from the bottle. Finally, we poured all the wines back into their appropriate stemware and tasted them again. Sheer perfection!

No matter how many times I do this taste exercise, I am amazed at the difference glass shape makes. Although this stemware is rather expensive, it is well worth the investment if you are a serious wine-lover. There are usually different series, in different price ranges, by any one producer. All series work equally well. What I recommend is this. If you, on average, spend ten to twenty dollars on a bottle of wine, that's what you should spend per stem. If you regularly purchase twenty- to thirty-dollar bottles, then that should be your price per glass. Your regular bottle purchase price should roughly equal what each glass should cost. Trust me on this one, you'll never go back to ordinary stemware again. Consider it an investment in good taste.

Dear Dr. WineKnow:
Does the thickness of a wine glass make a difference in perception? **Diagnosis:** It may not make a difference if drinking juice, pop, water, or other alcoholic beverages, but when it comes to wine, thickness is somewhat important. From the point of view of sheer comfort, thinner glass feels better in the hand and against the mouth. It also looks more aesthetic. But the real importance of glass thickness is realized in the appreciation aspect. Thinner glass allows the wine to warm up more quickly and give off more aromatics. This is a key note in what you perceive.

Prescription: Use thin glasses, if possible. Unfortunately, there are a lot of thick wine glasses out there, used merely as a deterrent against breakage. This "industrial-type" stemware, although very solid, does little to enhance the wine. Most better restaurants utilize thinner glasses. When dining out, you don't have a say in what glasses your wine is served in. For ultimate enjoyment at home, however, use glasses that are fairly thin, and you will notice a vast difference in what you perceive.

Dear Dr. WineKnow:

I have these lovely clay and silver wine goblets my aunt gave me for my birthday. When I use them, I never seem to be able to smell or taste much of anything. Why?

Diagnosis: Glasses are the most important tool in allowing the wine to communicate to the taster via the senses. Historically, of course, wine has been consumed from every possible type of container. Clay and metal were big back in medieval times. Of course, many people died from lead poisoning from drinking out of copper, largely because the wine was stored in the vessels and, as a result, the lead leached into the wine. Shape, size, and composition of glassware, in fact, evolved merely through ritualistic or cultural practices with very little regard for what they held. As long as the vessels contained the liquid and allowed the tasters to get at it, everything was copacetic. It really has been only in the last fifty years or so that glassware has come into prominence as the key vehicle of wine.

Prescription: Turn the clay and metal goblets into planters. Wine should be tasted out of glass and only glass. It is the most neutral environment to best show the nectar of the grape. You will find that your entire experience of wine will be totally different if you taste out of glass.

Dear Dr. WineKnow:

I bought some lovely, ornate, purple wine glasses at a department store. They look great on the dinner table, but one of my guests almost swallowed a fly at dinner because he couldn't see it in the glass.

Diagnosis: Ah yes, the old fly-in-the-glass routine! Wine appreciation is a sensual phenomenon involving the sense of sight, smell, and taste. By eliminating the visual aspect you really rob yourself of a third of the total experience. Simple, basic factors like colour, depth of colour, tint, luminescence, brilliance, viscosity, and, most importantly, clarity and cleanliness are made invisible. So you won't be able to see that fly doing the backstroke in your glass. The Exxon Valdez could have sunk in your glass and left an oil slick the size of Kentucky. The wine could have chunks of lumber floating in it. It might be murky, cloudy, or hazy. Coloured glassware reflects a traditional European fad, once developed to hide the oxidized colour of poor-quality wine.

Prescription: Make sure your wine glasses are clear, colourless, and unmarked. Forget about pictures of Donald Duck or writing on them. Many wine shows often have the show name plastered on the glass for advertising purposes. You are better off to bring your own clear tasting glass to events like these. As for the ornate, purple numbers, try putting them in a windowsill. I'm sure they'll look peachy with the sun shining through.

GRAPE FLASH

Did you know that glasses should never be chilled or warmed up before wine is poured into them? It is detrimental to whatever wine the glass holds. Warm glasses increase the rate of evaporation, forcing the alcohol to stick out. Chilled stemware "dummies" up a wine, masking its nuances. Chilling is especially hazardous to bubbly, as it kills the bubbles instantly as soon as the wine is poured into the glass. Make this a rule of thumb. Never chill or warm any stemware. If a wine needs to be chilled, that's what to do. If a wine needs warming up, because it just came out of the cellar, then it should be allowed to do so. Use glassware

> at room temperature (18 to 20°C) and allow the wine to raise or lower its temperature. So, if the glasses just came out of the dishwasher, give them some time to reach room temperature before using.

Dear Dr. WineKnow:

Why is it that people insist on using plastic wine glasses for parties? It makes me crazy.

Diagnosis: Insanity is a state of mind that boggles the wine. There is only one reason why anyone would use plastic wine glasses. They're great for clean-up. After use, simply file under "G," for garbage. However, this is not a good enough reason.

Prescription: Forget plastic, use glass. Wine consumed out of plastic tastes and smells like plastic.

Dear Dr. WineKnow:

What about lead-crystal stemware? I've heard so much negative press about them being a health hazard.

Diagnosis: The health concern here involves the leaching of lead into the wine and ultimately into the taster. Of course, the wine would have to sit in the glass for many months in order for this to happen, a very unlikely scenario. This is more likely to happen when wines or alcohol products sit for months in crystal decanters.

Prescription: Many of the better glasses on the market today contain lead crystal. The decision to use them is ultimately yours.

Dear Dr. WineKnow:

Sitting in my china cabinet are some beautiful etched cut-glass wine glasses. How do these fare for tasting?

Diagnosis: Don't they look great on the dinner table? The light plays off of them like diamonds in a store window. In essence, they actually rob the taster of some of wine's visuals. It would be better to see the light play off the wine, rather than the glass. Besides, these glasses tend to be bulky, heavy, and often poorly balanced.

Prescription: Nice to look at, but poor for tasting! My advice is to keep them displayed in the china cabinet and use plain, unetched glasses instead for optimum appreciation.

Dear Dr. WineKnow:
I find that when I sip bubbly at home in my large-barrelled glasses, the bubbles disappear very quickly. Are my glasses dirty?
Diagnosis: Chances are your glasses are clean, but are the wrong type for bubbly. The key to sparkling wine, my friend, is the bubbles. Large-barrelled glasses have too much surface area, allowing the bubbles to disappear very quickly. Too often, we are influenced by movies, where Champagne is often enjoyed in large, wide glasses. To this I say, "It's fantasy; it's phony; forget it."
Prescription: Enter the "flute." These elongated, thin-barrelled glasses have a very small surface area, maintaining the bubbles the longest. Forget the movies – invest in a few "flutes" to enjoy your bubbly and reserve the "big guns" for other wines.

GRAPE FLASH

Did you know that a clean glass is a happy glass? In order for a wine glass to do its job properly, it must be impeccably clean. Any kind of residual detergent can form a film on the inside of the glass, causing not only bad smells but lack of viscosity (thickness or richness of a wine displayed in the way it adheres to the side of the glass). Residual detergent in stemware robs bubbly of its bubbles very quickly and makes the head on a beer disappear promptly. To avoid possible residual detergent on tasting glasses, wash all your stemware in extremely hot water without detergent. Only air dry them by hanging or standing them up. Avoid towel drying them on the inside as this leaves lint and dust particles, which affect perception. Following these procedures will ensure you are not robbed of pleasure in your wine when sipping at home.

Dear Dr. WineKnow:
Does the amount of wine poured into a glass affect what is tasted?
Diagnosis: This matter of fill is very important. From a strictly physical point of view a full glass doesn't allow one to swirl the wine in the glass and it makes for more spillage. It can also affect appreciation by altering what is perceived visually and aromatically. The fuller the glass, the deeper the colour, the smaller the surface area, and the slower the rate of evaporation of the wine. Since the wine takes longer to warm up and aerate by virtue of its sheer volume, the less revealing the nose may be. Besides, a partially filled glass just looks better.
Prescription: Stemware should be filled with no more than one-quarter to one-third with wine for best appreciation, regardless of the size of the glass.

Dear Dr. WineKnow:
Although I wash my wine glasses very carefully without detergent they always smell funny. I can't figure it out.
Diagnosis: Perhaps the problem with your stemware is storage. Like wine, glassware can absorb and maintain strange "off" odours. They should not be stored near cooking areas, strong-smelling food, or chemicals. Many modern homes and restaurants keep their glasses in the kitchen area, often very close to the stove or food-preparation area. It's a common practice to have them hanging upside down in special racks over the cooking area. This just traps aromas in them. Even china cabinets or kitchen cupboards have been known to make stemware smell of excessive wood.
Prescription: Neutrality is best. Try storing your glasses in a relatively neutral place in your home, even if it's away from the dining area. The fresh glassware will make up for the small inconvenience. Never lay your glasses upside down on a towel, paper, or cupboard shelf either, as this can cause a musty, papery, dull, "off" smell in them.

Dear Dr. WineKnow:

Is there a proper way to hold a wine glass when tasting?

Diagnosis: Keep in mind that a wine glass is not like any other glass. Its shape and design really emphasizes this.

Prescription: Handle with care. Unlike water, juice, soda, or other alcoholic beverages, wine displays much about itself through what it looks like. Therefore, you never hold the glass by the barrel, since it obscures the wine. Also your hand will warm up any wine that should be chilled. Hold the glass by the stem or the base.

CHAPTER
6

HEDONISM
Enjoying It

*L*et's face it. Taste is the part of wine that is by far the most fun. Sure, how it gets from the grape to the bottle is fascinating stuff, but the real pleasure comes from indulging in it.

Wine appreciation is a sensual phenomenon, a real treat for sight, smell, and taste. Each aspect of these senses plays a key role in what is perceived overall. Eliminate any one of these senses and a certain part of the experience is lost.

Because human beings are so complex and so different from one another, there are many physical, psychological, and emotional variables that can affect appreciation. Even a taster's health plays a large role. Add to this the abundance of other elements such as environment, where you taste, and the effect that food has on your perception and it's a wonder any of us can agree on a wine's merit at all.

The Human Condition

Generally speaking, who you are, your makeup, and your life history all affect your experience of wine and what you perceive in it. Since we all differ in these ways our individual perception of wine has a uniquely personal character. What you perceive in wine is not necessarily the same what as the person next to you perceives.

Let's Get Physical

Lace up those old aerobic shoes and let's get busy. We're about to exercise our understanding of how our physical selves, our personal life experience, and our socialization affect our enjoyment of wine.

Dear Dr. WineKnow:
I'm having a mega-argument with my girlfriend. She says women are the best wine tasters. I say men are. What do you think?
Diagnosis: I could really be opening up a can of worms in answering this question. However, certain evidence indicates that gender *does* play a part in the ability to taste wine. One of the main differences in men and women, other than the obvious, is chemical, and more specifically, hormonal. Hormones are carried in the blood, which supplies all our senses and affects our brain activity. Women, generally, have a more acute sense of smell. This is directly related to the female hormone, estrogen.

Sorry, guys. Since wine appreciation is about 70 to 75 per cent smell, this one factor would potentially make women better tasters than men. Notice I use the word "potentially," though. Many other factors play a part in the battle of the sexes and determining who's the better taster.

Dear Dr. WineKnow:
I'm the only woman wine buyer my company has. All the rest are men. At buying sessions, I notice I smell much more in wine at certain times than others, and I constantly get ribbed about it by my male colleagues. It's really weird.

Diagnosis: Although this may sound rather unusual, it really is not. We can blame our old friend estrogen again here. Science shows that, although women's sense of smell is more acute overall, it tends to be variable at different times and can really affect sensitivity. Sensitivity is most acute when estrogen levels are highest. Therefore judgement calls can vary due to estrogen levels in women.

Dear Dr. WineKnow:
I often taste wine with my wife. It astonishes me how she has such a great handle on describing a wine's colour. To me, it's either red or white.

Diagnosis: There's a very sound reason for this. As a rule, women tend to be more colour-conscious than men. In fact, scientific research shows that 8 per cent of all men are colour blind, while less than one half of one per cent of all women are afflicted. This could account for differences in visual judgements of wine. Add to this the fact that, due to socialization, women, right from childhood, seem to get more practice matching colours when buying clothes and accessories, choosing cosmetics, etc. They simply possess better visual judgement in this area.

Prescription: Taste wine with your wife more often. Maybe some of that colour/visual judgement will rub off on you. It's always a good idea to taste with people who are more advanced than you. It creates a great environment in which to learn.

GRAPE FLASH

Did you know that women show a stronger preference for the sweet component of taste than men? They sometimes crave sweets more often than men, and find most dessert wines wonderfully rich and unctuous. This is all due, once again, to estrogen. Therefore, women might sometimes have a hard time accurately evaluating the sweet component in wine.

Dear Dr. WineKnow:

In my experience, women are better at describing a wine's body, weight, or mouth feel than men. They just seem to have a knack for it.

Diagnosis: Truer words were never spoken. Women generally show a superior sensitivity to touch than do men, and this sensitivity increases with age, according to science. So it follows that they would be better evaluators of body, weight, or mouth feel and overall richness of wine.

Prescription: Keep in mind that the body or weight of a wine has to do with the tactile sensation in the mouth. This is strictly how it feels on the palate. Richer or fuller wines are more oily or creamy on the palate. Lighter wines are thinner and don't have an oily, creamy feel to them. By rubbing your tongue over your gums while a wine is in there, you can get some idea of its richness.

Dear Dr. WineKnow:

Will I become a better taster as I get older?

Diagnosis: I'd like to tell you that age is a state of mind, but there are certain medical effects as a person ages. There is a simple physical deterioration of sensitivity and, ultimately, of perception. At around age forty, there is some reduction in sensitivity, due to ageing sensory receptors and the decline of neural efficiency. This brings about a noted decrease in sensitivity to such components as sweetness, bitterness, and saltiness. These are key components of wine, so they become harder to detect. There is a gradual deterioration in colour vision, due to a reduction of the pupil size in the eye, which lets in less light. Odour sensitivity becomes greatly reduced. What you could smell in a wine when younger becomes harder to decipher.

Prescription: You can teach an old dog new tricks. These are but a few of the downfalls of ageing. However, there is a positive note to be found here. Hopefully, as one ages, one logs up more tasting experience. So what is lost through ageing can be somewhat balanced by experience.

Dear Dr. WineKnow:

I'm sixty-three years old and have a very hard time identifying flavours in blended wines I taste. Single varietal wines are no problem for me.

Diagnosis: Sense of taste also changes with age. There's no doubt that ability to identify flavours, especially when blended, as in Bordeaux, Rhône reds, and Meritage, is reduced. Simple medical science has proven this. The palate has a much more difficult time separating and distinguishing individual flavours.

Prescription: Although not much can be done to alleviate this, more tasting of blended wines might help. Increased tastings of individual grape varieties to build up a real solid library of their characters should help you pick them out when they are blended.

GRAPE FLASH

Did you know that "dry mouth" syndrome can affect tasting prowess? As one ages, the inside of the mouth dries up, requiring more moisture on the palate for it to work efficiently. Everything from simple talking to wine tasting will be affected. This common affliction usually kicks in as you enter your seventies. Sipping lots of water while drinking wine to help lubricate the palate should add more moisture and keep the "whistle wet," as it were.

Dear Dr. WineKnow:

I've been drinking a glass or two of wine with dinner since I was twenty-one. Now in my mid-eighties, I'm healthy, and I still enjoy it, but I can't pick out as much in wine as I used to. Can you explain why?

Diagnosis: Kudos to you. As you get older, reaction times become slower. It's only natural as neural efficiency declines. This becomes evident when several wines are presented quickly or are complex

in structure. You may have difficulty in focussing or dividing attention. Even motor control and activity are lessened, affecting tasting technique and ultimately, perception. We simply slow down.
Prescription: Don't change a thing. It's obviously keeping you in good shape. Enjoy whatever you get out of wine. It'll probably keep you going forever.

Dear Dr. WineKnow:
Does a person's height or weight affect wine tasting?
Diagnosis: I don't think there is any scientific evidence that suggests either of these two variables affect perception, even if the wine is swallowed. Just because someone is taller or larger doesn't necessarily mean they will be more or less affected by wine even if ingested. It's a matter of tolerance.

Dear Dr. WineKnow:
I belong to a tasting group made up of many ethnic groups. When we discuss the wines after tasting, we never seem to agree on anything. Could this have something to do with our cultural backgrounds?
Diagnosis: You bet your stemware it could! Given that all tasters are created equal on a physical level, there are definitely certain cultural elements that would account for differences in perception. Within the physiological chemistry of every person from a particular culture, there may be inherent genes governing specific aspects of their being. Certain sensitivities, tastes, and physiological handicaps that have evolved over centuries, and have become characteristics of that group of people, might make it very difficult for them to perceive certain components in wine. The cultural mores of specific groups may treat alcohol in unusual ways and these can create attitudes towards it and ultimately inhibit perception of taste.
Prescription: Although rising above these inherent, individual characteristics that may affect tasting ability can be difficult, it can

be done. Recognition of your specific tasting handicap is the start. Then you need lots of practice in tasting wines that highlight the problem area. Even palate-training exercises can help. It's also a great idea to continue tasting with folks from other cultures, who have neutral or different palates, so you can play off them.

GRAPE FLASH

Did you know that religious denomination can affect wine appreciation? If people taste only sweet sacramental wine during religious ceremonies, then they might never develop a taste for drier wine. It can become a conditioned reflex, as well as a psychological one. If a person in this situation actually has a desire to enjoy drier wine, a weaning process must take place. By tasting wines with slightly less sweetness and reducing that sweetness over a long period of time, you can retrain yourself to appreciate drier styles.

Dear Dr. WineKnow:

Can your diet play a part in what you perceive in wine?

Diagnosis: Diet is one of the most aggressive manipulators of the palate and can play an extensive part in what you taste in wine. This can be seen quite clearly when it comes to ethnic foods. If, for instance, spicy food is a regular part of your daily diet, it could hamper your identification of spice in wine, as well as numb your palate to other complexity. In fact, your taste buds could be burned out to the point that appreciation of subtle spice and other elements in wine will never be fully realized. Alternately, if a bland diet is your norm, your sensitivity to any strong flavours and components could be intense. A fatty diet could rob you of your appreciation of body in wine. A highly acidic diet could obscure balance in wine.

Prescription: You are what you eat. Palate training and conditioning again are the keys to all of these diet-related problems. It's certainly much easier to go in the other direction. To develop a taste for spice one need only taste wines regularly with increasingly spicy characters.

Dear Dr. WineKnow:
I'm sure lifestyle affects wine appreciation. Any thoughts on this?
Diagnosis: Although this is not obviously an issue, it can play a part. Folks with an affluent lifestyle may find themselves exposed more to wine, and so develop a better understanding of it. Certainly, more disposable income to purchase wine is an important factor, allowing you to experience more widely. Even the pace of a person's lifestyle could make some difference. A laid-back lifestyle might allow someone's approach to wine to be more systematic and detailed.
Prescription: Whatever your lifestyle, you should always take time to "smell the roses." This includes sitting down and enjoying the nectar of the grape. If you do so, you have a better chance to develop an appreciation of wine.

Dear Dr. WineKnow:
Most tastings take place in the evening. However, I notice that I pick up far more things in a wine when I taste earlier in the day. Why is this?
Diagnosis: The time of day when you taste wine certainly plays a part in what you perceive. Although most people would not even dream of coming near wine before midday at the earliest, the palate is sharpest and most sensitive in the morning, since it is fresh, with little to taint it. As the day passes, food and drink coat the palate, making it harder for you to pick up nuances.
Prescription: If you are tasting wine to make buying decisions, try to restrict this to the morning hours and reserve the latter part of the day for pure hedonistic enjoyment.

GRAPE FLASH

Did you know that whether you're a "day" or "night" person can affect your palate sensitivity? Let me explain. It's a fact of life. Some people perform better in the earlier part of the day and fade quickly in the evening while others are the opposite. Because it's simply not your "time of day," cognitive problem-solving ability can be affected, and ultimately, what you perceive when tasting wine is altered. Recognizing what kind of individual you are and when you are at peak performance during the day can aid in tasting ability and what is perceived.

Dear Dr. WineKnow:

When I order wine to accompany a meal, it always tastes more complex to me before I actually start eating. Isn't that odd?

Diagnosis: This really isn't unusual. Your tasting senses are more acute on an empty stomach or when you are hungry. When food is in the stomach, blood is forced there to help digest, and concentration suffers somewhat. Any boss knows better than to call a staff meeting directly after lunch.

Prescription: To get the most out of wine when ordering it in a restaurant or having it at home, taste the wine first, before involving food. This way, as well, the wine gets a chance to stand alone, without the complication of food flavours.

Dear Dr. WineKnow:

Why is it that Champagne seems to go to my head faster than still wine?

Diagnosis: This age-old question is posed by many people. This is quite interesting as the majority of sparkling wines are not overly alcoholic, most a maximum of about 12 to 12.5 per cent alcohol by volume. It's all in the bubbles. The bubbles allow the wine, and more specifically, the alcohol, to oxygenate in your blood quicker.

Therefore, you feel its effect over a shorter period of time and usually with just a minimal amount.

Prescription: Keep this in mind when enjoying it. You may want to drink much slower, consume less, nibble food, and sip on water to combat its attack on your system.

GRAPE FLASH

Did you know that some people taste more accurately while standing, while others get more out of wine while seated? It's all a matter of comfort. Standing while tasting gives more freedom of movement. It allows the taster to obtain a quicker and more accurate picture of a wine, especially in a clinical setting (no food). You can taste more wines, utilizing one glass, as you simply move down a line of wines sitting on a countertop. The drawback though might make this position distracting to others. If you taste better in this position, wine shows and fairs should work well for you, since walking and standing are the name of the game.

Sitting while tasting is certainly more comfortable. It allows you to concentrate on the wines, particularly in a clinical setting. As a result, your impressions and notes are a little more delayed, but more detail can be logged. However, you can usually taste fewer wines as the logistics of set up and glassware become tedious. If tasting seated is your thing, you had best stay away from wine shows. Sit-down, conducted tastings are for you.

The Healthy Taster

When asked why he consumed a glass of wine a day, the man simply replied, "I only take it for medicinal purposes." Believe it or not, there is a lot of truth to this statement. In the nineteenth century, wine was used extensively as a restorative for certain illnesses. As it turns out, today, wine still plays somewhat of the same role when moderately consumed.

Your physical health is a factor that definitely affects your wine appreciation and most everything in life. If you are not feeling well, it's hard to gain enjoyment from simple everyday tasks, let alone from wine. If you have a health problem, you may never have ideal tasting prowess. That is to say, a physically healthy taster presents a wine with the most neutral environment. If you are not in good physical health, you may want to forego tasting wine or at least be prepared to not get the most out of it.

Dear Dr. WineKnow:
When I have a cold, wine tastes like nothing to me. Is there anything I can do to overcome this?
Diagnosis: Most colds stuff up the nose. Breathing becomes laboured, and smelling is practically impossible. As wine appreciation is approximately 70 to 75 per cent nose, this is a real problem. Since taste is so much a large part of smell, it too would be drastically hampered. However, the sense of taste in human beings is relatively poor. Most of us attribute many things to taste that are really more a part of smell.

To prove just how poor sense of taste is, try the following exercise. Get hold of a raw potato and a delicious apple. Peel both and cut them into quarters. Cover your eyes and hold your nose. Have someone feed you one or the other. Chances are, if you can't see it and, more importantly, can't smell it, you won't be able to tell which it is.
Prescription: Unfortunately, there's not too much that can be done to aid in wine appreciation if a cold has you in its grip. It's probably not a good idea to be drinking wine anyway.

Dear Dr. WineKnow:
Unfortunately, I'm afflicted with sinusitis, hay fever, and allergies. They really "stuff up" my enjoyment of wine.

Diagnosis: You have my sincerest sympathy. These common maladies that block the olfactory senses are no fun and rob wine appreciation of its pleasure – big time. Besides, you may find yourself sneezing all over the wine and others.

Prescription: Try to reserve tasting for times when the problem is not bothering you. Perhaps the use of some nose drops before tasting might help to clear the old beezer. However, do check the drops to see that they don't have any precautions about mixing with wine (also, don't use antihistamines). If you do use drops, apply a half-hour before tasting. This will ensure no residual flavours hang in and affect your taste, as drops tend to spill over into the throat.

Dear Dr. WineKnow:

I often get headaches from red wine. Can you explain why?

Diagnosis: You are not alone in this problem. Many people experience headaches from red wine. Most of the time, they are reactions to something in the wine. Since red wine utilizes the skins of the grape in production, there are many more components present, such as phenols and tannins. Tannin is a major contributor to headaches, because the dry, drawing sensation on the palate puts a strain on the taste glands, causing one to tense up, thus producing a headache. (Allergies may cause headaches, but allergies are usually caused by other components in grape skins, such as sulphur.)

Prescription: Avoid overly tannic reds. You should seek out those that have been soft-pressed or produced through carbonic maceration. Since most wines do not indicate the method of pressing on the labels, you'll have to ask for assistance in picking them.

GRAPE FLASH

Did you know that wines fermented or aged in oak can cause headaches or stuffy noses? Although ye old barrel has a real affinity for wine, it does present some problems to certain people. It's the histamines in wood that do the damage. Histamines tend to foil the olfactory senses by filling them up

> with mucous, which in turn yields sinus headaches. Even if
> you adore that wonderful kiss of oak in your wines, you may
> want to steer clear of them if you are afflicted. Choose vinos
> that have not seen oak, or very little of it.

Dear Dr. WineKnow:

Even though red or oak-treated wines don't usually bother me, I
still occasionally get headaches from them. What else could be
the cause?

Diagnosis: Perhaps your wine-related headaches are caused when
you are presented with the bill after a meal in a restaurant.
Seriously, you may still be reacting to something in the wine. There
is a good possibility that you are sensitive to sulphur. You see,
grapes and winemaking equipment are often sprayed with some
sort of sulphur mixture to kill bacteria before usage. If you are sensitive or allergic to this substance, you could very easily develop
headaches after consumption. Even if excessive or residual sulphur
is not used in the vineyard or winery, it's really hard to avoid it, as
sulphur is a natural bi-product of fermentation.

Prescription: Look for wines that say "organic" on the label. This
means that at least no excess sulphur has been used in their production. It also implies that only natural pesticides and fungicides
have been used to combat pests and disease. Finding "organic"
wines may prove to be tedious, as most retailers don't market them
under designated signs. Do ask for help when looking for these.

Dear Dr. WineKnow:

My spouse tells me I snore while sleeping after drinking some
wine. What could cause this?

Diagnosis: Being a fellow sufferer, I can sympathize. Oaky wines
are the culprit. My wife always instinctively knows by my snoring
when I have been out for a business dinner and have had wine with
oak. The colour doesn't matter. If a wine has seen oak in any
format, it can induce snoring. The histamines in oak stuff up the

nose, making breathing difficult. So the mouth opens to assist and, voilá, snoring begins.

Prescription: Lay off the oaky wines. That is, if you don't want to spend your nights sleeping on the couch.

Dear Dr. WineKnow:

Can medication for health problems affect wine appreciation?

Diagnosis: Alcohol often negates most medication and the drugs can't do what they are supposed to. Chemically, alcohol and drugs cause adverse reactions. Certain drugs may exaggerate component sensitivity. Much relatively mild and commonly used medication dries the mouth out, affecting taste. A simple thing like Aspirin could alter sensitivity. Furthermore, there is a residual effect of drugs and alcohol together. Sometimes even after you stop taking medication, it can take a while until it is totally out of your system.

Prescription: Do not mix drugs and alcohol. If you are on medication, don't drink wine.

GRAPE FLASH

Did you know that smokers are just as good at tasting wine as non-smokers? This is rather interesting, since from a strictly physiological perspective there are certain things about smokers to consider. Medical science shows that they absorb several active chemicals like nicotine, tar, and carbon monoxide. These substances enter the body through the mouth and nose and, by nature of their coating action, have to affect the sense of taste. All one needs to do is examine a smoker's stained fingers, mouth, and throat, not to mention X-rays of his or her lungs, to see the coating action. Because of this the absolute thresholds of taste are higher for smokers than for nonsmokers. Nonetheless, it's interesting to note that some of the best tasters in the world are smokers.

Dear Dr. WineKnow:
I'm one of those people who is drastically affected by lack of sunlight in the winter months (SAD syndrome). As a result, I enjoy wine far more in spring and summer.
Diagnosis: Many people suffer from this condition and it does affect their enjoyment of wine and other aspects of life in the winter. Some people become depressed, lethargic, or develop headaches as a result.
Prescription: You could drink wine only in the warmer months, but this would truly be SAD. Seriously, if you are afflicted, try sampling wine at the midpoint of the day in winter, when the sun is at its highest.

Dear Dr. WineKnow:
I've read that there are health benefits to moderate consumption of wine. Is this true?
Diagnosis: Generally, moderate alcohol consumption, including that of wine, does have some health benefits. Overall, problem areas such as digestion, stress, and blood circulation can lead to heart attack and stroke, and wine can definitely aid you in reducing these liabilities. It does so by increasing the "good cholesterol" in your system that cleans up the arteries (that is, it acts as an antioxidant). Phenolics from wine, especially red, chemically modify the lipoproteins, the fraction of the blood fats that determine the development of coronary artery disease.
Prescription: The key here is MODERATE consumption. It's a fallacy to believe that if a little does you some good, a lot will do you more. It doesn't work that way.

Dear Dr. WineKnow:
I've heard that red wine is actually better for you than white. How so?
Diagnosis: It's all in the polyphenols. Similar to the types found in fresh fruits and vegetables, teas, grains, and seeds, these polyphenols

act as antioxidants. They reduce the speed and level at which our bodies are affected by oxidative stress. This stress can kill our cells and cause disease, especially cancer. Red wines tend to contain much larger amounts of polyphenols, because they have more tannin and colour. However, don't write off white wine entirely. Certain recent scientific research has discovered that white wine can prevent the development of diseases such as rheumatoid arthritis and osteoporosis that affect the bones and joints. Apparently, white wine is made up of smaller molecules than red, and contains not only some antioxidants, as well, but tyrosol and caffeic acid, which act as anti-inflammatories. (The smaller molecules containing these chemicals are absorbed into the system more efficiently.)

Prescription: Doctor's orders, drink a glass of red and white wine each day. Since red wines contain more polyphenols because of their colour and tannin, young, full-bodied selections should provide the most. Then simply chase the red down with a glass of white to ensure the anti-inflammatory benefits. Think of it as medication you can live with.

GRAPE FLASH

Did you know that wine drinkers have healthier habits, overall, than beer or liquor drinkers? Danish researchers have found that wine drinkers are less likely to abuse alcohol, thus reducing the risk of related illnesses. In fact, they concluded that wine drinkers generally have a lower mortality rate than beer or liquor consumers – or those who abstain altogether.

It's All in Your Head

Psychological and emotional factors that affect how and what we experience in wine are numerous and extremely complex. Without the psyche, there would be no appreciation, or for that fact, anything. It is our minds that assimilate information about the physical world around us and process it into something understandable. The mind receives the input from a wine, via the eyes, nose, and palate, and directs reaction.

The psychological, mental, and emotional health of the taster is a very touchy subject in wine appreciation. Whether you should be tasting wine at all if problems exist in these areas is questionable. However, examination of these factors may account for differences in enjoyment.

Dear Dr. WineKnow:

Do people with high IQs make better tasters?

Diagnosis: The basis of intelligence is a person's ability to perceive logical relationships and use their knowledge to solve problems associated with human reasoning. To taste, deduce wine quality, and put one's findings about the merits of the wine in understandable terms requires a certain amount of cognitive ability.

However, a high IQ alone will not guarantee that a person is a good taster. Many variables like experience, education, and drive can either reinforce and strengthen or detract from wine perception.

Dear Dr. WineKnow:

A friend of mine says people with more education or schooling make better tasters. Is this true?

Diagnosis: Piffle, I say. Is a taster with a Ph.D. better equipped to evaluate and get more out of a wine than someone with a high-school education? The answer is no. General education does not play any significant part in perception of wine, beyond increasing your ability to express what you are experiencing.

Prescription: Only one type of education makes a difference in perception and can improve wine appreciation: wine education. A better understanding of what wine is, how and where it is grown and made, grape varieties, service, storage, and the tasting art provide the best possible foundation for enhanced perception. Understanding is the key to knowing what to look for in wine. One need only add experience to flourish.

Dear Dr. WineKnow:
My memory is atrocious. I can taste a wine and a half hour later not remember what it was like.
Diagnosis: Sorry, what was the question? The bad part is that this problem seems to worsen with age. Memory is a real plus in wine appreciation. Remembering and recognizing certain sensory characteristics is crucial to judging wine. What good is building up that "wine library" of characteristic smells and tastes in the brain if you can't recall them when desired? A good memory saves time, promotes better results, and allows the taster to sample more products.
Prescription: Memory alone is not essential. Closely related is experience. It is impossible to remember, let alone identify, a characteristic that you have not previously experienced. To increase your memory in general and especially for wine, try shaking your brain cells up a bit. No, don't jump on some amusement-park ride that rearranges your molecules. You need to stimulate the brain. If you are right-handed, try brushing your teeth with your left hand. Instead of smelling coffee first thing in the morning, take a whiff of vanilla extract. These stimulating changes from the normal help fire your brain's neurons, strengthening memory. Of course, you should also make tasting notes. This way you have documentation that acts as a great reference tool.

Dear Dr. WineKnow:
I pride myself in being very logical. Will this aid in my tasting prowess?
Diagnosis: Being logical implies the ability to reason in a rational, organized order in which ideas and things fall into place naturally and sensibly, providing easier understanding. Logic can indeed enhance or detract from intelligence when it comes to wine appreciation.
Prescription: Make sure you follow the correct procedure when tasting. Always visually examine a wine first, then move on to the nose, and finally the palate. This logical approach should enable data about the wine to fall correctly into place.

GRAPE FLASH

Did you know that good powers of concentration are a real plus for a wine taster? Without them, it is very difficult to focus on and isolate specific senses and smells, thus increasing your sensitivity to them. Bringing past bad or good experiences and potential future ones into the tasting environment certainly gets in the way, as well. Since the biggest deterrents to concentration with respect to wine are distractions such as extraneous noises and smells, eliminating them is the key. Try finding a quiet tasting space at a big event to do your thing. Make sure it is away from food, so their smells don't interfere. When setting up tastings, try to avoid these bothersome stimuli. It is possible to train yourself to concentrate better on a wine through mental exercises, too. Some simple yoga mind-clearing exercises before tasting can help.

Dear Dr. WineKnow:

Sometimes I'm in the mood to taste wine and sometimes not. Can my mood play a part in what I perceive?

Diagnosis: Surely there is no one on this planet who is not familiar with the expression "I'm just not in the mood to do that." Mood plays a large part in complete appreciation of anything. This includes wine. It is, however, easy to enjoy some things, even though not in the mood. For me, it's chocolate. When it comes to wine, there are certain scenarios where this is applicable. In a relaxed, social setting, where superficial appreciation of wine is all that is required, mood doesn't matter. Quite the opposite is true in a clinical setting. Here alertness, focus, and the will to dissect a wine qualitatively are required. Given that, it is not hard to understand how being in a good or bad mood can affect your perception of wine.

Prescription: If you are in a positive mood, tackle quality judgements of wine. If not, restrict your appreciation to a social setting. Get together with friends, have some food, and simply enjoy a glass.

Dear Dr. WineKnow:
Does personality affect what is tasted in wine?
Diagnosis: Obviously, no two people are alike, and personalities are all over the map. Although personality alone has little impact on wine perception, it can presuppose an attitude, a style, or a way of looking at wine.
Prescription: I wouldn't get too hung up on this, but recognizing your own personality type could allow you to compensate for what you may or may not be doing.

Dear Dr. WineKnow:
I either like a wine or I don't. It's so hard to be objective when tasting.
Diagnosis: This is one of the most difficult parts of wine appreciation, the subjective/objective principle. It's really tough to put aside whether you like something or not and be totally objective about it. When it comes to wine, for most people, subjectivity rules. It dictates whether they like or dislike a wine based strictly on the pleasure they receive from drinking it, and not necessarily on its quality. Subjectivity simply doesn't allow them to look beyond their likes or dislikes to say whether a wine is well-made, for what it is, regardless of its appeal to them. In fact, subjectivity may force a taster to overlook quality and structural defects in a wine entirely.
Prescription: Remain objective. This allows you to determine quality based strictly on the merits or shortfalls in a wine's structure. The ability to do this does not come easily. Wine education and experience can help here, but lots and lots of practice is required.

GRAPE FLASH
Did you know that motivation plays a key role in why people taste wine? Basic psychology dictates that some form of reward is the basis for motivation in life. If we extend this to wine appreciation, there are several reasons why someone

would be motivated to taste a specific wine. In a social setting, the motivating factor or reward is the potential gastronomic pleasure derived. If pleasure falls short of expectations here, they might experience some disappointment, but really nothing is lost. Motivation in a clinical setting such as a competition or wine-buying session is much more complicated. There are usually other, more serious factors at stake. Often, in this case, a reputation may depend on the outcome. In this type of situation, the motivating factor is knowing the results of how accurate and how well one does.

Dear Dr. WineKnow:

Is it possible for someone to have a "knack," talent, or special ability for tasting wine?

Diagnosis: As far as wine appreciation goes, a "knack" or special ability is the extra power or skill one has to do the job of tasting. As in any field, some people are better equipped and have more ability than others to excel at a specific task. It's like learning to play a musical instrument. Most people can learn the technique, but those with talent will shine.

Prescription: Practise, practise, practise. Either you have a talent to excel at wine appreciation or not. However, education, practice, and experience can heighten any ability.

Dear Dr. WineKnow:

When I'm at a wine tasting, I don't comment on the wines for fear of making a fool of myself.

Diagnosis: Confidence is an all-important factor. Without it, you would never share your comments on the wine tasted. You have to feel comfortable with the subject material before voicing your opinions.

Prescription: Become a "confidence" man or woman. To gain it, taste wine often and take a wine-appreciation course to form a firm foundation that will lead to a lifetime of appreciation.

Dear Dr. WineKnow:

I know a fair bit about wine. However, I must admit that when I am around really knowledgeable tasters, I find myself faltering. How can I keep this from affecting or bothering me?

Diagnosis: No matter how adept we think we are at something, when in the presence of someone who is better, we tend to feel less adequate. In cases like this, our confidence gets a mite shaky and we are apt to make mistakes. Prime situations where this happens are in some restaurants dealing with very knowledgeable wine waiters or sommeliers and at group tastings.

Prescription: Don't be intimidated. Relax and use those opportunities to learn more about wine by asking questions and seeking advice.

GRAPE FLASH

Did you know that your emotional state can affect what you perceive in wine? Emotions can dictate your overall view of life in general, and wine is part of life. Emotions are the triggers for so many things, including health, attitude, mood, and motivation. Your emotional state might highlight positive or negative elements and components in wine, and you won't get the real picture. If you are feeling emotional, wine may not be the best thing to drink anyway. Waiting until emotions subside is probably best.

Dear Dr. WineKnow:

When I read tasting notes in wine magazines or hear professionals talking about wines, I have a hard time understanding what they mean. They seem to have a language all their own.

Diagnosis: Every profession and sport has a language unto itself with respect to terminology. Until you master the specific terminology of any of these, understanding and communication is jeopardized. The world of wine is no different in this regard. If you don't know the terminology of wine it may even alter your perception, simply because you don't understand what is being talked about or what you read. This is especially true when it comes to tasting notes.

Prescription: Flip to the back of any wine book – like this one – first. Consulting a glossary or index of tasting terms like the one you will find there can help. However, real understanding comes from knowledge. Learning all the basics of wine appreciation and much practice will bring the language to life and it will have more meaning for you.

Dear Dr. WineKnow:

At an event recently, I could not bring myself to taste a specific wine. As soon as I saw the label, I remembered it as the same wine that once made me really sick in my travels. Can I overcome this?

Diagnosis: This is simply a case of preconceived notions about a wine from its label. In this case seeing the label of the specific wine that made you sick reminded you of all the bad feelings associated with it. You assumed this wine would do the same again and, as a result, couldn't taste it. Perhaps after seeing a label, you remembered some negative or positive press you had read about the wine, producer, or property and you formed an opinion before tasting it. An initial taste of something like Retsina from Greece could set up a pattern of conditioned reactions to all wine labelled Retsina. The same could apply to a wine's packaging. You might automatically assume that wine with a screw cap would be of inferior quality, since they are normally used on inexpensive wine. Even bottle shapes, sizes, and colours can trigger something in your memory that affects the way you experience wine.

Prescription: The old adage, "never judge a book by its cover," is very appropriate here. Keep an open mind. Again, the only sure way to combat preconceived notions is to serve wine "blind." The wines are covered, so that preconceived ideas are avoided. This is actually the most objective and fair way to evaluate a wine.

Dear Dr. WineKnow:

How do I build up a library of descriptors in my brain to apply to wine when I taste it?

Diagnosis: It's impossible to recall something from your brain if you have never experienced it. How could you describe the nose of a wine as smelling like lychee if you have never smelled or tasted lychee?

Prescription: To become a really good taster, you need to get out in the world and smell as much as possible. Get out in the garden and smell the trees, flowers, shrubs, and bushes. When at the supermarket pick up fruits, veggies, herbs, and spices and smell them. Inevitably, all of these will make an appearance in a wine's nose or palate at some point in your life. This is the only way to build up a decent library of wine descriptors in the brain.

Dear Dr. WineKnow:

I attend many tastings, and sometimes find that where a particular wine is positioned in a tasting can influence how it shows.

Diagnosis: This very valid point is often not given enough credit. Order of presentation of wines in a tasting can influence the taster. Let me elaborate. When two or more wines are presented for tasting, the first wine tasted is generally evaluated less critically, because there is no frame of reference. Once the first wine is tasted, a frame of reference is established, and the next wine will undoubtedly be compared to the first. If the first wine tasted is exceptionally good or bad, the second wine tasted might be rated lower or higher than it really should be in comparison. A good wine following a great wine may be shafted for marks just because of where it sits in the lineup. A poor wine might make the mediocre wine that follows appear better than it actually is.

Prescription: Taste the questionable wines out of sequence. Reserve final judgements until this is done.

Dear Dr. WineKnow:

How do wine drinkers compare to beer and liquor drinkers psychologically, emotionally, and socially?

Diagnosis: A definitive answer to a question like this is hard to come by. Far too many variables come into play. However, we could look to some Danish and Dutch research for input.

Prescription: Comparatively speaking their results suggested that wine drinkers tended to have overall healthier psyches than those who consumed beer or liquor. They found that wine drinkers generally had higher education, scored higher on IQ tests, possessed higher socio-economic status, and were better adjusted. The Dutch even went as far as to claim that regular, moderate wine consumption helps ward off dementia. What do you think of that?

Tasting Is Believing

Knowing and understanding the role of each of smell, sight, and taste is imperative to your enjoyment of wine. Proper tasting technique, as well, can surely enhance or detract from your appreciation. The technique of tasting is defined as the actual, physical, motor procedure involved in looking at, smelling, and tasting wine. Correct technique allows wine to best show its stuff, providing the taster with all the vital information to totally evaluate and enjoy it. This technique can be learned.

To become really good at tasting, you need a lot of experience. However, the old adage "experience is the best teacher" is only partly true when it comes to wine. Experience can provide the taster with practice. It aids in familiarity with a multitude of wine styles, allowing the taster to better appreciate the differences. It also helps detect complexity and structure in wine beyond superficial aspects. For experience to be really effective, though, education must be added.

Every Picture Tells a Story – Visuals
Although taste is the defining point for most people when it comes to wine, the wine's appearance displays much important information. It almost always determines whether you are going to proceed

to actually taste it or not. We human beings live with our eyes. When you order a dish in a fancy restaurant, doesn't it always come to the table beautifully displayed on the plate, like a work of art? You don't even want to put a fork into it, because it would destroy the symmetry. Imagine if it came to you looking like they had simply plopped some chili on the plate – but it wasn't chili. I doubt very much if you would be enticed to put it in your mouth. The same applies to wine. It must look good enough to ingest. Visual examination is the first step in wine appreciation. It can tell you a lot about the wine before you even smell or taste it. Get used to doing it. It's an important part of the big picture.

Technique
The technique is easy. Hold the glass by the stem or base, not the barrel. You don't want to hide the viewing area. Examine it for clarity, cleanliness, luminescence (the way light plays off the wine), and reflectiveness (usually seen on a wine's surface). These are all aspects of the wine's stability. Now hold the glass on an angle against a white background. Look for colour and depth of colour. Then examine the colour in the rim, or shallower portion of the glass. This will provide information about the wine's age. Finally, swirl the wine in the glass and let it come to rest. Check out the way the wine beads around the sides. This is an indication of the wine's viscosity (thickness).

Dear Dr. WineKnow:
Certain red wines are very deeply coloured or opaque. Does this mean anything?
Diagnosis: Colour and depth of colour of a wine are good indications of its richness. Deeper-coloured wines tend to suggest better concentration and extract. This can be accomplished by extensive contact with the grape skins and "pumping over." This means the floating skins are periodically or continuously pushed down and immersed in the fermenting must and juice to maximize colour extraction. Another way to gain deep colour is to hard press. The

juice is squeezed out of the grapes utilizing a press in which metal pushes against metal.

There can be a downside to hard pressing or excessive skin contact. Too many of the bitter elements from the skins are released into the wine, causing puckering tannins or a very austere mouth feel. Characteristically, certain grape varieties like Cabernet, Zinfandel, Syrah, and Nebbiolo tend to produce deeply coloured wines anyway.

Dear Dr. WineKnow:
What do golden or browning colours in a wine mean?
Diagnosis: Golden or browning colours indicate age in a wine. Generally, the more they are present, the older the wine. White wine, when young, is often very light in colour, almost water-like. As it ages, it becomes golden, then amber, and eventually brown. Red wine starts out looking like Welch's grape juice. As it matures it becomes garnet, brick, and eventually brown, as well.
Prescription: Observe a wine's age in the rim of a glass. Browning starts to show itself here first, before moving to the deeper portion of the wine. By examining a wine's rim in a glass, you can approximate its age.

Dear Dr. WineKnow:
I sometimes notice greenish highlights in some white wines. What can this be?
Diagnosis: This phenomenon actually exists in red wine, too, it's just harder to see, because of the colour. Greenish tinges in a white wine usually indicate cool-climate production. Most whites produced in cool-climate viticultural areas display this until they mature. These areas include Canada, the United States, and most of Europe. Certain southern-hemisphere countries that are far enough away from the equator and affected by the ocean and mountains will display this, too. Places like Chile and New Zealand fall into this category. Occasionally, some warm-climate-produced whites show some green, but they are usually grown at higher altitudes.

GRAPE FLASH

Did you know that a white wine that is deeply coloured was probably extensively oak treated or produced in a warm climate? Wines that are barrel-fermented or aged for six months or more in new or small oak barrels will possess a deeper yellow colour because of the extract from the wood. In warm climates, where the grapes get almost sunburned from the heat, the fruit is harvested much riper, translating great colour to the juice. So, warm-climate whites like those from Australia, South Africa, and certain parts of South America and California are deeply coloured because of the intense sun and heat. Sometimes certain wines get a double whammy of colour by being produced in a warm climate with long oak contact.

Dear Dr. WineKnow:
At tastings, wine experts talk about "legs" in the wine. What exactly causes them and what's their importance, if any?
Diagnosis: "That wine's got legs and it knows how to use them." "Legs" are a vital indication of a wine's richness, especially when it hits the palate. They are an extension of the beading on the sides of the glass. It's all due to glycerol. After a glass of wine is swirled and gravity pulls the liquid down the sides, what is left clinging to the walls is glycerol. The thickness, three-dimensionality of the beading, and rate of decline of the "legs" down the sides indicates viscosity, or how rich or thin the wine will be in the mouth. Look for things that cause high viscosity in wines. Wood contact, especially new oak, adds viscosity to a wine. Higher fermentation temperatures could do it. Residual sugar left in a wine would increase the glycerol content. Aren't sweet wines always syrupy in the glass? Since alcohol is one of the heaviest components of wine, higher alcohol content could increase viscosity. By simply examining viscosity in the glass, you can project possible mouth feel, body, or weight.

Dear Dr. WineKnow:
When I use only one wine glass at a tasting, rinsing it with water between wines seems to rob each wine of beading and legs. Is there anything else that I can do so this doesn't happen?
Diagnosis: I know what you mean. Residual water from rinsing stemware does infringe on glycerol's ability to adhere to the sides of the glass (viscosity). Since much about the palate can be discovered from the beading and legs, you are missing out on something.
Prescription: Forget the water and purge the glass with a little of the next wine about to be tasted. Swirl it around, coating the glass before dumping. Then pour yourself a taste portion. I believe you will find this method works much better in maintaining and displaying each wine's viscosity.

The Nose Knows

The sense of smell is the most important factor that affects one's perception of wine – or of any food, for that fact. Wine appreciation is approximately 70 to 75 per cent smell and smell affects taste greatly. The sense of smell contributes great richness and variety of experience to your enjoyment of wine. Without it, there would be no pleasure in drinking wine, only consumption of liquid. It is important to keep in mind that all odours in wine are volatile and, in order to stimulate the sense of smell, materials must be airborne, usually in a gaseous state. Much can be discovered about a specific wine by smelling it.

Technique

Smell the wine first unswirled, or at rest in the glass, to decipher its cleanliness. If there is a defect or "off" smell in the wine, it will show itself while the wine is at rest. Swirling the wine only hides a potential problem. A couple of short sniffs should be enough. Don't overdo it, as the olfactory sense can become numb from too much stimulation. When you are convinced that the wine does not smell bad, swirl the wine in the glass. This aerates the wine and increases the surface area, allowing the volatiles and nuances to come to the surface. I guarantee, you will perceive a lot more after the wine is swirled. Determine how intense the attack on the nose is. More specifically, is the nose of the wine aggressive or subtle? Now look for the aroma (the smell of the grapes themselves). Each grape variety has characteristic smells, so you may be able to pick out the grape. The bouquet (the smell evolved through fermentation and wood ageing) usually follows in examination. The bouquet may very well include the aroma as well, but is complicated by such things as oak contact and other influences of processing. Perhaps most important is the balance between the aroma and bouquet. They should be in harmony, without either overwhelming the other. If you are experienced enough, you might be able to tell what part of the world a wine was produced in by smelling it. Warm-climate wines tend to possess much riper fruit qualities and produce jammier reds and tropical fruity whites. Certain regional characteristics might reveal themselves by smell.

ODOUR RECEPTOR

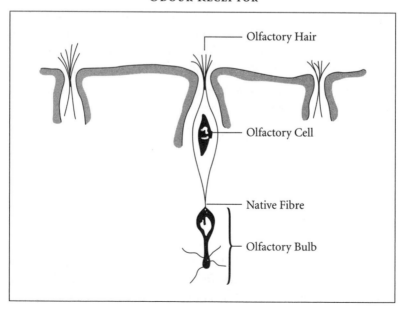

BASIC AROMA CHART

These are the common categories of aromatics that most people smell in wine. As one becomes more proficient, further breakdowns of the specific aromatics are experienced. For example, citrus might be experienced as grapefruit, lemon, orange, lime, etc.

COMMON CATEGORIES	SPECIFIC AROMATICS
Fruit	Citrus, berry, tree fruit, tropical fruit (fresh, cooked, canned, dried)
Vegetable	Green, red, brown (cooked, canned)
Flower	Violet, rose, orange blossom, honeysuckle
Spice	Licorice, black pepper, white pepper, cloves, mint, eucalyptus, herbs (exotic)
Nut	Walnut, hazelnut, almond
Wood	Vanilla, cedar, smoke, toast, coffee, biscuit, creamed corn, butterscotch, butter
Earth	Mushroom, gravel, dust, tobacco, tar, grass
Carmel	Honey, molasses, chocolate
Chemical	Sulphur, plastic, petroleum, alcohol, rubber, yeast
Off-odours	Oxidation, cork, garlic, mould, skunk, vinegar

Dear Dr. WineKnow:
What exactly does oak smell like in a wine?
Diagnosis: Whether the wine is barrel-fermented or simply aged in it, oak adds richness and complexity to the nose of a wine. It is almost always picked up by the olfactory senses. The newer the oak, the smaller the barrels, and the longer time wine spends either fermenting or ageing in it, the stronger the oak character imparted to the smell.

Prescription: You don't have to be a beaver to know the answer to this one. Oak in wine usually smells like vanilla, toast, biscuit, nuts, caramel, butterscotch, or even creamed corn. American oak will give more vanilla, spice, and tannins than, say, French or other European oak. Toasted, charred barrels will impart more of a toasty, smoky note to a wine.

Dear Dr. WineKnow:
Some wines say on the label that they have spent time in barrel, but have no oak complexity when smelled. What's the point?

Diagnosis: Remember that the most wood complexity, especially on the nose, comes from using new oak or smaller barrels, or leaving the wine in oak for longer fermenting or ageing. Perhaps the wine spent a short period of time ageing in it, or the barrels were very large. Maybe the oak was older, some three or four years' worth. In any of these cases, not a lot of oak complexity would be picked up.

If a wine has come in contact with oak but doesn't really display its character, there may be another reason why the wine was oaked. Some winemakers use oak merely to give it some additional mouth feel, a little roundness or creaminess on the palate. Big, rich, vanilla toastiness is not always the sought-after result.

Prescription: The next time you taste a wine that says it has some oak influence but don't smell it, pay particular attention to the mouth feel or body. The oak may be working its magic here.

Common Wine Defects

Since wine appreciation is approximately 70 to 75 per cent nose, the majority of wine defects are perceived through odour or smell.

Odours resulting from extensive use of sulphur-containing compounds:

sulphur dioxide – a pungent smell which leaves an unpleasant effect on the tissues of the nose and throat.

hydrogen sulphide – a rotten egg smell.

mercaptan – a very unpleasant odour that is rubbery or garlic-like, often confused with hydrogen sulphide.

Odours resulting from the action of bacteria:

mousey – a sharp and pungent odour of mouse, best smelled after rubbing a few drops between your palms or fingers.

butyric – an odour of rancid butter or spoiled Camembert cheese.

lactic – a sauerkraut or goaty odour.

acetic – an odour and taste of vinegar, from leaving wine open and exposed to air.

acetone – an odour of nail polish, sometimes in old reds.

ethyl acetate – the smell of nail-polish remover.

Odours resulting from other sources:

oxidized – stale, tired odour and flat taste in a wine that has been exposed to too much air. The wine might even have turned brown.

maderized – browning colour and dull, caramelized taste from exposure to warm temperatures.

cooked – a cooked or baked odour present when a wine has been baked or to which reduced must or concentrate has been added.

stemmy – the bitter or green odour of grape stems.

woody – the odour of wet wood.

green – an odour of leaf alcohol and leaf aldehyde from unripe grapes.

yeasty – a pronounced odour of yeast, which could indicate fermentation is still taking place or there is still some active yeast (expected in Champagne).

lees – a pungent odour resulting from yeast being allowed to remain too long in contact with the wine.

musty – a dank odour of dirty barrels or rotting grapes in a wine.

mouldy – the odour of mould, resulting from the use of mouldy grapes or mouldy cooperage.

corked – an odour of cork in a wine, due to a tainted cork.

rubbery – the odour of rubber or old tires, sometimes associated with very high pH.

filter-pad – a chalky or cardboard odour, resulting from dirty filter-pads used in filtration.

geranium – the odour of geranium in a wine.

Dear Dr. WineKnow:

When I'm at wine tastings, it drives me crazy when I can smell people's cologne and perfume over the wine. Don't they know any better?

Diagnosis: Hey! I detect nuances of Chanel No. 5 on the nose of this wine. Aromatic fragrances such as perfume, aftershave, some shampoo, and other beauty and hygiene aids interfere with other tasters' perceptions and appreciation of wine, not to mention your own. They get in the way and mask the wines' subtle delicacies.

Prescription: Women, as well as men, should carefully choose beauty products that do not have strong odours when going to attend a wine event. Since the wine is probably the main attraction, let it put on the show with its own aromatics. Besides, it's impolite to rob someone else of the olfactory enjoyment, even if it doesn't matter to you. Some invitations specifically ask that neither men nor women wear fragrances to an event.

Dear Dr. WineKnow:

When I'm at a wine tasting I get quite bothered when I can smell cigarette smoke on someone. It really hampers my appreciation.

Diagnosis: This is a common pet peeve among wine tasters. Even though smoking is not allowed at wine tastings, that tobacco smell lingers indefinitely and is a real detriment to smelling wine's nuances.

Prescription: Unfortunately, there is not much that can be done. Try and find a part of the tasting environment that is away from people smelling of smoke.

Dear Dr. WineKnow:

At a recent tasting, the person conducting it said one of the wines smelled "foxy." I give up. What the blazes did she mean?

Diagnosis: Surely you're familiar with the fragrant smell of fox? I remember it well. Chances of getting to sniff a fox these days are pretty slim, however, this perfect descriptor epitomizes the characteristic aroma of Labrusca grapes. This species of North American vines produces juice and wine that has a pronounced grapey, candy-like, almost wild-animal-fur character to the smell. One of the most heavily scented is the Concord (grape, not the airplane). Although these grapes make great drinking juice, reasonable brandy, and some sweet, fortified wines, most quality wines do not utilize them.

Taste – The Final Frontier

For the majority of people, taste is what wine is all about. This statement may be true but it is surprisingly inaccurate. In fact, if one was never able to taste wine at all, for whatever reason (God forbid), about 75 to 80 per cent of a wine's totality would be experienced thanks to taste buds at the back of the olfactory (smell) glands. So, to a lesser degree, you can actually taste wine without putting it in the mouth. Certainly you've smelled a bowl of fresh, ripe strawberries at some point and could literally taste them that way. In reality, the tasting of wine merely reinforces what the nose is telling us, and is directly related to the efficiency of the nose.

Simple science explains that experiencing a substance in wine via taste depends on a number of variables, among them solubility, concentration, temperature, and basic chemical composition. The wine is assimilated by the taste buds. Not only do taste buds differ from person to person but within each taste bud of any one person, individual cells are continually developing. Each cell has a very short lifespan, of only a few days. Therefore, each taste bud changes continuously, and possesses some immature, mature, and dying cells at all times. This accounts for variance in taste, not only from person to person, but within the same person. Alcohol tends to deaden or numb taste buds. Regardless of all these factors, much can be achieved by tasting a wine.

Technique
Take a sip of the wine. Determine the intensity of taste as the wine attacks the palate. Now look for the fruit or sweetness, followed by the acid or sourness. This balance between fruit and acid or sweet and sour is all-important in whether a wine works on the palate or not. This relationship is the key to a wine's structure. A wine must possess balance in order not only for it to taste right but for ageing ability. Next, if it's red wine, experience the bitterness or astringency. This will be the puckery feeling on the gums. Now decipher the tactile (touch) sensation called body, weight, or mouth feel, usually described as light, medium, or full. Finally, check out the finish or aftertaste. It's what's left in your mouth after swallowing or spitting out the wine.

TASTE RECEPTOR

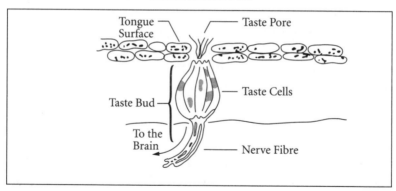

Dear Dr. WineKnow:
I see professional tasters who look like they are gargling the wine before they spit it out. What's this all about?
Diagnosis: It is important to note that, as human beings, we are pretty limited in our ability to taste components. All we are physically capable of tasting are the components of sweet, sour, bitter, salt, and a newly discovered component called umami (savouriness or deliciousness), caused by amino acids. These components are experienced on the tongue at different locations. What professional

tasters or "wineknows" are doing when they gargle wine is letting it touch all those sensitive parts of the tongue in order to get a total picture of it. The term used for doing this is "chewing" the wine.

Prescription: Sweetness is experienced at the tip of the tongue. Sourness is tasted along the edges of the tongue near the tip. Bitterness is realized at the back of the tongue near the middle. Saltiness (although not too common in wine) usually makes itself evident along the edges of the tongue halfway back. The newly discovered umami can be detected by an amino-acid receptor on the tongue. However, the contribution and location of this component cannot yet be precisely calculated as compared to the other components of taste.

THE TONGUE

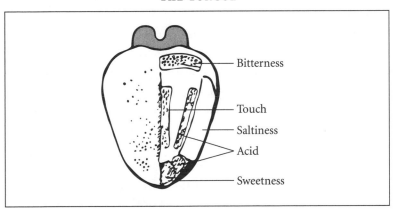

Dear Dr. WineKnow:
Everyone talks about how hard and green or soft and ripe tannins in wine are. I haven't a clue as to what they mean. Please shed some light on this for me.

Diagnosis: For those of you who aren't that familiar with tannin, let me enlighten you. In red wine, tannin is the dry, drawing, puckery sensation usually experienced in the mouth when you taste. It's the same feeling you get when you leave a tea bag in your cup too long. When grapes ripen on the vine, the tannins don't always ripen along with the pulp. In long, warm, dry growing seasons, tannins usually ripen equally with the rest of the grape. Other times they do not. It can also be a matter of how the grapes are pressed. Hard pressing yields much more aggressive tannins than soft pressing. This state of the tannin is usually displayed in the finished wine when you taste it.

Prescription: Pucker up. If the tannins cause you to pucker excessively, are kind of vegetative in character, and are experienced on the upper and lower gums, they are generally hard, green, or unripe. This wine may require further ageing to soften them. If they cause little puckering, are not vegetative, and are experienced on the sides of your cheeks, they are usually soft and ripe. As far as the tannins go, this wine is ready to drink.

Dear Dr. WineKnow:
I understand that wine can acquire tannin from oak barrels. Does this taste different to grape-skin tannin?

Diagnosis: Oak barrels can also impart tannin to a wine. A sappiness of sorts is transferred into a wine that has spent considerable time in oak. It is usually not as aggressive as grape-skin tannins. The main difference between grape-skin tannins and wood tannins is where in the taste of wine you experience them.

Prescription: Grape tannins are usually appreciated up front when the wine is first put in your mouth. In my experience, wood tannins are experienced at the back end of the wine, usually in the finish or aftertaste.

Dear Dr. WineKnow:
Why is it that I find some red wines very tannic and other people don't?

Diagnosis: A very interesting question! It's all about tolerance. Not just any tolerance, but tolerance of certain things! Due to individual differences in physiology, people have different thresholds for certain components and elements in wine. These include tannin, acid, sugar, bitterness, and salt. Say, for example, two people are both eating a chocolate-covered doughnut. Contestant number one, says, "Umm, good," whereas contestant number two, might say, "This is really too sweet for me." So you may very well have a hard time enjoying a specific red wine because of the tannin, while another person loves the mouth-puckering bitterness. These thresholds could apply to any of the aforementioned components or elements of wine.

Prescription: All human beings are not alike. These tolerances or thresholds are different for each of us. That's just the way it is. The way around it, though, is this. The first step is recognition. You must recognize your individual threshold to certain components or elements. By being aware that you are over- or under-sensitive to specific components, you are in a better position to correct it. Then a palate adjustment is necessary. This can be achieved by component-tasting exercises. These exercises help the palate decipher different degrees of a specific component. Here's what to do for tannin and bitterness. Get hold of five coloured glasses or cups. Mark them one to five on the bottom. Using a tea bag in the glasses or cups, mix five different dilutions of tea, ranging from extremely weak to incredibly strong (one the weakest, five the strongest). Dipping and squeezing the bag to varying degrees should accomplish this. Have someone shuffle them around so that they are mixed up and not in the right order. Then, by tasting them, put them in the correct order from weakest tannin to strongest. Repeat the same thing with lemon juice for acid, sugar for sweetness, and salt for saltiness. Exercises like this will not only help you overcome your threshold deficiencies, but make you a better objective taster.

GRAPE FLASH

Did you know that an over-tolerance to certain components in wine can affect perception and enjoyment? Someone can be so tolerant to acid or sourness as to not detect the obvious lack of fruit or sweetness in a wine that puts it totally out of

balance. In this case, definite palate compensation is required
to make objective evaluation more beneficial. The same can
apply to an under-tolerance. Again, component-tasting exercises can make the difference.

Dear Dr. WineKnow:

When I taste a number of wines at a tasting, I find that the flavour
of one wine tends to carry over to another. Is there any way to
avoid this?

Diagnosis: Components such as tannin, oak, and sugar from a
specific wine can remain in the mouth after tasting. Even elements
like excessive alcohol and body can put your palate off for the next
wine. You aren't really sure which characteristics are coming from
the specific wine being tasted. It could be residual flavours or components from the previous wine or the one before that.

Prescription: There are some general rules about order of tasting.
Taste white to red, dry to sweet, light-bodied to full-bodied, low
alcohol to high alcohol, and unoaked to oaky, for best results. If you
taste out of sequence, you can count on your palate being confused
and put off. Even if you follow this format, some flavours or components may still linger. To eliminate this, try cleaning your palate
between wines. A nibble of plain, dry bread or a cracker should do
the job nicely. Alternately, try a sip of water between wines.

Dear Dr. WineKnow:

When I taste wine after brushing my teeth or eating certain foods,
it tastes horrible. What's the story?

Diagnosis: Certain foods or flavours have a tendency to stick to the
palate and take a while to wear off. Any wine tasted after these
things have been put into the mouth will no doubt taste weird.

Prescription: Strong medicinal flavours from such things as
toothpaste and mouthwash should also be avoided before tasting
wine. Stay away from kippered snacks, chocolate, and coffee. Steer
clear of excessively smoky flavours as well.

Dear Dr. WineKnow:
Sometimes I buy wine that has a sugar code of (0) but tastes slightly sweeter. Other times I buy wine with a sugar code of (2), but it tastes slightly drier. What's going on? Is there something wrong with my tastebuds?

Diagnosis: Don't fret. Your palate is alive and well. The sugar code numbers that some retailers use to indicate the dryness or sweetness of wine can be slightly deceptive. They actually represent, through laboratory analysis, the residual sugar present in a wine at the time of bottling. Generally, the higher the number, the more sugar present. Since we don't have laboratories in our mouths to measure sugar, we must go by perception. When it comes to wine, perception is nine-tenths of the law.

Prescription: Don't totally ignore sugar codes, but keep the following in mind. High acid or hard tannins will pull a wine's perception to the drier side. Ripe, fruit flavours and the use of new oak can easily make a wine appear sweeter. A simpler, more accurate (as far as our perception goes) method of indicating sweetness or dryness in a wine would be to just use the terms extra-dry, dry, medium-dry, medium, medium-sweet, and sweet. I believe these would relay the overall sweetness designation of a wine in a way that is more in line with how it is perceived on the palate.

GRAPE FLASH

By now you should know that the "flavour" of a wine is actually experienced in both the nose and the mouth. What most people generally express as taste in wine is really flavour. Although independent, the nose and mouth work in harmony when it comes to wine's flavour. The mouth experiences components such as sweet, sour, bitter, salt, and umami, as well as sensations like temperature, texture, and astringency. The nose adds flavour and aroma to the mix and transforms simple acceptance into flavourful appreciation. Human beings are constantly trying to taste sensations in wine that really belong to smell. To best experience the flavour of a wine, the nose and mouth must be in perfect working order. They are a team that depend on each other to deliver the goods.

COMMON GRAPE VARIETIES
AND THEIR WINE CHARACTER

WHITE VARIETY	WINE CHARACTERISTICS
Aligoté	Pale, soft, and crisp. Like a simpler Chardonnay. Short-lived.
Alvarinho	Pale, crisp, minerally, slightly spritzy. Short-lived. In Vinho Verde.
Auxerrois	Fresh, clean, and crisp. Short-lived.
Bacchus	Floral, peachy, and simple. Short-lived.
Bual	Figgy, pruny, rich, and sweet. Long-lived.
Chardonnay	Cool climate – appley, nutty, flinty. Warm climate – tropical fruity. Great affinity to oak. Can age fairly well.
Chasselas	Delicate, crisp, and light. Short-lived.
Chenin Blanc	Melon, honeyed, and crisp. Long-lived.
Colombard	Floral and soft. Short-lived.
Emerald Riesling	Fragrant, fruity, and soft. Short-lived.
Furmint	Appley, floral, and apricot. Short-lived, except in Tokay.
Gewürztraminer	Perfumy, spicy, lychee, peach, and rose petal. Long-lived. Best from Alsace.
Grüner Veltliner	Fruity and fresh. Short-lived.
Hárslevelu	Fragrant and spicy. Long-lived.
Jacquère	Herbaceous and light. Short-lived.
Kerner	Fruity, spicy, and crisp. Long-lived.
Malvasia	Floral, fruity, and crisp. Long-lived in sweet wines.

Marsanne	Lanolin, wet fur, and floral. Short-lived.
Morio-Muscat	Fragrant, spicy, and peachy. Long-lived.
Müller-Thurgau	Fruity and soft. Short-lived.
Muscadelle	Fragrant and floral. Short-lived.
Muscadet	Light, minerally, and crisp. Short-lived.
Muscat	Fragrant, peachy, and floral. Long-lived.
Palomino	Floral and simple. Low acid. Short-lived.
Pedro Ximénez	Neutral and alcoholic. Short-lived.
Picolit	Rich and somewhat bitter. Long-lived.
Pinot Blanc	Fruity, crisp, and clean. Short-lived.
Pinot Gris	Spicy, fruity, and floral. Long-lived.
Riesling	Floral, fruity, petrol, and crisp. Long-lived.
Rkatsiteli	Floral, spicy, and crisp. Long-lived.
Sacy	Lively, crisp, and forward. Short-lived.
Savagnin	Nutty, full, and rich. Long-lived.
Sauvignon Blanc	Herbaceous, gooseberry, and crisp. Short-lived.
Scheurebe	Fragrant, fruity, and crisp. Long-lived.
Sémillon	Fruity, honeyed, and fat. Low acid. Short-lived.
Sercial	Delicate, dry, and crisp. Long-lived.
Seyval Blanc	Floral, plummy, and herbaceous. Short-lived.
Silvaner	Neutral and forward. Short-lived.
Trebbiano	Floral, crisp, and clean. Short-lived.
Verdelho	Nutty, medium-dry, and soft. Short-lived.
Verdicchio	Floral, crisp, and slightly bitter. Short-lived.
Vernaccia	Full, austere, crisp, and slightly bitter. Long-lived.
Vidal	Floral, fruity, and crisp. Short-lived when dry.

Viognier	Floral, peachy, full, and rich. Long-lived.
Viura	Fragrant, fruity, and crisp. Long-lived.
Welschriesling	Floral, fruity, lively, and crisp. Long-lived.

RED VARIETY	WINE CHARACTERISTICS
Aglianico	Tarry, tannic, and full. Long-lived.
Alicante	Good colour, but neutral. Short-lived.
Baco Noir	Blackberry, dill, and crisp. Short-lived.
Barbera	Cherry, leathery, crisp, and austere. Long-lived.
Cabernet Franc	Herbaceous, black currant, and medium-bodied. Long-lived.
Cabernet Sauvignon	Black currant, tobacco, cedar, tannic, and full. Long-lived.
Carignan	Good colour, alcoholic, tannic, and austere. Short-lived.
Cinsault	Good colour, meaty flavours, and low tannins. Short-lived.
Dolcetto	Good colour, mulberry, soft, with low tannins. Short-lived.
Gamay	Violet, cherry, fruity, and light. Short-lived.
Grenache	Spicy, fruity, soft, with low tannins. Short-lived.
Grignolino	Delicate, floral, berry, and slightly herbaceous. Short-lived.
Kadarka	Slightly spicy, fruity, and full. Long-lived.
Lambrusco	Fruity, juicy, light, and medium-dry. Short-lived.
Malbec	Blackberry, soft, with low acid. Short-lived.

Maréchal Foch	Good colour, plummy, spicy, tobacco, and crisp. Long-lived.
Merlot	Blackberry, full and round. Long-lived.
Mourvèdre	Good colour, spicy, blackberry. Long-lived.
Nebbiolo	Violets, mushroom, tarry, tannic, and austere. Long-lived.
Petite Sirah	Good colour, spicy, leathery, and full. Long-lived.
Pinot Noir	Strawberry/raspberry, barnyard, and earthy. Long-lived.
Pinot Meunier	Fruity, crisp, and low alcohol. Short-lived.
Pinotage	Robust, herbaceous, and somewhat baked. Short-lived.
Primitivo	Good colour, fruity, and powerful. Long-lived.
Sangiovese	Cherry, leather, earthy, and crisp. Long-lived.
Syrah	Spicy, blackberry, earthy, leathery, and powerful. Long-lived.
Tempranillo	Strawberry, round, and low acid. Short-lived.
Touriga Naçional	Good colour, rich, berry, and tannic. Long-lived.
Xynomavro	Good colour, tannic, and crisp. Long-lived.
Zinfandel	Brambleberry, strawberry, rich, and sometimes slightly spicy. Long-lived.

Dear Dr. WineKnow:

I'm really quite confused about this thing called the "finish" of a wine. Can you explain it?

Diagnosis: Finish, or aftertaste, is what's left in the mouth after the wine is swallowed or spit out. It's an important indicator of a wine's quality. There are two parts to finish or aftertaste: intensity and persistence. How strong is the aftertaste? Is it weak or distinctive? How long does it linger on the palate? Is it short or long?

Prescription: If a wine, after you swallow it or spit it out, retains mouth-filling flavours, it can be said to have a distinctive finish. If it lingers on the palate for only a couple of seconds, it might be called short. If it hangs around for eight seconds or so, it could be referred to as medium length. If it lasts any time beyond thirteen to fifteen seconds, it has good length or a long finish. If you are driving home a half hour after tasting it, and you pull up to a stoplight and are accosted by wine flavours – Wow!

Dear Dr. WineKnow:
I'm a smoker and find I can handle very tannic wines where others can't.
Diagnosis: Tar makes cigarettes bitter-tasting, thus desensitizing the palate to the bitter component in wine, especially tannin in reds.
Prescription: Until smoking is reduced, or better yet, avoided, you will probably not be a great judge of tannin in wine.

Dear Dr. WineKnow:
I recently gave up smoking, and now I find wine tastes much better.
Diagnosis: Smokers claim that when they give up the habit, food becomes more flavourful to them after a while. So why should this not apply to wine? Elements and components that coated the taste buds are diminished or have disappeared, leaving the palate free to experience all the subtleties that wine has to offer.
Prescription: Give up the habit. Gain a broader experience of what wine is all about. Provide the most neutral environment in your nose and palate for wine to do its thing.

Dear Dr. WineKnow:
I prefer to taste wines when I don't know what they are. I find I learn a lot more and my senses get a good workout.

Diagnosis: It's interesting that you should say this. This type of tasting is known as "blind" tasting. No, the tasters are not blind-folded, but the wines are. They are usually poured in another room, presented in the glass, decanted, or the bottles are covered as they are poured. You can't see the label and don't know what the wine is.

Prescription: Challenge your taste buds. Although most difficult, this is by far the best and most objective way to evaluate a wine's quality. The senses do all the work. It's a wonderful learning tool. Just to make things a little easier, the style or grape variety might be divulged, so the taster knows what category the wine falls into. This is the only way that wines can be truly judged in competition. It's also a great test for the senses.

Vertical Tasting vs. Horizontal Tasting

These two terms refer to themes by which most wine tastings are organized. Contrary to popular belief, they have nothing to do with whether the taster is lying down or standing up. "Vertical" tastings provide much narrower focus. A number of vintages/years of the same wine are tasted. It's a great way of seeing how a specific wine performs over a period of time and is reflected by individual growing seasons. It's also a great barometer of the quality of a specific winery and the ability of its winemaker. "Horizontal" tastings are somewhat looser in scope, utilizing different wines all with the same vintage/year, country, region, grape variety, price range, style, and so forth. It shows how wines perform overall compared to others in a broader category. This theme will provide you with much supporting information for purchasing one winery, country, or region over another.

Dear Dr. WineKnow:

Many tastings I attend never include food of any sort and are very serious. I find that I am much harder on the wines in this situation.

Diagnosis: Get serious. Tasting wine straight up is very different than having it with food. The wine is the focus, and must stand on its own merits without the benefit of food to play off. Often food can mask or diminish problems in a wine. This type of tasting or evaluation is known as "clinical." The wine is literally torn apart componently and structurally, and evaluated for quality. It's not dissimilar to looking for a husband or wife; one tends to look for the downfalls first. It's no wonder you are much harder on the wines in this setting, as their bare bones are exposed to your senses for judgement. Retaste the wine with food. Although wine shines with food, clinical evaluation is the real test of its greatness. If it comes across decently here, it is sure to be wonderful with food.

Dear Dr. WineKnow:
I tasted a wine recently at a tasting, and I didn't think much of it. Then I had it again at a friend's place with dinner, and it was much better. Why is that?
Diagnosis: This is the difference between "clinical" and "social" settings. More than likely, when you first tasted this wine, it was alone, without food, in a relatively serious environment. Then in a social setting, where the wine wasn't the focus, there was food to play off, people talking, music, and a relaxed setting. In other words, the wine could fade into the background and complement the situation. It's magic. Wines can taste much better in a social setting. Often wine that seems only mediocre in a "clinical" tasting comes across much better in a social setting. Its ability to "socialize" situations and its wonderful affinity to food are the keys.

Dear Dr. WineKnow:
I have the white-wine blahs. Everywhere I go, people are constantly serving me Chardonnay. It's driving me crazy. What's the prescription, Doc?
Diagnosis: Oh my, it sounds like you have a bad case of "chardonnitis." It arises from sipping too much of the world's most popular white wine. The first choice of wine lovers among white grape

varieties is Chardonnay. It's affinity to oak, its versatility, and its likeable, easy-going nature make it number one.

Prescription: Your prognosis looks good. Here's what to do. Apply the "ABC" principle (Anything But Chardonnay). Drink only non-Chardonnay whites for a while. Take two glasses and call me in the morning. I'm sure you'll regain your taste for Chardonnay.

GRAPE FLASH

Did you know that a "wine schmooze" is the most popular get-together these days? The unabridged Dr. WineKnow dictionary defines "wine schmooze" as a gathering where people chitchat, network, meet and greet, nibble, and otherwise socialize, all while sipping on some wine. You too can "wine schmooze" with the best of them. Here are Dr. WineKnow's seven golden rules for "wine schmoozing" par excellence. 1) Don't use plastic wine glasses. 2) Serve only finger foods. 3) Make nonalcoholic drinks like soda, juice, and water available. 4) Provide a designated driver, if necessary. 5) Although chairs should be provided, it is better to stand, allowing people to network and move about freely to socialize. 6) Look good. This is a great opportunity to strut your stuff and a good reason to stand. 7) Most importantly, always have a wine glass in your hand, one-third full of wine, juice, or water, even if you're not sipping. The glass filled with liquid is a vital part of the "schmooze" look.

What's the Score? Evaluating It

Every time you enjoy a glass of wine, you are making some sort of value judgement about it. It doesn't have to be in a formal setting or wine competition. You could be out for dinner with some friends or at home. Whether consciously or not, value judgements take place. This is only human nature. You like a wine or you don't.

Here are some common concerns about the process of evaluating wine's quality.

Dear Dr. WineKnow:
What exactly is a quality wine?
Diagnosis: The question of quality when applied to wine has plagued professionals for decades. In fact, there may very well be no definitive answer. If there is, it's certainly not a simple one.
Prescription: Perhaps the best indication of quality in wine must first be objective, then subjective. From an objective point of view, a wine should possess certain characteristics. It must be clean and free of defects. It should look appealing and smell aromatic from the grape variety used and the process of production. It should have depth, breadth, and length of flavour. All components should be balanced and harmonious. Finally, it should have a distinct personality. The subjective factor is that it should give pleasure. Some would argue that this point is not that important. However, we are subjective animals. No matter how great a wine is, if you don't like it, that may detract from the quality for you.

Dear Dr. WineKnow:
How does someone judge a wine fairly if he or she doesn't like that particular style?
Diagnosis: Evaluating or judging a wine that you don't particularly like merely because of its style is a difficult task. Subjectivity plays a big part in everyday life. We all can't or don't like the same things, and unfortunately wine that doesn't appeal to us usually gets a bad review.
Prescription: To become a good taster and evaluator of product takes intense objectivity. In other words, leave your subjectivity out of it. Even though you may not like a specific style of wine – like a bone-dry sherry, for instance – you should know what a good, bone-dry sherry tastes like. So you must appreciate all styles of wine strictly from a qualitative point of view. You can achieve this only through much tasting practice and wine education.

Dear Dr. WineKnow:
When evaluating a wine, is it better to judge it alone or in comparison to others of its kind?

Diagnosis: Ideally speaking, every wine should be evaluated as it sits in front of you, without comparison to others. It should not be compared to what came before or after. However, human nature is such that, unless some frame of reference in a grouping is present, most people find it difficult to assign a value to a wine. Experienced tasters already have a good mental image of what a specific wine or grape variety should taste like, and find it easier to judge outside a grouping.

Prescription: Drink wines in groups. For reference and comparison's sake, most wines are presented in groupings of styles, grape varieties, regions, etc. to make the job of evaluation easier. Comparing wines this way is also very educational. In competition, wines are usually presented in groupings of styles, varietals, or vintages.

GRAPE FLASH

Did you know that, in order to get an accurate picture of the quality of a wine, you should evaluate it initially without food? Wine and food are like husband and wife. They are a team. Together, they act a certain way and play off of each other. However, you don't know what the real man or woman is like until you get them alone. It is then that their true personality and colours show. Wine and food are no different. Regardless of the setting or situation, wine should always be evaluated first without food. In competition, this is not an issue, but in social settings, like tastings and dinners, food or nibbles are generally part of the ritual. Before complicating flavours with the introduction of food, always taste the wine, so you know what it is like on its own. This way, no matter what else you put in your mouth, you will have an independent,

> objective picture of the wine. The same principle should be
> applied when restaurant wining and dining.

Dear Dr. WineKnow:
People who buy wine seem so hung up on its tasting score. In fact,
most tasting sheets at events have a column for the score. Is it really
necessary to grade wines when you taste them?
Diagnosis: The world is really obsessed with wine scores. Some
people purchase wine based solely on the score given it by an
expert. A wine's score becomes its marketing tool. The higher the
score, the better it sells. It all stems back to our schooling and
grades. Remember how important "As" and "Bs" were to you and
your parents?
Prescription: You don't have to play teacher. Although grading
wines is a good idea in categorizing and dividing wines into great,
mediocre, and poor groups, it's not the be all and end all. A simple
asterisk next to a wine you particularly liked should suffice. After
all, there's not much difference between a wine scoring 85/100 and
one scoring 82/100. What remains important are tasting notes.
Herein lies a wine's value to you.

Dear Dr. WineKnow:
In tasting, there seem to be many wine grading systems out there.
Is any one better than another?
Diagnosis: Answering this question is like deciding whether it's
better to be graded utilizing a letter or a number. What's the
difference? It's still a grade, whichever way you look at it. Aside
from the actual grading systems, there are certain things a tasting/
grading sheet should contain: the name of the wine, vintage date,
region, producer, and price. There should be three general areas of
perception for each wine: sight, nose, and taste. As for grading
systems, you're right. There are a number: 10 and 20 point, 100
point, 5 and 10 star, and so forth. The 100-point system seems to be

the most widely used because it carries over from our schooldays, when all grading was done out of 100. The highest proportion of points or stars are attributed to the nose of a wine, because that's the most important aspect of appreciation.

TWENTY POINT SYSTEM

(Modified system utilized by the University of California at Davis.)

Date ————————————

Wine Name	Appearance & Colour (3)	Aroma & Bouquet (6)	Total Acidity (1)	Balance (2)	Body (1)	Flavour (3)	Finish (2)	General Quality (2)	Comments	Total

SIMPLER SYSTEM

Wine	Appearance	Nose	Taste	(Score)
1.				
2.				
3.				
4.				
5.				
6.				

Prescription: No one system is better than another. However, certain benefits are derived from specific kinds. The more overall points allowed to a wine in its score the harder the judging or evaluating job. So a 100-point system breaks a wine down into its components in more detail. For novices, the fewer overall points allowed, the easier it is to judge.

Dear Dr. WineKnow:
Why do wine consumers feel it necessary to have numbers attached to wines anyway?
Diagnosis: We live in a complex society, where numbers dictate almost everything. School grades, sport scores, merchandise and grocery prices, temperature, body weight, calendar years, and age, are but a few examples. Why should wine be any different, especially when you are trying to place one above or below another in respect to quality?

Prescription: Plain and simple: numbers sell wine. There are two important reasons for applying numbers to wine in evaluation. Unlike tasting notes, descriptors, and comments, which are variable, numbers are exact and precise. The number 95 means pretty much the same thing to most people. Numbers can also be averaged out. In other words, the marks of several tasters can be averaged out to come up with a mean score, representing a group of people. This makes numbers really handy.

Dear Dr. WineKnow:
Most grading sheets contain different columns for varying aspects of a wine, with a point allowance. How do you know how many points to award a certain component?
Diagnosis: Wine is like a car. You buy a specific car because of many things you like about it: its looks, options, cost, and performance. The same applies to wine. It's the overall wine that pleases, not just its appearance or smell. However, the whole is made up of integral parts, and evaluating the component parts is essential to understanding why a wine is good or not.
Prescription: The best approach when trying to score a specific component in a wine is to focus your attention on that element. Before addressing it, assume that its score is average, right in the middle. For example, if six points are allowed for aroma and bouquet, assume that it is automatically a three. Then address the component. If it is better than average, mark it up. If it is worse, mark it down. By doing this for each element or column and then adding them, you come up with a total score for the wine.

Dear Dr. WineKnow:
I notice some grading sheets have an area for "potential." What is meant by this?
Diagnosis: Some grading sheets do provide a space for a wine's potential. It's meant for you to note the wine's "drinkability." Is it mature and drinkable now? How much longer will it need to reach

maturity? How long might it be aged? Although it can be helpful, filling in this area is usually optional.

Prescription: If you are a wine collector, then this area of the grading sheet becomes very important to you. This is where you make your notes as to how long a wine should sit in your cellar and the best time to consume it. Without some notation here, a wine could easily languish in your cellar until it's over the hill.

Dear Dr. WineKnow:
Can a wine score poorly in some area and still end up with a decent mark?

Diagnosis: It is possible for wine to score low in one area and still end up with a reasonable mark, but it depends on what that area is. Certain components of a wine are absolutely essential to how it smells and tastes. They are integral parts of the overall structure. Without them being intact, a wine smells or tastes awkward and even bad. A very slight deficiency might be acceptable, but anything more and the wine is doomed. However, certain areas like appearance, body, flavour, and finish are perhaps not as detrimental to the overall quality, and deficiencies here might not weigh as heavily on the general structure. It's not that they aren't important, but a little more play in these areas won't make or break a wine.

Prescription: Since wine appreciation depends mostly on the sense of smell, the aroma and bouquet are areas that should score reasonably well. The same applies to balance – that symmetry between the fruit (sweetness) and the acid (sourness). This is the most important aspect if a wine is going work in the mouth and taste right or not.

GRAPE FLASH
Did you know that the most important thing to do when tasting, evaluating, or judging a wine is to make notes? As the number of wines you taste regularly rises, it gets increasingly

difficult to recall all of them, no matter how great your memory is. The best and the worst stick out, while all the others become a homogeneous mess. Documentation is a great idea for reference. Say you taste something at an event that's fabulous. If you have it documented, you can purchase it later. By the same token, if you taste a wine that's just terrible, and you don't have it documented, you may very well end up buying it by mistake at a future date. Always make notes on wine you taste, even if a tasting sheet is not provided. Try carrying a small pad around for this purpose. Aside from documentation, making notes on wines you have tasted is a great learning tool. You can always refer back to them, especially when tasting the same wine some time later.

Dear Dr. WineKnow:
If I only make tasting notes and don't score wines, what should those notes include?

Diagnosis: Not everybody is into grading and scoring wines. However, making notes so you remember what you have tasted is extremely important. Tasting notes are great references for buying and ageing wine. There is essential information that should always be included to make the tasting note useful to you.

Prescription: Here's a general guideline:

1) Date of Tasting
2) Name of Wine (include region, district, estate, and vineyard)
3) Vintage Year (if applicable)
4) Name of Bottler
5) Price
6) Description of Appearance (include colour, depth, clarity, viscosity)
7) Description of Nose (include aroma, bouquet)
8) Description of Taste (balance, body, flavour, finish)
9) Conclusions (include quality/value, ageing ability, food matches), and whether you liked it.

Dear Dr. WineKnow:
What happens when you are given a wine to evaluate and it is "off" or defective?
Diagnosis: It's funny how you can go along and not experience a defective wine for months. Then, all of a sudden, you get three or four in a row. This is even more likely when you are tasting many wines at one time. Unfortunately, this is a very real problem these days, and one must be prepared for it.
Prescription: If you discover a wine to be "off" or defective, you can request that another bottle be opened. It's possible that an occasional bottle is defective for whatever reason, and one hopes the new one will be fine. If the new one is problematic, then it's possibly not an isolated case. Perhaps a whole shipment is infected. This could be very serious for the producer/distributor/agent. Sometimes, the only bottle available to taste is the one that is "off." Too bad!

Dear Dr. WineKnow:
Do you have any tips for quickly evaluating many wines in a short time?
Diagnosis: It's extremely interesting that you should pose this question. I tend to be a very quick taster. In fact, my colleagues constantly rib me about it. Sometimes when you're confronted with many wines to taste or evaluate in a short period, it's hard to spend an inordinate amount time tasting and retasting any one for different components. This luxury is restricted to situations where only a small number are available. What is required are quick impressions. At times like these one must rely solely on first impressions. Usually they're pretty good. It's simply a matter of trusting them.
Prescription: The Dr. WineKnow method of quick tasting involves three easy steps. Look at the wine. If it's clean, bright, shiny, and free of any obvious sludge or suspensions, move on to the next step. Many wine buyers in Europe won't go any further with a wine if its appearance is substandard. Nose the wine. If it

smells the way it should, without any foul odours or overwhelming oak character, you're ready for the final step. Again, if you are accosted with some "off" odour, move on to another wine. Finally, if appearance and nose are acceptable, taste it. If sweet (fruit) and sour (acid) are in harmony, generally, the wine is fine. Experience will fill in the missing blanks.

The Space Is the Place

The physical set up of the space one tastes in can play havoc with your enjoyment of wine. There are many variables that we have no control over, and these variables affect and alter our behaviour and can direct how we approach and perceive wine. In fact, they may even affect the way wine itself behaves. Even who you taste with can make a difference in your perception. These effects can be both positive and negative.

Most of us appreciate and consume wine in one of three places: at wine fairs, at home, and in restaurants. Each environment is unique and provides its own set of interesting variables which affect our perception and enjoyment.

Atmosphere
Feeling physically comfortable in a tasting space is essential to your appreciation. Not only does the environment or atmosphere affect your functioning, it can also change the way wine shows. Atmospheric elements like temperature, humidity, lighting, pressure, and altitude all make a difference. Both people and wine act certain ways under different conditions.

Dear Dr. WineKnow:
At a recent wine tasting, it was so hot in the room that the discomfort got in the way of my enjoyment of the wine.
Diagnosis: Comfort level is an important factor for ultimate enjoyment of wine, and for that matter, of anything. If it's too hot

or cold it becomes difficult to concentrate on much else. Besides, it can be so extreme as to actually alter the temperature of the wine, making it taste different.

Prescription: The ideal room temperature in which to taste wine is approximately 18°C.

Dear Dr. WineKnow:
The other day I had dinner at a restaurant that was so dry my nostrils virtually stuck together when I sniffed the wine. It didn't have much of a nose either. Can humidity affect what I perceive?

Diagnosis: Humidity is even more important to wine appreciation than room temperature. It not only affects the functioning of the taster, but the wine itself. The olfactory senses in the nose dry up, inhibiting smell, and wine odours are less easily perceived in dry conditions than in moist. If it is too humid, glassware can fog up, making visual examination difficult, especially with chilled selections.

Prescription: Ideal humidity in which to taste wine is approximately 70 per cent.

Dear Dr. WineKnow:
I buy a fair amount of wine for my cellar. Lately, I've noticed that, if the space I'm tasting in is colourful, brightly decorated, or highly furnished, I am distracted and don't make good buying decisions. Does this make sense?

Diagnosis: Surprisingly, this makes a lot of sense. Oh, what a monodimensional world it would be if we had few visuals to stimulate our emotions. There would be no need for paint stores, interior decorators, or clothiers. The world would truly be a boring place. Experience has shown that bright colours and shiny surfaces tend to arouse one set of emotions, while dull colours and muted surfaces bring forth others. Certain things such as wine are perceived differently in various colour schemes, merely because of reflection. Bright colours make certain components in wine prominent. They also make tasters feel a certain way – such as cheerful – and they are led down a path to a particular conclusion.

As for furnishings, a crowded environment invades your personal space and makes it hard to move about freely. It is also a source of distraction, so the focus is not on the wine but on whether you'll knock into the chair next to you.

Prescription: Wine shows more realistically in an environment that is least stimulating, with colours that are pale, uniform, and neutral. Utilize a white placemat, a white sheet of paper, or a white tablecloth to provide a neutral backdrop for examining a wine's visual attributes. Finally, a sparsely furnished space works best, as fewer distractions allow the wine to show its stuff.

GRAPE FLASH

Did you know that it is very hard to determine a wine's colour under different lighting conditions? We often drink wine in settings with dim lighting, such as candles. Under this illumination it's sometimes hard to find your mouth, let alone determine the exact colour or clarity of a wine. In fact, it might even prove difficult to see if something is floating in your glass. Since wine appreciation involves the sense of sight, and much can be determined about a wine by visual examination, it is important how well you can see the wine in the glass. Lighting can and does affect your perception of colour, depth of colour, and clarity, not to mention your mood. Harsh or fluorescent lighting dulls and falsifies colours. The best possible light to highlight the visuals of wine is daylight. If it were not so impractical, it would make sense to taste outdoors. Alternately, tasting near a window is a good idea. Since the character and dimension of daylight changes throughout the day, for consistency of examination, wine should theoretically be tasted at the same time each day. Keep in mind that sunny and cloudy conditions could conceivably illuminate wine slightly differently.

Dear Dr. WineKnow:
I seem to really feel the effect of wine when sipping in an airplane. It also doesn't seem to taste as good.
Diagnosis: Most people will agree that alcohol, in any format, gets to you quicker while flying. When it comes to wine, it's a matter of its physical chemistry. Let's not forget that wine is a rather complex liquid. It contains alcohol (ethanol), water, hydrocarbons, aldehydes, ketones, and phenols as well as sugars, acids, and gases. How all these components work together and under certain atmospheric conditions is probably sufficiently complex for an entire book on its own. To address this query, though, let's focus on the component in wine that affects us most . . . alcohol. Consider this. At very high altitudes, such as in a plane, air is thinner, containing little oxygen, and air pressure is low. This causes the alcohol in wine to evaporate quicker, entering the blood stream faster and more potently. You'll notice that wine appears more alcoholic and forward on the nose in the sky. However, the sensitivity of the palate is reduced at such heights, causing subtle flavours to disappear and making wine less flavoursome.
Prescription: Although this gives a whole different perspective on getting "high," the best approach to avoiding wines' alcoholic aggression in the sky is abstinence. If you do indulge, try drinking plenty of water for dilution in the system. As for the fact that wine tastes "blah" up there, try choosing wines with loads of fruit and strong aromas.

Dear Dr. WineKnow:
I don't know what it is but wine tastes better to me on sunny days than on cloudy, rainy days. Does the weather affect wine?
Diagnosis: Only the grapes in the vineyard, I'm afraid! There is no evidence that suggests wine behaves differently under high or low pressure. It sounds to me like you, yourself, are affected by barometric pressure. Low-pressure systems are often accompanied by overcast, rainy weather, causing many people to feel depressed or headachy. This could certainly affect your concentration, and your

perception and enjoyment of wine. High pressure usually indicates clear skies and sunshine, creating a state of well-being and clear thinking.

Prescription: Isolating and recognizing your individual problem is the key. What you need to do is monitor this a little closer and note the results. Chances are that barometric pressure affects other aspects of your life as well. You could indulge in wine only on sunny days. Otherwise, try tasting under a bright overhead light on cloudy, rainy days, and see if that makes any difference.

GRAPE FLASH

Did you know that you can experience different things in wine, depending on who you taste with? Assuming that the wine is not defective or suffering from bottle variation, there is a sound reason for this. Puzzling as it may seem, most of this can be attributed to non-verbal stimuli. A simple facial expression, a moan, or a grunt while tasting can affect another taster's perception and reaction to a certain wine, both positively and negatively. Chances are, if friends turn up their noses and wrinkle their faces while smelling and tasting a wine in front of you, your impression of that wine will lean to the negative side. A moan of pleasure might induce a positive impression of the wine. The best thing to do is try to block out the reaction of others to the wine and use your own judgement. Every person's palate is different, and likes and dislikes in wine vary. You might want to enjoy sipping with those who seem to have the same tastes in wine as you do.

Dear Dr. WineKnow:

I love wine. However, when I sip with people who only mildly enjoy it or have a less developed palate than mine, I don't get as much out of it.

Diagnosis: Nothing new here! It's called "contact high." Enthusiasm is contagious. Tasting with people who are really keen and knowledgeable about wine makes for a positive environment. It creates excitement about the product and initiates some great communication and wine dialogue. It also aids in learning and perception.

Prescription: If serious wine knowledge is what you are after, join a wine club or taste with people who are enthusiastic and from whom you can learn. Reserve tasting with others to social gatherings and perhaps you can pass on some of your new-found wine knowledge and excitement to them.

Dear Dr. WineKnow:
My wife and I found the same wine at a local wine shop that we enjoyed at a little French bistro on the Left Bank, in Paris. When we opened and tasted it at home, it wasn't quite the same. Something was missing. I can't, for the life of me, figure out what it is. Can you help?

Diagnosis: Certainly! I'll simply sprinkle some fairy wine dust over both of you. Untold numbers of people experience this after visiting a foreign country and tasting wine there. It's called the "romance factor," and it plays a large part in your enjoyment. There is nothing quite like tasting a wine in the place of origin. In your case it was a small bistro on the Left Bank of Paris. Sure, the wine itself may be the same at home, but what is missing is all the other extraneous stimuli that made the tasting in Paris that much more wonderful. What's missing are the beautiful locale, the street sounds, the smells, the ambiance, the French cuisine – in other words, the romance.

Prescription: Since the hedonistic experience is really the point here, the best you can do in a situation like this is to recreate, as much as possible, the scene of the original tasting. Try some candlelight, and soft French music, maybe watch a video depicting some Paris street scenes, to get in the mood. This should help. Vive la romance!

Show and Tell – Wine Fairs

What can I say about wine fairs? They are great venues for show-casing a multitude of product at one time and, I suppose, they provide a certain amount of market presence for producers. However, as ideal environments to taste wine – they're not. There is just too much stimuli for you to focus properly on the wines. There are, nonetheless, some tricks available to you, so you can get the most out of wine in these environments.

Dear Dr. WineKnow:

I find it very difficult to taste any wine properly at a wine show or fair. The crowds, noise, and food smells all get in the way of my enjoyment. I'd rather sip wine at home.

Diagnosis: This is a point well taken. We are all aware of how much our surroundings affect the way we see things and the world around us. It can easily alter our moods, colour our perceptions, and ruin our concentration. It's very tough to really enjoy a glass of wine if people are bumping into you or it's so noisy you can't hear yourself think. Furthermore, it's almost impossible to smell the subtleties of a specific wine if the air is permeated with a cornu-copia of extraneous smells like garlic or smoke from cooking.

Prescription: Generally, the best place to enjoy wine and get the most out of it is free of people traffic, loud, constant noise, and strong smells. Wine shows do not qualify as optimum environ-ments. For the record, most professional "wineknows" don't like seriously tasting at wine fairs. As far as wine awards given out at these shows, you can be sure the wines have been judged in a more ideal space at a different time.

Dear Dr. WineKnow:

When I go to a wine fair, I'm all over the map. I move from booth to booth, tasting anything that is offered. I try to taste as many different products as possible, too. At the end of the day I wonder how much I really got out of the show. Is there anything I can do to make my experience more worth while?

Diagnosis: It's a good thing you consulted a doctor. Strolling and tasting aimlessly through a wine fair is definitely not the way to go. If confusion is your ultimate goal, then this is the way to achieve it. Vinous chaos is the result. There is far too much product to taste and trying to taste everything is not only impossible but crazy. You simply can't get anything out of it.

Prescription: Focus, focus, focus! Before you actually enter the show, sit down with the show guide and look it over, getting an overview of who and what is there. Then plan your attack. Pick a wine style, a grape variety, a country, a region, a vintage, and concentrate only on wines that fall under that category. At the end of the day, you'll find you got a lot more out of the fair and have a real sense of accomplishment. You should end up with a pretty good sense of your chosen subject.

Dear Dr. WineKnow:

I have a real problem at wine shows. After trying several wines, I start to get buzzed and tired, which affects my tasting ability. Any suggestions?

Diagnosis: Rule number 1: DON'T SWALLOW! After the alcohol kicks in, your ability to decipher the complexity of wines and to think clearly goes right out the window. The effect of alcohol in the system tends to make you tired, as well.

Prescription: Here's what to do, aside from spitting all wine out. Take lots of breaks. Don't taste any more than four or five wines at a stretch. Drink lots of water and nibble food often. This should prevent you from doing a "horizontal tasting."

GRAPE FLASH

Did you know that the best time to take in a wine show is right when it opens? Say the show opens on a Friday at noon, for instance. If you can, book off of work and get to the show when the doors open. This way the exhibitors are fresh and willing to chat, and it's certainly not crowded. Ensure that, by five

> o'clock, you are on your way home, before the rest of humanity hits the show. If taking time off work is not an option, try arriving at the show as it opens on the weekend. Do your thing and vamoose. There are some definite times to avoid. Since most wine fairs run for long hours or for several days over a weekend, don't arrive near the close of the show. It's also not great around dinnertime. Most fairs become a mobile buffet around this time. The worst time is Friday or Saturday night. This is when all the "party animals" are out. They tend to be the least serious about wine. It's also the most crowded time.

Dear Dr. WineKnow:

Although I try spitting wine out at wine fairs, places to dispose of it are few and far between. Booths rarely have spittoons available. This is a problem.

Diagnosis: It's funny. You would think that organizers of these shows almost want to encourage you to swallow. Then they wonder why at peak times there seems to be some people who have simply imbibed too much.

Prescription: If no spittoons are available, use a rinsing station. Rinsing stations, the only other possible place to dispose of wine, are sporadically scattered throughout the show.

B.Y.O.S. There is only one real solution to this dilemma. Bring Your Own Spittoon. A container with a lid of some sort will do nicely. Perhaps you can rig up some sort of string or cord so the unit can hang from your neck leaving your hands free. At least this will allow you to taste and spit out a number of wines freely without having to seek out a rinsing station to dispose of it.

Dear Dr. WineKnow:

Many wine shows give you these small, industrial glasses with the name of the event on them. Why is that?

Diagnosis: Because they are inexpensive and sturdy. Industrial stemware is used strictly as a deterrent to breakage. The size that is chosen often helps determine the pour. You can only pour so much into a small glass. This takes the guesswork out of it for the exhibitors. It's also not hard to understand why producers of such shows plaster the name of the event on the glass. It's great advertising and the glass usually goes home with the attendee as a keepsake. However, these hinder appreciation.

Prescription: Again, the solution is obvious. Bring your own tasting glass.

Home on the Range

Ah, home! It's where the heart is and usually the place you're most comfortable, especially when it comes to wine enjoyment. The majority of people find this environment the ideal place to indulge, mainly because they don't have to travel and worry about alcohol's effect. Of course; although your comfort level may be at its ultimate here, the home does present its own variables, which can affect your appreciation.

Dear Dr. WineKnow:

Where's the best place to hold a wine tasting in one's home?

Diagnosis: For some reason, wine always tastes better at home. There's no muss or fuss, or dressing up. It's also the cheapest place, too, as you only pay the retail price for the wine.

Prescription: Choose a place in your home that is relatively quiet with little traffic. A windowed or well-lit back room, away from the kitchen, washroom, stairs, and so forth will do nicely.

Dear Dr. WineKnow:

I live in a small place and would love to host a wine tasting. However, it won't accommodate a large table, placemats, many chairs, or numerous glasses for each person. Should I forget about it?

Diagnosis: The only thing you need to forget about is a formal, sit-down tasting. Since this type of tasting requires a fair amount of space for furniture, chairs, and lots of stemware, it's simply not practical for your space. However, an informal one would work just fine. **Prescription:** Utilizing the kitchen counter, simply place the opened bottles, lined up, and allow tasters to move down the line, pouring themselves taste portions. One glass per person is all the stemware required as people can rinse between wines. Just make sure you provide buckets for dumping and water for rinsing. Enjoy!

Dear Dr. WineKnow:
I live alone and love a glass of wine with dinner. If I recork a white wine right away after opening it, how long will it last in the refrigerator? What about red?
Diagnosis: One should never waste a good bottle of anything. Air is wine's worst enemy. Regardless of colour, as soon as a bottle is opened it starts to oxidize. Short of using a wine preservation unit, its lifespan is fairly limited – a day or two at most.
Prescription: Try pouring the remaining wine into a smaller bottle, so the air pocket (ullage) between the cork and surface of the wine is minimal. To further slow down the deterioration process, refrigerate the bottle. When you're ready to drink it, let it come up to its appropriate serving temperature before pouring.

GRAPE FLASH

Did you know that those pump-type units for keeping wine fresh at home that are sold in wine shops are generally misused by most people? I'm sure you're aware of the item I'm referring to. It allows air to be sucked out of a wine bottle through a rubber stopper, thus preserving the wine. The rubber stopper is placed in the mouth of the bottle like a cork or plug. The pump unit, similar to a bicycle pump for filling your bicycle tires with air, is placed on top and pumped. Instead of putting air in, it basically vacuums the air out. The problem is most people pump too much. They pump beyond the point at which they feel resistance (usually when the air is out of the bottle). If you can smell the wine, then you've pumped too much. However, there are some models on the market now that actually click closed when all the air is out. If you purchase one of these units, try to get this version. In my experience, both of these work well if the air pocket, or "ullage," is minimal and the wine is young.

Dear Dr. WineKnow:

Short of having a nitrogen system to keep wine fresh at home, like they do in restaurants, is there anything out there that comes close? **Diagnosis:** The nitrogen system is the ultimate wine-preservation unit. It does a perfect job of keeping wine fresh. In this case, a tank of inert gas, mostly nitrogen, is attached to a single wine bottle, or many, via hoses. A regulator, not dissimilar to the one found on most gas BBQ's, controls the flow. Every time some wine is withdrawn from a bottle, the space within is replaced with this inert gas, thus keeping air away. If air can't reach the wine, it can't oxidize it. A bottle or many can be kept fresh indefinitely this way.

Some real wine aficionados have these at home, so they can keep a great wine going for a long time. For most of us though, they are cumbersome, take up space, and are aesthetically unappealing. **Prescription:** Enter a little aerosol spray can that's God's gift to wine lovers. This little baby is filled with inert gas and does the same thing that a nitrogen system does for a fraction of the cost. Besides, it doesn't take up much space and can be hidden away after use. After opening a bottle of wine and pouring some, you simply use the attached straw to spritz three or four shots into the bottle and recork it. The inert gas keeps air at bay, and the wine stays fresh for weeks. You simply reapply it every time you open and pour some more wine. If you refrigerate the bottle after spraying, I find that it will stay fresh even longer. You should get approximately one hundred and twenty sprays out of a can. This is enough for numerous bottles of wine, depending on how much you use it.

Some larger liquor stores sell these. One brand is called Private Preserve.

Dear Dr. WineKnow:
I love to peel wine labels off bottles and paste them into a book with my tasting notes. I usually soak the labels off, but this often ruins them. Is there any other method of removing them intact?
Diagnosis: I used to know a chap who constantly peeled labels off of beer bottles. However, I believe his habit was a nervous tic. Many people like to remove wine labels and keep them in a book. Getting them off the bottle is never an easy task. The glue used to stick them on is heavy duty and meant to hold through most anything.
Prescription: There is a product on the market that lifts labels from wine bottles relatively quickly. It's a clear, adhesive piece of plastic that is placed over the label, rubbed firmly, and peeled off, taking the label with it. The longer you leave it on the label, the greater the sticking power. For larger labels, two overlapping pieces of plastic will do the job. One brand is called Label Lifters, produced by Vintage Niagra Adventures (905) 708-0159 or www.vna.on.ca.

Dear Dr. WineKnow:
I always bring a special bottle of wine from my cellar when I'm invited for dinner. However, I'm upset that most of the time it doesn't get opened and I don't get a chance to taste it. Is there anything I can do?
Diagnosis: The gift of wine is always appreciated. However, expecting the bottle to be opened at that specific dinner may be unrealistic, since the wine choices for the meal may have already been made.
Prescription: Put a sticky note on the bottle saying "stale date – best before 9 p.m." There is no guarantee that the wine you bring will be opened, but here's something you can do that might make it more likely. Call the host beforehand, and politely ask what is on the menu, so that you might bring a wine to complement the meal. This will be seen as thoughtful and helpful. Chances are that they will use the wine you bring for the meal, and you will get to taste it.

Restaurant Wining

For many people, dining out at restaurants would not be complete without wine to enhance the meal. For others, it may be the only time they actually have wine. Restaurants are well aware of wine's role as an enhancer of the dining experience. This is perhaps the most important venue where wine is really showcased, and presentation and service generally take centre stage. Of course, the extent to which wine is highlighted depends on the individual establishment and their commitment to it. It's also the place where the consumer's wine knowledge and comfort level is put to the test – the most. Yes, the restaurant environment presents a whole set of variables when it comes to understanding and enjoying wine.

Wine Lists
The wine menu can be one of the most fascinating, yet frightening and intimidating, aspects of enjoying wine out in a restaurant. There can be so many names, countries, and regions represented that the average consumer is totally overwhelmed. Pricing is another story altogether. For many people who are dining out and ordering wine, price is usually the barometer that dictates what will be ordered. People have a dollar amount in their head that they are willing to spend on wine. Unfortunately, for many, this dollar amount is relatively small compared to what they are willing to spend on food. The smart consumer would be wise to consult the waiter for the best buys on the wine list that will go with their food of choice.

Dear Dr. WineKnow:
To me, simple is better. What would you consider the simplest way for a restaurant to list their wines?
Diagnosis: For many people, looking at a wine list and deciding what to drink can be very confusing. So many wines, so little time!
Prescription: The simplest way restaurants list their available

wines is usually geographically. Under general headings of red and white or grape variety, they appear under country or region in ascending order of price. So you simply look at the country or region you like and order according to price.

Dear Dr. WineKnow:
I don't know from names of wine at all, so spelling them out on the wine list does nothing for me. Can't they use some other method?
Diagnosis: It's quite true. Unless you are an oenophile, the names of wines don't mean too much to you. It might as well be another language. This type of list caters to the wine-knowledgeable.
Prescription: To combat this problem, some establishments utilize a rather fashionable format on their wine lists. They list the wines by style. You'll see headings like light-bodied whites, or full-bodied reds. So, even if you don't know the names of the wines, you can get some idea of what their character is like merely by the heading they fall under. This also makes them infinitely easier to match to food, especially if you don't want to ask for assistance in ordering.

Dear Dr. WineKnow:
Is there a way restaurants can make their wine lists a little more user-friendly with regards to food they offer?
Diagnosis: Restaurants that take the mystery and intimidation out of ordering wine deserve much credit. If a restaurateur can make the customer feel totally at ease with choosing wine, then the dining experience is elevated to another level. The customer can concentrate purely on hedonistic, gastronomic enjoyment, without any discomfort about wine.
Prescription: More and more dining facilities are adopting progressive, innovative ways of presenting their wine lists. Many are actually combining the food and wine on a list as one, matched up. So a particular dish would have the appropriate wine choice right next to it on the menu. This novel approach is being met with great success. Of course, anyone, at any time, can stray from the listed matches and order separately.

GRAPE FLASH

Did you know that the best wines to order in an ethnic restaurant are those of the country of origin of the restaurant? Most ethnic eateries are owned and operated by someone from that country. Italians usually own Italian restaurants; Greeks usually own Greek restaurants; Spanish usually own Spanish restaurants. These people were raised with this cuisine and most probably know it best, along with the wines.

Dear Dr. WineKnow:

I'm a new restaurant owner and would like to learn some ways of promoting my wine and helping the customer make selections. Can you help?

Diagnosis: It's no secret that wine can be a pretty overwhelming and intimidating subject for restaurateur and customer alike. Anything a restaurateur does to make the average customer more comfortable with ordering wine is promotion in itself. As far as the customer is concerned, the simpler and easier, the better.

Prescription: Wine displays near the main entrance and throughout the restaurant are a good start. This displays the establishment's focus on wine. It is also helpful to have specialized themes, highlighting new wines, specific countries, regions, wineries, or producers. Try offering all-inclusive dinner packages that pair specific wines to certain menu items. Have special "in-house" promotions, where agents and distributors come to the restaurant and offer tastings. Make use of tent cards and newspaper reviews on tabletops. Display wine labels on the wine list. Include menu inserts, highlighting specific wines. Staff training is also one of the best catalysts for promoting and selling product. Far too many restaurants lose out on better wine sales simply because of laziness or lack of interest.

Dear Dr. WineKnow:
Dining establishments seem to come and go these days. What do they do with all the wine they must have in their cellars when they go out of business?

Diagnosis: You would like me say they have one hell of a party and drink it all, wouldn't you? Unfortunately, there is usually a ton of money tied up in wine inventory if a restaurant goes belly-up. In some cases, this can amount to a fortune. They often will sell it off to other restaurants, hotels, or collectors.

Prescription: If a restaurant with a good wine list is going out of business, there is perhaps a great opportunity here for individuals to purchase some wine at decent reduced prices. The restaurant may have in its possession product that is unusual, no longer available, rare, or old. Try approaching the owner to see if he or she is amenable to this idea. They may already have made a deal with another restaurant or individual to take it off their hands, but it's certainly worth a try.

GRAPE FLASH

Did you know that many restaurants offer literally hundreds of wines you've never heard of or seen for sale in wine shops? To stand out and to lure people in with unusual and diverse wines that are not readily accessible to the average consumer in retail outlets, many will bring wines in privately or directly through agents and distributors. This gives them an edge over their competitors. It also allows them more flexibility in setting prices for those wines on their lists.

Dear Dr. WineKnow:
What are some of the things included in the markup of wines in restaurants?

Diagnosis: Aside from the actual cost of the wine the restaurant pays, certain things must be covered.

Prescription: Such items as the service involved, the use of glassware, and corkage are all included. The markup usually starts with a basic 3 per cent of the cost price increase to cover loss from overpouring, spillage, and breakage.

Dear Dr. WineKnow:

What would you say is the fairest method a restaurant could use to mark up their wines?

Diagnosis: This is a tough question. There are many who believe that no matter what method is utilized, it's just too much. However, you must realize that restaurants have to go out and buy wine, store it, serve it, use and dirty stemware, wash the stemware, and maybe train staff to be knowledgeable about it. It's only logical that they should be charging for it.

Prescription: Perhaps the method of markup that appeals most to the consumer, because they tend to know what many wines cost retail, is the flat markup. In this case, a reasonable, fixed dollar amount is simply added to the cost of each wine.

GRAPE FLASH

Did you know that in many restaurants more expensive wine has less of a markup than less expensive wine? Many restaurants like to act as educators and introduce their clients and customers to better wines. Enter the sliding-scale markup. Here the pricier the wine, the less the markup. This encourages the consumer to drink better-quality product. So, overall, the wine may cost you more, but the actual restaurant markup is less. Thus, better wine on these wine lists represents better value.

Dear Dr. WineKnow:

Are there any other methods of marking up wines – other than the straight markup – that restaurants use?

Diagnosis: Restaurants are always trying to figure out ways of making more money from alcohol. For most, this is where they make the major profits. There really isn't much profit to be had from the food.

Prescription: The old dartboard method works well for many. Wherever the darts land is what is charged. In reality, one other method is used by dining establishments, the cost-plus markup. The cost-plus markup involves increasing each wine's price by a certain percentage, then a fixed dollar amount is added on.

House Wine

"House wine" originated in restaurants as a way for the owner to bring in special wine that he or she bought in barrel, self-labelled, and offered to customers inexpensively. This was usually fairly decent, and the restaurant's clientele came to rely on the owner's judgement. Although there may be the rare proprietor who still does this, especially in Europe, times have changed. Today, "house wine" is the least expensive wine available in the restaurant. Because of intimidation, lack of desire to study a wine list, or a wish for a single glass of wine, many average consumers choose this route.

Dear Dr. WineKnow:

Why is it that restaurants sell "house wine"? Wouldn't it be more profitable to sell only better bottles? Also why is house wine sold by the glass usually not great?

Diagnosis: Ideally, if "house wine" is not available and the diner wants some wine, he or she will order something off the list. However, experience has shown that, in reality, wine will not be ordered at all if some sort of inexpensive vino is not offered. "House wine" offers the diner an alternative.

Prescription: For most who order "house wine," all they want is a simple, inoffensive drink to wash down a meal. The average consumer is satisfied. If you do decide on "house wine," remember that it is far more economical to order a half-carafe than two single glasses.

Another point here is that the restaurant may end up being stuck with remaining wine in the bottle at closing time. It's certainly easier, more economical, and less painful to forfeit some leftover inexpensive wine than a high ticket number. If you are seeking out better-quality wines by the glass, try better restaurants. They generally offer higher quality. Your other alternative, and probably a better one, is a wine bar. Since, as the name implies, their focus is wine, they usually offer the best selection by the glass.

Dear Dr. WineKnow:
There are so many reasonably good wines under cork on the market it is beyond me why any restaurant would want to serve something under a screw cap as a "house wine."
Diagnosis: Amen, brother! With the vast amount of good-quality/value wines coming out of South America, Portugal, the Balkans, and the south of France, today, there seems to be no reason for it. But there are some reasons. First of all, they're inexpensive. Secondly, screw-cap selections usually come in larger sizes, making them more economical. Thirdly, there is no fuss or muss in opening them. No special, strength, skill, training, or corkscrew is required. Finally, believe it or not, a screw cap is a better seal on a bottle of wine than a cork and will keep wine fresher, longer.

There is no doubt that wine selections with a cork rather than a screw cap are much more romantic.

GRAPE FLASH

Did you know that, if you want a single glass of wine with dinner in a restaurant but are unhappy with the selection, there are other options? You could probably order a bottle, have only one glass, and take the rest home. However, unless you plan to consume it very shortly thereafter, the wine will most probably go bad. Ask the waiter if there are any half-bottles available. This amounts to two decent-sized glasses of wine. If not, a discreet word with the owner or manager might persuade him or her to open something better for you to have a glass. More than likely they will be able to sell off the rest of the bottle the same way. This works well if you are a regular customer. If this fails, forget wine and order a beer or a cocktail.

Dear Dr. WineKnow:

How do restaurants keep wine fresh if they are pouring many by the glass?

Diagnosis: This is a really good question. Consider this. Air is wine's worst enemy. Once a bottle is opened, it starts to oxidize. It's only a matter of time until it's no longer good. Simply recorking the bottle continuously after opening and pouring will really not slow down its demise. As a result, many wines by the glass appear tired or stale when ordered.

Prescription: Only order wine by the glass in restaurants that utilize some sort of a preservation system. Many, like wine bars, use the nitrogen system mentioned on p. 218. Ask!

Dear Dr. WineKnow:

What do restaurants do with wine that they've opened to pour by the glass when it's left over at closing time?

Diagnosis: Most restaurants open a bottle of wine and pour by the glass throughout the day. The bottle just keeps being opened, poured, and recorked until it is empty. The owner may be stuck with opened leftover wine at closing time. This is not a great situation if the wine is expensive, since whatever remains most probably will be pitched out.

Prescription: Do yourself a favour. Never, ever order wine by the glass just before closing time in a restaurant. You're liable to get the dregs of a bottle. Also, be careful when doing the same at opening time. Request that the pour come from a freshly opened bottle.

Dear Dr. WineKnow:
Some wine lists don't tell you the size of the pour of the "house wine" by the glass. I'm always embarrassed to ask.
Diagnosis: Isn't that bothersome? For some people, asking the size of the pour can be a bit intimidating or embarrassing.
Prescription: A word of note to restaurateurs! The size of the pour should be clearly indicated on the wine list. If it isn't, ask, and don't feel bad about it.

GRAPE FLASH

Did you know that the average pour for a glass of "house wine" in a restaurant is about 6 oz.? However, I have seen less. Considering the cost of most wines by the glass, you'd think you would get much more. However, most people who order a glass of wine as opposed to a bottle, make that glass last the whole meal, and it's generally more than you would pour out of a bottle for yourself.

Dear Dr. WineKnow:
Would the size of pour differ for an aperitif, sweet, or fortified wine?
Diagnosis: In some cases the restaurant likes to act as your liquor-control board, dictating how much you should drink. Most people don't consume large quantities of sweet wines anyway, because they are just too rich to handle in quantity and are generally higher in alcohol. Therefore, the restaurant passes this lifestyle statement on to the consumer in its pours.
Prescription: Average pour for aperitif, sweet, or fortified wine is around 2 to 3 oz. The pours don't look so small, though, because they are usually served in smaller glasses.

Dear Dr. WineKnow:
How do restaurants mark up "house wine," and wine by the glass?

Diagnosis: "House wine," like other wine, gets marked up. Sometimes it takes more of a beating and is marked up higher than other wine on the list, mainly because it is poured by the glass or litre. **Prescription:** It usually works this way: the size of the portion is calculated as a percentage of the overall cost of each bottle. Then the 3 per cent is added to cover loss from overpouring, spillage, and breakage. Finally, one of the various markup systems is implemented.

Wine Rituals

There are certain behaviour patterns that go on in restaurants all focussed around wine. In better restaurants, where wine really matters, this behaviour takes on an almost religious significance.

Dear Dr. WineKnow:

When I arrive at a restaurant for dinner, they sometimes seat me near the kitchen or front door. Either way, the smell of food cooking or the people coming and going interferes with my enjoyment of the wine I ordered. What do I do?

Diagnosis: Many restaurants, especially small ones, have simple layouts or dining facilities that don't allow for ideal seating locations. In others, the best tables are usually given to regular customers or large groups.

Prescription: Slip the waiter a bill or two when he or she greets you at the door. Surprisingly, this happens quite often, not just in the movies. Alternately, when making your reservation, request a table away from the kitchen, entrance, and restroom. If this is done well in advance, most establishments should be able to guarantee prime seating. A corner table is often a good suggestion. If you are already in the restaurant and unhappy with your location, ask your waiter to relocate you.

Dear Dr. WineKnow:

Why do some restaurants have wine waiters (sommeliers) and others don't?

Diagnosis: It's usually a matter of dollars and cents. Sommeliers go through extensive schooling and training. As a result, they have to be paid more.

Prescription: Most restaurateurs would rather hire experienced waiters with reasonably good wine knowledge, who can handle both food and wine service. The really enlightened few will either hire a pro to do staff training or run regular in-house wine tastings, where the staff can actually try the wines on the list. Often, the more upscale restaurants with well-known chefs and extensive wine lists have sommeliers on staff. In these establishments, wine is an extremely important part of the dining experience. One thing is certain; if a restaurant does have a sommelier on staff, wine will cost a bit more there, as his or her expertise demands a higher salary.

Dear Dr. WineKnow:

Most waiters in restaurants ask about drinks before they ask about food. It's hard to know what to drink before I decide on what to eat.

Diagnosis: The "offer the drink before food" phenomenon is a carryover of the cocktail ritual. An aperitif supposedly helps relaxation and prepares the palate for food by getting the gastronomic juices flowing. Often, people will order something other than wine as an aperitif before the meal. In reality, any spirit or highly alcoholic drink before wine will kill the palate.

Prescription: Rule of thumb: choose your food first, then a wine to complement it.

GRAPE FLASH

Did you know that the historical reason the waiter or sommelier in a restaurant gives you the cork when the bottle is opened is to prevent fraud? The presentation of the cork originated to curtail fraudulent dealers from passing off a wine for something it wasn't. Usually, the cork was stamped with the producer's name. When it was extracted from the bottle, it was presented to the purchaser to prove it actually was the wine stated on the label that was requested. Today, the presentation of the cork continues that tradition, but goes much further. If the cork is mouldy or defective in some way, the diner can immediately see this and question the health of the wine. One is supposed to smell the cork, as well, to see that it is void of any funky "off"-smells. If so, the bottle can be rejected. Do examine the cork when the waiter presents it to you. Check to see that the winery's name is on it and that it is relatively clean. A knowledgeable word of advice is called for, when you are given the cork to smell. To me, corks always smell like cork. If they are clean, not much can be determined from them. Have the waiter pour you some wine in a glass, instead.

Dear Dr. WineKnow:
What should I be looking for when the waiter opens a new bottle of wine and pours me a little in my glass to try?
Diagnosis: Wine, when opened, can display many different problems. There might be something doing the backstroke in the glass. It could be cloudy, hazy, dirty, or oily. The possibilities are endless. The smell could be awful. The stability, cleanliness, and clarity are what's important here.
Prescription: Cleanliness and health! Visually examine the wine to make sure it looks good enough to ingest. Then sniff it for "off" or bad odours. If it smells like your gym bag, then something is wrong. Finally, taste it to see that all is copacetic in the mouth. Any problem, simply let the waiter, who is poised and ready to pour for all, know immediately. If in doubt, have someone else at the table or the waiter taste it to confirm.

It's trickier to send back wine you simply don't like. Although it may not be "off," most reputable places won't argue – they will just sell it off "by the glass."

Dear Dr. WineKnow:
I ordered a bottle of white wine in a restaurant recently. When the wine was poured and the waiter left, I noticed some shiny crystals sitting at the bottom of the bottle. Thinking they were pieces of glass, I sent the wine back.

Diagnosis: Most people would probably do the same in this situation, but these really were not shards of glass. They are what we in the profession call "wine diamonds," and they occur in certain whites and even some reds. Sometimes they adhere to the cork. They are potassium bitartrate crystals that result if a wine is not cold-stabilized. Believe it or not, they are actually a good sign in a wine, implying reasonable quality. Their appearance means the wine hasn't been pasteurized (heated) and then quickly chilled before bottling.

Prescription: Although unsightly, they are totally harmless with no colour or taste. Next time, merely have the waiter decant the wine.

GRAPE FLASH

Did you know that many people end up drinking wine they are unhappy with in a restaurant because they don't want to create a scene? Here's what happens. In a majority of cases someone has ordered a wine with which they are not really familiar. In other words, they don't know what to expect from the taste. It may simply be that they don't like the wine because it is unusual, odd, or not what they anticipated, and are embarrassed to say anything. This can be avoided by asking your server for advice on what to drink before committing yourself, and on what aromatics and flavours can be expected from specific wines. This will cut down on unexpected surprises and reduce the risk of disappointment. Other times someone thinks a wine is "off" (bad) but is unsure or lacks the confidence to speak up. Unless you are a pro or a very experienced amateur, deciding whether a wine is faulty or not is a tough call. If you really think the wine is defective, ask someone else at your table or another to taste it to confirm your results. Then discreetly hail the waiter and state your case. Life is far too short to drink bad wine.

Dear Dr. WineKnow:

When dining out at restaurants, waiters fill my wine glass to the rim. No sooner do I take a sip, than they are back, topping it up.

Diagnosis: Wine glasses should be poured one-quarter to one-third full. Servers must keep in mind that the glass is not for water or juice and that wine is not ordered to quench one's thirst but to complement and enhance food. Restaurateurs should spend more time training their staff on wine service. It makes a huge difference in enjoyment.

GLASS FILL

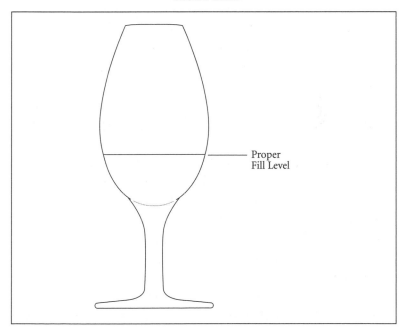

Proper
Fill Level

Prescription: If after the initial opening and pouring of the wine to check its stability, the server keeps topping up your glass, tell him/her you will deal with the wine pouring for the rest of the meal.

Dear Dr. WineKnow:
My buddy and I disagree on a specific wine-service procedure in restaurants. He says that, if you order a second bottle of the same wine, it's all right for the waiter to pour the newly opened wine into the old glasses. I say we should be given new glasses as if it were a different wine altogether. Who's right?

Diagnosis: It depends on the situation. Are the old glasses empty or is there still wine from the first bottle in them? Protocol should dictate that the new bottle be checked for defects, either by the waiter/sommelier or someone at the table. If it is healthy, you could simply pour away, but any bottle variation from the first to the second might go undetected. The bottom line is this. Unless in a very wine-savvy restaurant with knowledgeable staff, don't count on the waiter to know exactly how to handle wine service in general and this situation in particular. It's up to you to ensure that the new wine is handled the way you like.

Prescription: Personally, I would prefer new glasses.

A Marriage Made in Heaven – Wine and Food

The marriage of wine and food is truly one made in heaven. They do so much to enhance each other. Some wines on their own taste okay, but when meshed with food, become something special. Wine and food play off each other. They feed on each other's positive points and elevate the whole to something far better.

A perfect wine and food match is indeed a treat for the senses. Knowing and understanding the individual structure of both the wine and the food is essential to matching the two.

The art of matching wine and food can be extended to cooking, as well. Not only does a wine mingle with certain foods, but actually using wine in cooking can further pull the two flavours together and add pizazz.

The Art of Compatibility

When it comes to wine and food working together, there are definitely some rules involved of which every person should be aware. Certain "dos" and "don'ts" govern matches. Much of this has to do with key elements in the food and/or wine.

Dear Dr. WineKnow:

How is it that some wines just match certain foods perfectly and others don't?

Diagnosis: Wine and food generally go together because they either share a similar characteristic or opposite characteristics play off one another. These characteristics fall into three categories: components, flavours, and textures. We, as human beings, are pretty limited in our scope. We can experience only five components: sweet, sour, bitter, salt, and umami (savouriness or deliciousness). There are a zillion flavours to be tasted as well as many different textures to be appreciated.

Prescription: By simply matching a similar component in a wine to the same component in a food product, harmony should be achieved. The same flavour in a wine should blend with the same flavour in a food choice. Finally, a textured wine should integrate with a similarly textured food. More difficult but equally enticing are opposite components, flavours, and textures in wine and food that pull them together. Trial and error plays a major part in learning what works together or doesn't. One eventually builds up a sixth sense about wine and food compatibility. Certainly, the art of association will kick in, too. If one match works, similar wines and food will probably work.

Dear Dr. WineKnow:

I don't like red wine. What am I to do with all the dishes that call for a red as the perfect match?

Diagnosis: You make a very good point here. The old adage "red wine with meat and white with fish" is still important, but it doesn't hold as much water as it used to. Much more innovation exists today. If, for instance, the perfect wine match to a roast lamb calls for a red like Cabernet Sauvignon, but you don't like red wine, then the match means nothing to you. The key is to match the lamb on a different level.

Prescription: Try matching on a flavour level with the seasonings and spices used on the lamb. The other alternative is to link it on a textural level. Lamb is richly textured, so pick a richly textured white wine.

Dear Dr. WineKnow:

I've heard the expression "food wine" used to describe a specific vino. What exactly does this mean?

Diagnosis: Some wine just cries out for food when tasted. Perhaps it is rustic, hard-edged, tannic, or contains a lot of earthy tones. In other words, the fruit or sweetness of the wine is in the background or subdued. What's upfront are the "terroir" flavours, which make the wine less easy to drink on its own. However, with food, it comes across much better, since it has other components to play off. More reds than whites tend to be "food wines," because reds usually contain more bitter elements due to skin contact for colour. Also, more wines from the "Old World" than the "New World" tend to fall into this category.

Prescription: Always taste a wine before serving it to your guests. This will ensure its health and tell you whether it would work better with food. If deemed a "food wine," serve some food or nibbles with it. Some "food wine" becomes easier to drink with age, as its hard edges are rounded off.

MATCHING WINE STYLES AND FOOD ENTRÉES

SPARKLING   fish, white meat
Champagne
Prosecco
Sekt
Crémant d'Alsace
Crémant de Bourgogne
Spumante
Cava

LIGHT, CRISP WHITES   oysters, mussels, clams
Muscadet
Frascati
Riesling
Vinho Verde
Auxerrois
Pinot Blanc
Trebbiano
Pinot Grigio

LIGHT TO MEDIUM-BODIED WHITES   shrimps, scallops
Sauvignon Blanc
Seyval Blanc
Entre-Deux-Mers
Aligoté
Grüner Veltliner
Malvasia
Soave
Müller-Thurgau
Verdicchio
Vidal

MEDIUM-BODIED WHITES   white fish
Chablis

Chenin Blanc
Orvieto
Some Chardonnay
Sémillon
Unoaked Spanish Whites

FULL-BODIED, OAKY WHITES   lobster, salmon, crab
White Burgundy
Warm-climate Chardonnay
White Rhône
Pinot Gris
Viognier
White Rioja
Pouilly-Fumé

AROMATIC WHITES   hot, spicy, exotic food
Gewürztraminer
Muscat
Scheurebe

ROSÉ   fried fish, white meat, cold cuts, pork
Blush
White Zinfandel
Tavel
Blanc de Noirs
Spanish Rosados

LIGHT-BODIED REDS   chicken, veal, turkey
Beaujolais
Gamay
Bardolino
Dolcetto
Minervois
Grignolino

LIGHT TO MEDIUM-BODIED REDS   pork, hamburger, ham
Valpolicella
Loire reds
Cru Beaujolais
Dornfelder
Merlot
Malbec

MEDIUM TO FULL-BODIED REDS   beef, lamb, duck
Red Burgundy
Châteaux-bottled Bordeaux
Cabernet Sauvignon
Sangiovese
Chianti
Brunello di Montalcino
Vino Nobile di Montepulciano
Red Rioja
Dão
Pinotage
Cabernet Franc

RICH, FULL-BODIED REDS   game, spicy food
Northern Rhône reds
Shiraz
Amarone
Zinfandel
Nebbiolo
Châteauneuf-du-Pape
Aglianico
Petite Sirah
Syrah

SWEET WINES   desserts, fruit, veiny cheeses, nuts
Icewine
Sauternes

Barsac
Late-harvest German
Tokaji Aszú
Muscat

FORTIFIED   smoked meats, soups, nuts, desserts
Sherry
Port
Marsala   .
Madeira

Dear Dr. WineKnow:
When I was at a friend's place for dinner the other night, she served
a heavy Cabernet Sauvignon with a rather light torte. It did not
work at all. Can you shed some light on why?
Diagnosis: It's all a matter of weight and character. Obviously the
Cabernet overpowered the torte. It was simply too much wine for
the torte to handle. With much more flavour and body, it over-
shadowed the flavour and body in the food and pushed it into the
background. I'll bet the food was totally lost in the richness of the
wine. Certainly not a good match!
Prescription: Here's another rule for imprinting on your brain.
Always match the character of the wine with the character of the
dish. A delicate wine with a delicate dish and a heavier wine with a
heavy dish. Keeping these structural elements in sync will help
wine and food matches attain affinity.

Dear Dr. WineKnow:
I like my steaks rare and bloody, while my wife likes hers well done.
I know that red wine works so well with red meat. Is there one wine
that will work for both of us?
Diagnosis: The answer in a nutshell is "no." Let me explain. The
reason red wine and red meat go so well together is because the
tannin in the wine meshes with the blood in the meat. So, for your
rare steak, a tannic wine plays off it perfectly. However, too much

tannin will overwhelm your wife's well-done portion, making it taste bitter.

Prescription: Rare-meat lovers should choose tannic red wines like young Bordeaux, Burgundy, or Italian. Well-done meat lovers should opt for fruity reds with as little tannin as possible. Try Beaujolais, Gamay, Merlot, or mature reds in which the tannin has subsided.

Dear Dr. WineKnow:

I matched what I thought was the perfect wine to an entrée, but my side dish of garlic mashed potato destroyed that match. Can you explain it?

Diagnosis: Overdid the garlic, did we? Plain and simple, the garlic mashed potato overpowered the flavour of the entrée and became the focal point of the dish.

Prescription: Make this an ironclad rule. Always match the wine to the strongest flavour on the plate, even if it isn't the entrée. In this case, you should have matched the wine to the garlic mashed potato.

Dear Dr. WineKnow:

I noticed that, when I add certain spices or herbs to an entrée, the wine I usually serve with it, which is supposed to be an ideal match, no longer works. Why?

Diagnosis: This relationship between wine and food involves a delicate balance of elements. If strong spices are added to a dish, the wine ends up ultimately competing with the spice, as opposed to meshing with the entrée.

Prescription: Herbivores beware. Always match the wine to the spice of an entrée, as opposed to the entrée itself. Otherwise, affinity can be lost.

Wine and Herbs

WINE MATCH	HERBS

WHITE WINE

Chardonnay	Chevril, Fennel, Hyssop, Lavender, Sage, Tarragon
Chenin Blanc	Dill
Gewürztraminer	Chervil, Coriander, Hyssop, Mint, Winter Savory
Muscat	Coriander, Lavender
Muscadet	Chives, Sorrel
Pinot Grigio	Thyme
Pinot Gris	Coriander
Riesling	Chervil, Dill, Hyssop, Parsley, Winter Savory
Sauvignon Blanc	Basil, Bay Leaf, Chervil, Chives, Dill, Fennel, Oregano, Parsley, Sage, Sorrel, Tarragon, Thyme, Winter Savory
Sémillon	Tarragon
Trebbiano	Oregano, Thyme
Vidal	Tarragon
Vinho Verde	Sage

ROSÉ

White Zinfandel	Basil, Chervil, Mint

RED WINE

Baco Noir	Fennel, Sage, Dill
Cabernet Franc	Parsley
Cabernet Sauvignon	Basil, Bay leaf, Hyssop, Lavender, Mint, Rosemary, Sage, Tarragon, Thyme, Winter Savory

Gamay	Basil, Parsley
Maréchal Foch	Dill, Sage
Merlot	Basil, Fennel, Parsley
Nebbiolo	Fennel, Oregano
Pinot Noir	Lavender, Rosemary, Thyme
Pinotage	Bay leaf
Sangiovese	Bay leaf, Oregano
Shiraz	Tarragon, Winter Savory
Syrah	Lavender, Rosemary, Winter Savory
Zinfandel	Basil, Bay leaf, Chives, Fennel, Mint, Rosemary, Sorrel, Winter Savory

Dear Dr. WineKnow:

I'm crazy about spicy food, but I always have a hard time matching wine to it.

Diagnosis: Spicy food can present wine with a most difficult task. Often, very aggressive and exotic flavours deal a death blow to wine; the flavours and seasonings are just too much for it. If the spice is hot, as well, it becomes even harder to successfully match wine. The strong flavours in the food would seem to dictate the use of strong flavours in the wine choice.

Prescription: Try it hot, hot, hot. If you enjoy foods like Cajun, Indian, Szechwan, Mexican, or chili, you have three options for wine choices. You can either pick a wine that is equally spicy with peppery notes, like a Rhone red, Syrah, Shiraz, or Zinfandel. You might pick something that is aromatically spicy, like a Gewürztraminer, Muscat, or Traminer. Your final wine choice could be something sweeter, like a late harvest Riesling or Vidal. If all else fails, there's always beer.

Dear Dr. WineKnow:

I love to dine "al fresco" in the nice weather. Will this affect what wine I sip with my meal?

Diagnosis: Dining outside in the warm weather is such a treat. However, there are so many extraneous smells, like those of grass, trees, lawn-mower fumes, and car exhaust, that can overpower the nuances of fine wine.

Prescription: My advice for "wining" outdoors in the warm weather is to keep it simple. Forget about pulling your best bottles from the cellar, since they won't show very well in the great outdoors – there's too much competition in the way of other olfactory stimulation. Young, forward, fruity numbers are more appropriate.

Dear Dr. WineKnow:

I love to BBQ and eat outdoors in the warm weather. What wines work best with BBQ food?

Diagnosis: I can almost smell those steaks grilling now. There's nothing quite like barbecued food. The flavours of smoke and charcoal on the food just drive me wild. However, this can be a bit of a problem for wine matches. These aromatics and flavours are generally aggressive and rob delicate, complex wines of their subtleties.

Prescription: For barbecued food, choose wines that are relatively simple, fruity, young, robust, lighter in body, alcohol, and oak. Try Sauvignon Blanc, Vidal, Seyval Blanc, Pinot Grigio, Riesling, Pinot Blanc, and some softer Chardonnay for whites. Red-wine lovers should vie for Merlot, lighter Cabernet, Gamay, Zweigelt, fruitier Zinfandel, heartier Shiraz, and Barbera.

Dear Dr. WineKnow:

If I decide to use a sauce on a dish, will that affect the wine match?

Diagnosis: Sauces on food are very much like seasoning, often aggressively flavoured. They also possess a textural element. A thick, rich, creamy sauce would certainly change the direction of the wine match. So a simple grilled chicken dish becomes somewhat sweeter and fatter with the addition of a buttery, creamy sauce. The wine match now requires a richer wine, with more fruit.

Prescription: No need to get saucy! Sauces will alter the wine match. If you want the wine match to remain close, use a sauce that is lightly textured and seasoned. Otherwise, you'll have to start looking at the big guns as far as the wine match is concerned. Another option is just to serve the sauce on the side and let people add as little or as much as desired. They may choose to pass entirely.

WINE AND VEGETABLES

Matching wine to veggies can be problematic, as most vegetables tend to be somewhat herbaceous.

BROWN VEGETABLES:

Robust, oakier whites	Pinot Gris/oaked Sauvignon Blanc/Viognier
Fuller, earthier reds	red Bordeaux/red Rhônes/Pinotage, Cabernet Sauvignon/Nebbiolo

GREEN VEGETABLES:

Crisp, herbaceous whites	Sauvignon Blanc – unoaked (Loire, California, South Africa)
Fruity reds	Gamay (Beaujolais)
Herbaceous reds	Cabernet Franc (Loire, Canada)
Rosé	Rosé (white Zinfandel)

RED VEGETABLES:

Crisp whites	(Vinho Verde, Muscadet, dry Riesling, Pinot Blanc)
Crisp, robust reds	(Sangiovese/Zweigelt/Baco Noir)

RICHLY SEASONED/SAUCED:

Fuller, oakier whites	(Chardonnay, Sémillon)
Fuller, oakier reds	(Cabernet Sauvignon/Zinfandel/Nebbiolo)

SPICY/HOT (SEASONED/SAUCED):

sweeter whites	(late-harvest Riesling/medium-dry Vouvray)
aromatic whites	(Gewürztraminer/Muscat)
spicy reds	(Syrah/Shiraz)

Dear Dr. WineKnow:

How does one deal with fried food when it comes to wine matches?

Diagnosis: Think about what fried food feels like on the palate. There's usually an oil slick the size of Montana that literally forms a coating on the inside of the mouth. If you run your tongue along your gums after this kind of food, it's greasy. In fact, the grease is often very difficult to get rid of. You've probably noticed that, if you drink a soda with this type of food, it's not as bad. The bubbles help remove it.

Prescription: Sparkles work. You have two options in matching wine to fried or greasy food. Like the soda with bubbles, you could choose a sparkling wine. This works well in cleaning the palate. Alternately, try a wine with good acidity. The sourness of the wine does a nice job in cutting through the oiliness to clean up the palate.

Dear Dr. WineKnow:

When I have salty food I end up drinking beer because I can't figure out what wine would work with it. I also get extremely thirsty, and wine doesn't quench that thirst.

Diagnosis: Why do you think most bars put peanuts, pretzels, and the like on tables? It's to promote a thirst, so you drink more. And yes, you're right, wine is not thirst quenching. It's not supposed to be. Salty food coats that portion of the tongue where both saltiness and sourness are perceived – along the sides, near the tip. Something is needed to clean it off. Beer and soda do a great job because of the bubbles.

Prescription: If you want to indulge in wine with salty food you'll have to try bubbly or something with high acidity. Since salt and sour are experienced at the same location on the tongue, abundant acid is required to clean the salt away. Although very crisp wines will not necessarily quench your thirst, they will deal with the saltiness nicely. Choose wines from cooler, northern wine-growing regions like New York State, Germany, Austria, Ontario, or Alsace for best results.

Dear Dr. WineKnow:
I absolutely love tomato-based food. Perhaps that's why I'm crazy about Italian. What's the best type of wine to serve with tomato-based dishes?
Diagnosis: Italiano, senore! When it comes to Italian food, the best wine match is Italian. Generally, tomato-based dishes tend to be aggressively tomato flavoured. Rarely do they just hint delicately. The key to matching tomato-based dishes to a wine is in the acid.
Prescription: Wines best suited for tomato-based food are those with good acidity to balance the acid in the tomatoes. If you choose Italian wine, it is best to make selections from the north of the country rather than the south. Better acid levels are achieved in the north, as it is slightly cooler, due to hilly or mountainous terrain.

Dear Dr. WineKnow:
What about wine and soup? Do they work together?
Diagnosis: Like fire and ice! Most soup is hot. Cold wine and hot soup don't really set the world aflame. However, it is far easier to marry wine with a cold soup, especially in the warmer weather. It also makes a big difference if the soup contains substantial chunks of food like meat, fish, vegetables, or beans.
Prescription: For cold soups the best choices would be dry, fortified wines like sherry, madeira, or port. To pull the flavours together add a touch of the wine to the soup just before serving. For big, hearty soups that eat like a stew, the best choice would be a young, fruity, crisp, robust red.

Soup – Favourite Matches

MEAT

Beef	Gamay (Beaujolais)
Chicken	Sylvaner (Alsace)
Consommé	Sherry (Fino or Amontillado)
Game	Port
Mulligatawny	Traminer
Turtle	Madeira (sercial or verdelho)

FISH

Bouillabaisse	Dry rosé
Clam Chowder	Wood-aged Sauvignon Blanc (Pouilly-Fumé)
Lobster	Chardonnay (white Burgundy)
Shrimp Bisque	Wood-aged Chardonnay (Australia)

VEGETABLE

Beans & Pasta	Valpolicella (Italy)
Borscht	Pinot Noir (California)
Cream	Riesling – medium dry (Germany)
Gazpacho	Pinot Gris (Alsace)
Minestrone	Sangiovese (Chianti)
Onion	Gamay (Beaujolais)
Tomato	Bardolino (Italy)
Vichyssoise	Muscat – dry (Alsace)

FRUIT (served cold)   Riesling – medium dry (Canada)

Dear Dr. WineKnow:
What's the best wine to serve with a salad?
Diagnosis: Salad can be devastating to a wine, especially if it has some sort of vinaigrette dressing. I guess wine instinctively knows that if oxidized to the extreme, vinegar is what it becomes when it dies. Maybe wine is clairvoyant. Therefore, wine is not usually served with salad for this reason.

Prescription: If you feel absolutely compelled to do so, then try this. Instead of some sort of vinegar in the salad dressing, use a crisp white wine or some lemon juice instead. This should provide the needed acidity in the dressing. If you simply must serve a vinegar dressing, then choose the crispest white wine you can find. Vinho Verde from Portugal might suffice. Good luck!

Dear Dr. WineKnow:
I'm a stinky-cheese lover. I've tried numerous wines with the cheese, but nothing seems to work. Either the cheese or the wine tastes funny. Help!

Diagnosis: Stinky-cheese lovers of the world unite! I, too, am a prisoner of those aromatic delights which turn many people off. These cheeses, including the veiny ones, are very aggressive, strong-smelling, and full-flavoured, requiring at least the same character in a wine. One of the key components of these is their saltiness, which suggests another approach to matching wine.

Prescription: If aggression is what you want in a wine match, try choosing big, full-bodied, full-flavoured reds like Nebbiolo, Syrah/Shiraz, Zinfandel, and Pinotage. For whites, pick on Gewürztraminer, Viognier, and Pinot Gris. However, the more interesting wine matches come from playing off the salty elements in the cheese. If you have not tried a sweet wine with some of these cheeses, you are missing out on one of life's truly incredible gastronomic experiences. The saltiness of the cheese and the sweetness of the wine play off of each other like two voices in a choir. The sweetness of the wine makes the cheese taste less salty, while the saltiness of the cheese renders the wine less sweet. Together the flavours are elevated to something ethereal, this side of heaven. Wines such as port, madeira, sauternes, and late-harvest selections should provide the religious experience.

Cheeses – Favourite Matches

Asiago	Nebbiolo (Barolo, Barbaresco)
Bel Paese	Medium-bodied Italian reds (Barbera, Valpolicella)
Bleu de Bresse	Gamay (Beaujolais)
Boursin	Gamay (Ontario) or dry rosé (Spain)
Brick	Sauvignon Blanc (Sancerre) or Pinot Grigio (Italy)
Brie	Cabernet Sauvignon (red Bordeaux, New Zealand)
Caerphilly	Dry riesling (Ontario) or dry sherry (Fino, Manzanilla)
Camembert	Cabernet Sauvignon (red Bordeaux)/Pinot Noir (red Burgundy)
Cheddar	Syrah (red Rhône) or Nebbiolo (Barolo)
Chèvre	Sauvignon Blanc (Sancerre) or red Rioja
Colby	Cabernet Sauvignon (red Bordeaux)/Nebbiolo (Barbaresco)
Cottage Cheese	Light Italian white (Soave) or sparkling Chenin Blanc (Vouvray)
Cream Cheese	Light Italian white (Verdicchio, Pinot Grigio)
Danish Blue	Sweet white (Sauternes, Port)/Pinot Noir (red Burgundy)
Edam	Medium-dry Riesling (Ontario, Germany) or light Italian red (Dolcetto, Grignolino)
Emmenthal	Medium-dry Riesling (Ontario, Germany)/unoaked Chardonnay (Chablis)
Feta	Retsina or unoaked Chardonnay (Chablis)
Gorgonzola	Big, spicy red (Syrah, Rhône, Zinfandel)
Gouda	Gamay (Beaujolais)/Cabernet Franc (Chinon)
Gruyère	Pinot Noir (red Burgundy)/Chardonnay (Australia)

Havarti	Light Italian white (Soave)/Sylvaner (Alsace)
Lancashire	Dry sherry (Amontillado)/Tawny port
Limburger	Syrah (red Rhône) or Gewürztraminer (Alsace)
Livarot	Pinot Noir (Burgundy)/Cabernet Sauvignon (red Bordeaux)
Mascarpone	Monbazillac or Müller-Thurgau (Austria)
Monterey Jack	Cabernet Sauvignon (Canada)
Mozzarella	Sangiovese (Chianti) or Valpolicella
Muenster	Gewürztraminer (Alsace) or dry Muscat (Alsace)
Oka	Light Italian white (Verdicchio) or white Rhône
Parmesan	Sangiovese (Chianti) or Amarone
Pecorino	Zinfandel (California) or red Rhône
Pont-L'Éveque	Cabernet Sauvignon (Bordeaux)/Pinot Noir (red Burgundy)
Port-Salut	Chardonnay (U.S.A.)/Cabernet Sauvignon (South America)
Provolone	Syrah (red Rhône) or Sauvignon Blanc (Fumé Blanc)
Romano	Sangiovese (Brunello) or Nebbiolo (Barbaresco)
Roquefort	Sweet wines (Sauternes, port)/Zinfandel (California)
Saint André	Chardonnay (St-Véran)/light Italian white (Orvieto)
Saint Paulin	Cabernet Sauvignon (red Bordeaux)/Chardonnay (white Burgundy)
Stilton	Sweet wines (port, Sauternes)
Tilsit	Gamay (Beaujolais) or Sylvaner (Alsace)

Dear Dr. WineKnow:

I'm a big fan of oysters, mussels, and any shellfish, but I'm always at odds as to what wine to have with it. I need to know.

Diagnosis: Shucks! You sound like a person after my own heart. I can eat a boatload of this stuff, myself. Most of this seafood has a rich, oily texture. Every mouthful coats the palate, requiring something to clean it off.

Prescription: What is required in a wine match is an unoaked white, with good, bracing acidity. This can be still or effervescent. In either case, that's a wine with a refreshing, tingling, lemon/lime tang that you feel on the sides of the tongue, like when you bite into a crisp Granny Smith apple. Bubbles in a wine have an added bonus, as they naturally clean the palate. Both styles cut through the oiliness like a hot knife through butter. So every mouthful of shellfish is instantly cleaned off by the acid and/or bubbles in the wine, preparing the palate for the next morsel. It's a match that can't be beat. Look for palate-cleansing wines. Still white wines that should do the job include Muscadet, Sancerre, Gavi, Soave, Verdicchio, and Vinho Verde. Among the grape varieties to look for are Riesling, Pinot Blanc, Sauvignon Blanc, Pinot Grigio, and Trebbiano. When choosing a bubbly, concentrate on non-vintage bottlings, as they tend to be younger.

FISH/SEAFOOD – FAVOURITE MATCHES

Coquilles St. Jacques	Sauvignon Blanc (Pouilly-Fumé)
Deep Fried Seafood	Chenin Blanc (Vouvray)
Fish & Chips	Soave
Frog's Legs	Sauvignon Blanc (Sancerre)
Gefilte Fish	Pinot Blanc (Alsatian)
Gravlax	White Rhône/Champagne
Lobster Newburg	Chardonnay (California, Australia)
Oysters	Champagne, Muscadet, Chablis
Prawns	White Bordeaux
Sardines	Vinho Verde
Smoked Salmon	Gewürztraminer (Alsace)/oaky Chardonnay (Australia)
Smoked Trout	Pouilly-Fumé or Fumé Blanc

POULTRY – FAVOURITE MATCHES

CHICKEN

Cacciatore	Sangiovese (Chianti, Brunello, Vino Nobile)
Cold	Gamay (Beaujolais)
Coq au Vin	Pinot Noir (red Burgundy)
Curried	Gewürztraminer
Kiev	Chardonnay (white Burgundy)
Tandoori	Shiraz

TURKEY

Dark meat	Cabernet (red Bordeaux)
White meat	Chardonnay (Australian)

DUCK

A l'orange	Medium Riesling (German Auslese)
Paté	Muscat (Alsatian)
Peking	Gamay (Cru Beaujolais)

PHEASANT   Merlot

QUAIL   Cabernet

MEAT – FAVOURITE MATCHES

BEEF

Beef Bourguignon	Pinot Noir (red Burgundy, Oregon)
Beef Wellington	Pinot Noir (South Africa, Burgundy)
Calves' Liver	Pinot Noir (red Burgundy, Ontario)
Chili Con Carne	Amarone
Goulash	Bull's Blood (Hungary)/Zinfandel (California)
Pepper Steak	Rhône red/Barolo
Roast Beef	Cabernet Sauvignon

Shepherd's Pie	Gamay (Beaujolais, Canada)
Spaghetti Bolognaise	Nebbiolo (Barbaresco)
Steak Tartare	Sangiovese (Brunello, Vino Nobile)
Veal Cordon Bleu	Chardonnay (Burgundy, New Zealand)

LAMB

Couscous	Rhône red
Irish Stew	White Bordeaux
Leg	Merlot (California) or red Rioja
Rack	Cabernet Sauvignon (red Bordeaux)
Shish Kebab	Zinfandel

PORK

Bacon	Gamay (Beaujolais)
BBQ Spare Ribs	Barbera (Italy)/Portuguese red
Frankfurters and Beans	Shiraz (Australia)
Ham	Riesling (Ontario)/Cabernet Franc (red Loire)
Hot Dog	Gamay (Ontario)
Prosciutto and Melon	Italian red/LBV port
Roast Pork	Chenin Blanc (Vouvray)
Salami	Nebbiolo (Barbaresco)

GAME

Bear	Syrah (Northern Rhône)
Grouse	Sangiovese (Brunello)
Hare	Bairrada (Portugal)
Moose	Pinot Noir (red Burgundy)
Partridge	Red Bordeaux (Médoc)
Pheasant	Shiraz (Australia)
Pigeon	Sémillon (Australia)
Rabbit	Red Rioja (Spain)
Venison	Sangiovese (Vino Nobile)
Wild Boar	Syrah (Northern Rhône)
Wild Duck	Pinot Noir (Oregon)

Wild Goose   Riesling (medium dry) (German Spätlese)

Dear Dr. WineKnow:
Matching wine to dessert is a real problem. Everything is so sweet.
Diagnosis: For many people, a sweet wine is dessert after a meal.
Having both is akin to having two desserts. Nonetheless, hordes of
people love this experience and expect it when dining out, where
wine is important. Not too many wines can stand up to massively
sweet foods. Sugar overdose can destroy the palate.
Prescription: For those with a sweet tooth, follow this advice. If
you simply must serve a sweet wine with dessert, please ensure that
the wine is sweeter than the dessert. If not, the wine will be lost,
and its acidity will stick out like a sore thumb.

DESSERTS – FAVOURITE MATCHES

Apple pie/Streudel	Riesling – late harvest (Canada, Germany)
Baked Alaska	Sweet sparkling (Asti Spumante, Clairette de Die)
Cake	Madeira – sweet/tawny port
Cheesecake	Chenin Blanc – sweet (Vouvray, Coteaux du Layon)
Chocolate	Port or framboise
Christmas pudding	Muscat (Beaumes-de-Venise)/semi-dry sparkling (German sekt)
Crême brulé	Sweet white (Sauternes, Barsac)
Crêpes	Sweet sparkling (Asti Spumante, Clairette de Die, Doux Champagne)
Fresh fruit and fruit pies	Eiswein/Sauternes
Pastries	Medium-dry sparkling (German sekt)
Pumpkin pie	Tokaji Aszú/cream sherry
Strawberries and cream	Dry sparkling (brut Champagne)

| Strawberry shortcake | Beaumes-de-Venise/dessert Muscat (Australia) |
| Sweet soufflés | Riesling (Canada, Germany) |

Dear Dr. WineKnow:
I'm a "chocoholic." What do you suggest for a wine match?
Diagnosis: It is written in the great book of Dionysis that wine and chocolate should never come together. They are foes. Chocolate has a real coating effect on the palate, with which most wines can't compete. One does see this unusual marriage in such places as California, where wine and chocolate do exist together, especially in such things as Cabernet-filled chocolate bon bons. Although certain wines do possess chocolate nuances, the coating action of chocolate usually kills the wine's other flavours and texture.
Prescription: Okay, if I were forced to match the two, I would probably vote for sweet fruit wine (other than grape) to best do the job. Raspberry and strawberry wine should work well. As for grape wine, try dessert Muscat, old Amarone, both bottle and wood-aged port, or sweet sparkles.

Dear Dr. WineKnow:
One of my best treats while watching TV is nibbling on some nuts. I would love to sip some wine with them, but have no idea of what to choose.
Diagnosis: Nuts, like other food, are very individual, possessing unique tastes and characteristics. Believe it or not, they are a very substantial food product, as they are packed with protein, carbo-hydrates, and vitamins. Most importantly, they are quite fatty.
Prescription: The fatty nature of nuts require wine that is quite substantial. Fortified, sweet, or powerful selections will be needed. Choose selections like sweeter sherries, Tokaji Aszú, madeira, tawny or vintage port. If salty nuts are your downfall, pick drier variations on the above. Try Fino and Manzanilla sherry or white port. Get crackin'.

Nuts – Favourite Matches

Almonds	Sangiovese (Chianti) or semi-sweet Italian white (Orvieto Aboccato)
Brazil	Nebbiolo – mature (Barolo) or Pineau des Charentes
Cashews	Sylvaner (Alsace) or German Rhine wine
Chestnuts	
roasted	Port or Recioto della Valpolicella Amarone
puréed	Sauternes or sweet bubbly (Asti Spumante)
Hazelnuts	Chardonnay (Burgundy) or bottle-aged port (vintage)
Macadamia	Muscat – dessert (Setúbal) or Tokaji Aszú
Mixed	Sherry – medium dry (Amontillado) or Madeira
Nuts and Raisins	Muscat – dry (Alsace) or Amarone
Pecans	Port – wood aged (Tawny) or Madeira
Pistachio	Sweet Italian white (Picolit) or Asti Spumante
Smoked	Gewürztraminer (Alsace) or Syrah/Shiraz (Rhône, Australia)
Walnuts	Sherry (sweet Oloroso)/wood-aged port (tawny)/Madeira

Cooking with Wine

Many people love to use wine in cooking. It adds additional flavour and complexity to dishes. It's also a sure way to guarantee wine and food affinity and enhance a meal. Like matching wine and food, however, certain rules must be applied in order to make it work.

Dear Dr. WineKnow:

When I add wine to cooking, my dishes always taste too much of the wine. What am I doing wrong?

Diagnosis: Using wine in cooking is wonderful, because it adds delicate flavour to food. It enhances most dishes. Provided you serve the same wine with the dish that you are adding to the cooking, it ensures a perfect match. However, when the wine is added and how much is the key.

Prescription: Always add wine during the cooking. This way most of the aggressive flavours burn off and all that is left is the delicate flavour of the wine. If you observe chefs in the kitchen, they are constantly tasting their creations (maybe that's why many are so large). You'll see that whatever they add to a preparation is in very small amounts. They keep tasting and adding until the hit is just right. The same format applies to wine. Add small amounts, allowing the flavours to mesh, then taste it. More can always be added. If you put too much in, there's no turning back. Sugar can be added to soften the blow, but this is not where you want to be. Start modestly, adding approximately one tablespoon wine to one cup of liquid.

Dear Dr. WineKnow:
I never throw wine away at home. If it's old or bad I simply use it for cooking.

Diagnosis: Bite your tongue. Nothing, and I do mean nothing, will ruin a dish faster than using old or bad wine in it. The tired or old flavours will blend into the food, making it taste weird.

Prescription: Have this statement tattooed onto your forehead. If a wine is not good enough to drink on its own, it certainly is not good enough to cook with. Throw it away. Use only sound, healthy wine in cooking, regardless of the quality or price.

Dear Dr. WineKnow:
I buy and use that "cooking wine" available at supermarkets. What are your thoughts on this product?

Diagnosis: I'm not exactly sure why they call this stuff "cooking wine." It doesn't resemble wine in any way. It doesn't even contain alcohol. Whether it did at one time or not is questionable. Without alcohol, many other elements in wine will be affected, because it helps preserve the product.

Prescription: Don't use it. You are much better off buying some inexpensive wine to keep in the kitchen. At least it contains alcohol, meaning it will be "correct" and have all elements in check. Just ensure that it is healthy and not old or defective.

GRAPE FLASH

Did you know that different ways of cooking the same food can alter the wine match? Such preparations as boiling, broiling, roasting, braising, barbecuing, and stewing all alter the texture of food, pushing the wine match in a different direction. This really isn't so astonishing. By changing the cooking method or procedure, you have actually altered the molecular structure of the food, giving it a different texture. Thus, the same piece of beef braised or broiled will require a different wine match.

Dear Dr. WineKnow:

I'm on a calorie-restricted diet and love wine. It is really not on my menu though. Would it be bad of me to use it in cooking?

Diagnosis: Since wine contains alcohol, which is fattening, it's not surprising that it is not part of your diet. But there is some good news here. When wine is added during cooking, the alcohol burns off. Most of the calories disappear, as well.

Prescription: Take heed. "Thou shall not cook with wine when on a diet" is not the eleventh commandment. Using a little wine in cooking should not make you fat. No, you would not be a bad person if you used some wine, providing you limit the amount. Make sure you add it during the cooking to allow the alcohol to totally burn off, reducing the calories substantially. Beware, though. Using some wine in cooking may lead you to enjoy a bit with the meal.

Dear Dr. WineKnow:

I know this sounds silly, but when I was making a brown sauce for a dish, I used white wine because it was all I had. The sauce didn't taste of the wine at all.

Diagnosis: Why bother? Most brown sauces are heavy in nature. The wine was too light for it to make a difference. The character of the wine should match the character of the sauce. Lighter wines in light sauces and heavier wines in heavier sauces – that's the key.

Prescription: Generally, use white wine in a white sauce and red in a brown sauce. You wouldn't think of putting red wine in a white sauce, for obvious reasons.

GRAPE FLASH

Did you know that people not only marinate meat in wine for flavour but to tenderize it, as well? Marinating meat in wine has been practised for a long time. There is no finer way of adding and instilling a wine's flavour. But, more importantly, the acid in wine helps tenderize meat and improve the texture. This is especially beneficial to less expensive cuts. Generally, the longer a meat is marinated, the more wine flavour it will possess and ultimately the more tender it will be. Please do not use the same marinate to baste with, as it may contain bacteria, unless you boil the remainder on the stove first. Don't save it for another time either. Dispose of it. If you want to baste with the same marinate, simply mix up a fresh batch. Alternately, reserve some for this purpose when you make the first batch.

Dear Dr. WineKnow:

I marinated some meat in an aluminum pan. When the food was cooked, it had a funny taste.

Diagnosis: Essence of tin, eh? Certain materials leach flavours into food, especially if wine is present. The alcohol and acid tend to draw these out. Drinking wine out of metal did kill many ancients from lead poisoning.

Prescription: When marinating choose a neutral container. Glass or porcelain containers work best.

CHAPTER 7

THE ROAD AHEAD

*W*hat, you might wonder, does the future hold for wine? What do we have to look forward to, vinously speaking? Will the countries, regions, and grape varieties we enjoy today be popular tomorrow? Will the face of wine change? With all the turmoil in the world today, will wine even matter? These are all valid questions and concerns. Let me pour myself a glass and give you Doc WineKnow's fix on the wine world of tomorrow.

Fear not, folks, wine is here to stay. Let's face it, with the benefits of moderate consumption now a part of a healthy lifestyle, the road ahead looks bright. All the variables that dictate our individual enjoyment should continue to make each of our personal experiences with it unique. As long as there is a glass to be filled and food to enjoy with, wine will continue to flourish. Innovations in the field of viticulture, vinification, technology, and gastronomy should all continue making wine an exciting beverage that enhances our lives.

Countries, Regions, and Varietals

Old World

Interesting trends are now starting to take shape concerning what countries, wine regions, and grape varieties will be popular up ahead. Traditional "Old World" producers will continue to dominate the world wine scene with steadfast wine styles and historical grape varieties that have proven themselves over time.

One of the foremost is Italy. With many wines and varietals indigenous to that country, their popularity will persist. Nebbiolo- and Sangiovese-based wines will top the list. However, look to Sicily for some real moves forward, especially with a little grape called Nero d'Avela. This lovely grape produces delightful wines that are both oak friendly and age worthy. I've tasted a number of these, and they are wonderful and inexpensive. It's only recently that some wines produced from this grape are showing up on store shelves around the world. I see a lot more of this liquid gem being produced and exported.

France will continue to reign supreme for Bordeaux, the classified growths in particular. Although pricing, I believe, will go through the roof, this unique style of terroir-driven wine will still hold its appeal. Red Burgundy will maintain its allure and price escalation, mostly due to the elusive Pinot Noir grape and the French mystique. When they get it right, the wines are spectacular. Although Chardonnay will continue its run as the world's most popular white grape variety, I don't feel that white Burgundy will epitomize it. There is simply too much great Chardonnay being produced elsewhere. As for Champagne, it will remain the king of bubbly. The popularity of wines from Alsace, the Rhône (especially Syrah), and the south of the country (vins de pay) will flourish.

Spain should see some growth in the south with sherry. Aside from port, it is the most popular fortified wine in the world. I'd keep my eye on the northwest of the country around the Douro River. Varietally labelled wines are looking very good in this area.

The late harvest and noble-rotted, white wines of Germany should hold strong as they continue to meld delicacy and crisp acidity into unctuous numbers.

As for the world's most popular fortified wine, port, its legend should live on. Again, the very uniqueness of this incredible beverage ensures its future. Look for prices to rise as well, due to innovation and labour costs. You will also see a move to bring Madeira to the foreground. As absolutely one of my favourite sippers, I would love to see this nectar get its just reward. Watch out for up-and-coming table wines from the experimental and exciting region of Alentejo. Some great things are happening here. There are other non-demarcated regions in Portugal that I feel show lots of potential. Don't be surprised to see such areas as Aruda, Torres Vedras, Ribateja, Palmela, and Arrabida become demarcated down the road. Just remember where you heard it first.

If I were you, I'd really watch Hungary's Tokaji Aszú. It's about to take its place as one of the most wonderful dessert wines in the world.

New World

As for the "New World," there are lots of good things to look forward to. The wines of Canada will continue to garner awards in international competition. Icewine will continue in popularity, because it is so unique and indigenous to this cool climate.

California's wines will dominate the North American scene, especially with Zinfandel. If the crowds at the annual ZAP (Zinfandel Advocates and Producers) tasting in San Francisco the last couple of Januarys is any indication, this variety, in its purest form, is going to come on like gangbusters. If there is any drawback to the wonderful California wine scene, it will be in the ever-escalating prices.

Oregon will make a big statement with Pinot Noir. In blind tastings over the last several years, where Oregon counterparts teed off against red Burgundy, its Pinots have consistently come up in the top three, often for a fraction of the cost. Considering that Oregon's wine history, especially with this grape, is maybe thirty years old, compared to Burgundy's hundreds of years of tradition, this is quite astounding. Give Oregon another thirty, forty, or fifty years, and watch out, Burgundy.

Another Pacific Northwest wine region to monitor in the years ahead is Washington State. There are some really good wines coming out of this region today and it can only get better.

On the other side of the world, down under, Australia has come a long way in a relatively short time, and I see no reason why it should slow down. Some overproduction is causing a few problems, but this should iron itself out. Look for Australian Shiraz to grow in popularity.

The wines of New Zealand will gain in interest. The whites in particular should show best. Grapes like Sauvignon Blanc are paving the way for a new, rich style.

No one can deny the popularity of South African wines. South Africa's unique locale and topography are keeping it on the forefront of production. Pinotage should be bigger out of this country in the years to come.

One of the real shining stars of the future will be the South American continent. Chile's run as a prolific producer will continue, especially with a rather interesting grape called Carmenère. Originally from Bordeaux, this grape looks very much like Merlot in the vineyard. It's only recently that growers have been able to recognize it and propagate it separately. Now, much wine is being made from it in Chile with very exciting results. This deeply coloured, low-acid wine, with spicy, vegetal, black fruit, appears to have quite a future in this country. Look for great examples to start filtering into markets around the world.

The other gem of South America is Argentina. Great strides in grape growing and winemaking are at hand in this country. I predict that, before too long, it will catch up with Chile and maybe even surpass it. They're doing some fabulous things with Syrah. Take note.

From a general perspective, grapes like Riesling will see a renaissance everywhere. The versatility of this fine grape will be realized.

Viognier also will become fashionable. Although relatively obscure, except for the northern Rhône in France, this varietal is drawing new interest in the south of the country and in California and Canada. Sauvignon Blanc will gain more followers, as consumers detox from Chardonnay. There will be much more blending of grape varieties in wines of tomorrow. As for our old friend Cabernet Sauvignon, it will continue to be the "chocolate of wine," just as Chardonnay will proliferate as the "vanilla."

Trends

It's really difficult to predict trends in wine, but certain evidence does suggest some possibilities. I'm convinced that there will be much more collaboration between "Old World" and "New World" producers. Joint ventures on both sides will flourish.

The aggressive use of oak, I believe, will subside. Of course, there will continue to be producers who are really into it. However, worldwide use will be more delicate.

If you think prices, overall, will fall, you had better think again. As grape growing and winemaking become more innovative and complex, the cost of production will increase. You guessed it. That cost will filter down to the consumer.

Packaging and labelling practices will become more avant garde and experimental. As producers and distributors compete for shelf space and their need to stand out increases, presentation should be quite fascinating. Look for artistic labels and unusual bottles. Wine in cans, for instance, is on the horizon.

Hold on to your corkscrews but the "screw cap" will be making a comeback. Because there are so many problems with real cork enclosures, many producers already in places like Australia are reintroducing this on many of their wines. As much as its reputation is synonymous with inexpensive vino, it is an airtight seal that eliminates "corkiness" in wines entirely. You'll see many more wineries worldwide starting to use them. I suppose they will have to come up with some pretty nifty new marketing campaigns to change the consumer's mindset about these.

"The young will inherit the grape," especially women in the "Old World." That's right. More and more, the reins of production, including everything from grape growing and winemaking to marketing and sales, will be turned over to a younger generation, mostly women, in European winemaking. You already see much of this in the "New World," but up until recently wine production has been mainly the domain of men in "Old World" countries. In traditional wine-producing countries like Italy, there is a real metamorphosis going on in this regard. Women, and young ones at that, are the obvious choice. Science already shows that they potentially possess superior palates and have marketing savvy, a knack for meshing tradition with innovation, and fingers on the pulse of what Gen-X tastes are all about. Many producers are realizing that they are the prime candidates to carry their wine portfolio into this new millennium.

There's no doubt that wine in the years ahead will be a miraculous, fascinating product. In some ways, it will be easier to create than ever. In the world of tomorrow, quality wine will pretty much be a given. There will be no such thing as poorly made wine. Advanced grape-growing and winemaking knowledge, coupled with super modern technology, will put an end to that. However, certain new, external pressures could affect this area. Such environmental elements as global warming due to reduced ozone layers could influence grape growing in certain parts of the world. We see changes already in this regard. The overall climate in some regions is topsy turvy. Places that never received snow before now get it. Other areas that are prone to snow are receiving less. Water levels in many of the larger bodies of water are at an all-time low. World unrest and the war against terrorism is destroying potentially viable, grape-growing land, killing future grape growers and winemakers and making it more difficult to go about the business of wine. These are all-important factors that could have major influences on this delicious potable. If these weren't serious enough concerns, others loom over the vinous horizon like a dark cloud. Surprisingly, they have to do with the producers themselves and the direction they choose to go in regarding their wine styles.

As a result of global desire for wines that are consumable earlier and trends that see winemakers altering their countries' wine styles to appeal more to a mass market, there is an inherent problem developing. More and more, producers worldwide are molding their wines in a "modern" vein, which results in products that are not very different from each other. This heralds a potential loss of individual character in wine.

Advanced vineyard management and production techniques, the use of new oak, and, in some cases, the blending in of popular, nontraditional grape varieties are all robbing wine of indigenous qualities. While this metamorphosis provides wine with smoother, fruitier, more harmonious flavours, it reinforces sameness. If this continues, within twenty years or so, we will be floating in a sea of homogenized, similar-tasting, quality wine void of not only country but regional and varietal distinction.

This situation has not developed overnight. It has been slowly evolving. In attempts to neutralize indigenous local flavours, many producers are drastically changing their traditional "house" styles, much to the dismay of not only their countrymen but their loyal customers.

The following example is an indication. A huge proportion of the new wine-drinking generation has only experienced Zinfandel in its "blush" or "white" format. Most of these consumers have never tasted the big, blackberry spice that is Zinfandel in its purest form, and few are even aware that it is a worthy red grape variety.

Imagine all wine tasting basically the same in the future. Buying and selling it will merely be done by the colour and the label, not by flavour profile. This would be a real shame, since flavour is the single most important reason for drinking a particular wine. I fear that the few of us who are old enough and experienced enough to remember will reminisce about the days when a bottle of wine labelled, Chianti, for instance, actually followed through and tasted like a Tuscan red wine, rather than a Californian or Australian.

Wine is a hedonistic gastronomic experience to be enjoyed because of its individuality and its affinity to certain foods – not merely as an intellectual pastime.

A Final Word

There's no doubt that the more you understand about wine in all its complexity, the better the experience will be. However, you can get so hung up on the who, what, where, and why of wine that the real meaning of sipping it might be lost. This could be a mistake. As a professional, I'm in the business of analysing wine – sometimes to death. Occasionally, it can be difficult to take one's self outside it and simply enjoy. The beauty of wine, though, is that it can be appreciated on so many levels. Fortunately for me, I have a unique talent for doing just that. There is indeed a time and place for scrutiny and another for sheer vinous pleasure. I suggest you learn and nurture the same knack. It's actually quite easy. Forget for a moment all the information about how to taste, what to look for, and why food and wine work together or not. Pour yourself a glass and simply revel in the unique beauty of this amazing beverage. Just enjoy the taste and have fun with it. After all, no matter what anyone tells you about what you should get out of it, remember this. You are experiencing this, nobody else is. If you like a particular wine, for whatever reason or with a specific food that isn't recommended, it's not the end of the world. The fact that you enjoy it makes that experience special and in the end that's all that really matters.

GLOSSARY

The Language of Wine

There is a language or vocabulary used by most wine lovers to communicate to each other the specifics of a certain wine. Understanding this vocabulary will increase your appreciation. The following are some basic terms.

Acidic – A sharp taste on the palate due to too much acid.

Aftertaste – The taste left on the palate after the wine is spit out or swallowed. A long aftertaste is a sign of quality. (*See* FINISH)

Alcoholic – The hot, sometimes burning taste of too much alcohol in a wine. More evident in warm-climate wines.

Aroma – The smell of the grapes used to make a wine.

Aromatic – Grape varieties with a fragrant or spicy note.

Astringent – The dry, rasping taste of tannin in young, red wines.

Austere – The dryness in the mouth of a red wine, caused by the tannins.

Back blending – A method used to sweeten wine with grape juice or the blending together of different batches of wine (perhaps treated differently), made from the same grapes, for the final blend.

Baked – A roasted or cooked note perceived on the nose in wines from warm climates.

Backward – A wine that is less developed for its age.

Balanced – A wine in which all components or elements are in sync or harmony.

Barnyard – The smell of a farmyard, horse droppings, or rotting straw found in certain wines like red Burgundy and red Rhônes.

Barrique – A Bordeaux-style barrel of 225 litres.

Baumé – The French scale for measuring the sugar in the must (fermenting juice).

Bitter – Usually in the aftertaste, the taste of excessive tannins or young vines.

Black currant – The main aroma of Cabernet grapes.

Bloom – The whitish haze-like covering on the grape skin.

Body – The mouth feel or weight of a wine in the mouth.

Botrytis – A fungus or rot that affects grapes, concentrating the sugars and acids, often making sweet wines.

Bottle-age – The quality that comes from ageing wine in the bottle.

Bottle-sickness – A temporary condition of a wine that smells odd from bottling. It appears when the bottle is opened, and usually disappears after some air.

Bottle-stink – The smell of dank air escaping from an old wine once opened. Usually disappears after some air.

Bouquet – The smell of a wine, evolved through the processes it has been put through (fermentation and ageing). May contain the aroma.

Brix – The North American scale for measuring the sugar in the must (fermenting juice).

Buttery – The smell of butter, especially in oak-aged wines.

Caramel – A burnt-sugar smell in oak-aged wines from hot years.

Carbon dioxide – The gas or bubbles in all sparkling wines. Sometimes noted as a spritz on the tip of the tongue in still wines.

Carbonic maceration – A form of fermentation for light red wines where the grapes are uncrushed. Fermentation takes place within cell walls.

Cat's pee – The smell of herbaceousness in Sauvignon Blanc.

Cava – Spanish sparkling wine made by the champagne method.

Cedarwood – Part of the bouquet of Cabernet Sauvignon.

Cépage – French term for grape variety.

Chaptalization – The addition of sugar during fermentation to raise the alcohol level.

Character charmat method – The distinctive personality of a wine. A method of making sparkling wine in a large, sealed tank. Often called the tank method. (*See* CUVÉE CLOSE)

Chocolate – Perceived on the nose of some big, red wines.

Cigar box – Part of the bouquet of Cabernet Sauvignon, especially from the Médoc in Bordeaux.

Citric – The smell of citric fruit (lemon, lime, grapefruit) in the bouquet of wine.

Claret – British term for red Bordeaux.

Clean – A wine free from "off" smells or tastes.

Closed – A young wine whose nose and palate are unyielding or undeveloped and locked in.

Cloying – A wine, often sweet, with too little acid to balance the sugar.

Complex – A wine with many smells and tastes.

Creamy – The texture or smell of some wines that see oak. Often the texture of Champagne.

Crémant – A champagne-method wine with less pressure.

Crisp – A green-apple zestiness in white wines, denoting lively acidity.

Cru – The French term for "growth."

Cuvée close – A method of making sparkling wine in a large, sealed tank. (*See* CHARMAT METHOD)

Decant – To gently pour wine from its bottle into a larger vessel, leaving behind the sediment.

Depth – Used of a multi-dimensional wine.

Disgorged – A Champagne in which the sediment has been removed after second fermentation in the bottle.

Dosage – The adding of sweet wine to Champagne just before bottling.

Dry – A wine in which the sugar has mostly been fermented out.

Drying out – A wine in which the fruit is fading, giving way to more austere flavours of tannin, acid, and oak.

Dumb – A wine that is unyielding and closed, offering very little nose and palate.

Earthy – The smell of earth and minerals in a wine.

Eiswein – A rare, sweet, German dessert wine made from grapes naturally frozen on the vine.

Elegant – A wine that is well-balanced with finesse.

Eucalyptus – The smell of mint often found in warm-climate Cabernet Sauvignon.

Fat – A wine that is rich, full, and well-extracted.

Finish – What's left on the palate after a wine is swallowed. The aftertaste.

Flabby – A wine that lacks acidity on the palate.

Fleshy – A well-extracted, concentrated wine, especially in reds.

Flinty – The smell of struck flint or stone in some wines.

Floral – The smell of fragrant flowers in some wines, especially fruity whites.

Forward – A wine that is very yielding, showing more maturity than its age.

Foxy – The characteristic, grapey smell of "labrusca" grapes.

Fresh – A wine with good acidity, making it lively.

Free-run juice – The juice that runs from crushed grapes that haven't been pressed.

Fruity – A wine with good, fruity smells and flavours from ripe grapes.

Full-bodied – A wine with a rich mouth feel from concentrated grape extract, higher alcohol, or oak contact.

Glycerol – A bi-product of fermentation that adds richness and sweetness to a wine, especially observed in its beading and legs.

Gooseberry – The characteristic smell in Sauvignon Blanc.

Grapey – The smell of fresh grapes in wine.

Green – A wine that is young or made from unripe grapes.

Hard – A wine that is tannic and acidic, masking the fruit.

Harmonious – A wine that is well-balanced and integrated.

Harsh – A wine with excessive tannin.

Herbaceous – A wine with a grassy, vegetal character.

Hock – British term for all Rhine wines from Germany.

Hollow – A wine where the middle palate drops out. There is a good front and back end in the mouth but nothing in the middle.

Honeyed – The sweet characteristic of many dessert and late-harvest wines.

Hot – The impression of heat on the palate from high alcohol content.

Hybrid – A cross of two varieties of vines.

Icewine – A "New World" term for rare, sweet dessert wine made from grapes naturally frozen on the vine.

Lactic acid – A mild acid found in milk.

Lanolin – The smell of wet wool in some wines.

Lean – A wine with not a lot of stuffing, that is, body or mouth-filling flavour.

Lees – Dead yeast cell and grape particles that settle at the bottom of fermentation containers.

Legs – The small droplets or tears that ooze down the side of a wine glass after swirling.

Length – The duration of time the flavour of a wine stays on the palate after you swallow it or spit it out.

Light – A wine with little body.

Lively – A wine with good acidity, making it fresh.

Luminescence – The way the light plays off a wine when you examine it visually.

Luscious – The unctuous, mouthwatering characteristic of many sweet, dessert wines.

Malic acid – An apple-flavoured acid found in grapes.

Malolactic fermentation – A secondary fermentation that converts harder malic acid into softer lactic acid.

Meaty – A red wine that is chewy and full-bodied. A wine with firm tannins, and which is mouth-filling.

Medium-dry – A wine that is "off-dry" containing some residual sugar.

Méthode champenoise – A method of making sparkling wine in which the second fermentation takes place in the same bottle.

Minty – Often found in the smell of warm-climate Cabernet Sauvignon.

Must – The mixture of grapes juice, pulp, and skins prior to fermentation.

Noble rot – A fungus (botrytis) that eats out the pulp of some grapes, concentrating the sugars and acid in the dried-up pulp, and resulting in a sweet wine.

Nose – The bouquet of a wine.

Nouveau – A new wine, fermented and bottled a few weeks after harvest for immediate drinking.

Nutty – The smell of nuts in some white wines from barrel fermentation or ageing.

Oaky – The smell of vanilla, toast, coconut, or biscuit in a wine that has seen much oak.

Oechsle – The German scale for measuring the sugar in the must.

Passito – An Italian term in wine, indicating that the grapes were air-dried to concentrate the sugars prior to fermentation.

Péttilant – A wine with a naturally, light sparkle or crackle.

pH – A measure of the intensity of acid a wine contains.

Phylloxera – A pest or louse that attacks vine roots.

Pommace – The pulp remaining in the fermentation tank after the free-run juice has been drawn off.

Press wine – Wine made from the must after it is pressed.

Racking – Pouring wine from one container, tank, or barrel to another, leaving behind the sediment.

Rac – A wine with lively acidity.

Rancio – A Spanish term for the smell of sweet, nutty, decay from wine long wood-aged and open to the air.

Reflectiveness – The mirror effect of a wine as seen on its surface. This is a sign of stability.

Remuage – The process of rotating and tilting Champagne bottles in riddling racks to prevent the sediment from sticking to the sides, after the second fermentation.

Residual sugar – Sugar that remains in a wine after fermentation and processing.

Ripasso – An Italian term, describing wine that is placed on the lees of Recioto grapes to give it more body, flavour, and alcohol.

Schaumwein – German term for sparkling wine.

Sekt – German term for quality sparkling wine.

Sharp – A wine with excessive acidity.

Short – A wine with little aftertaste or finish.

Sinewy – A wine with good alcohol and acid, but less fruit.

Smoky – The smell of smoke in some wines from oak, soil, or grapes.

Soft – A wine that is round and mellow.

Spätburgunder – German name for Pinot Noir.

Spicy – The smell of spice in some wines.

Spritzig – A German term for a wine with a natural, slight sparkle on the tongue.

Spumante – An Italian term for sparkling wine.

Stalky – A wine with a green, raw taste from young vines, unripe grapes, or the use of some grape stems in fermentation.

Sulphur – A natural bi-product of fermentation. Also used as an antioxidant and antibacterial agent in winemaking. The smell of a burnt match in wine.

Supple – Soft, round, and smooth on the palate.

Sur lie – A wine that is left resting on its spent yeast cells (lees) and grape particles after fermentation.

Süssreserve – Unfermented grape juice used to sweeten the must or wine.

Sweaty saddle – The smell of leather and sweat in some red wines, usually older ones.

Sweet – The presence of sugar in a wine, either unfermented or back-blended.

Tafelwein – A German term for table wine.

Tannin – The astringent, puckery mouth feel from the skins, stalks, and pits of red grapes or from oak barrels.

Tart – A wine with sharp acidity.

Tartaric acid – The main acid in wine.

Tastevin – A small, shallow, silver cup used by winemakers and wine professionals to taste wine.

Terroir – The French term for climate, soil, and landscape in a vineyard, which give a region's wines their character.

Toasty – The smell and taste of a white wine fermented or aged in barrel.

Tonne – A measure of grapes producing approximately a thousand bottles.

Transfer method – A method of making sparkling wine where the wine is transferred to a large tank for cleanup after the second fermentation in bottle.

Ullage – The air pocket in a bottle between the surface of the wine and the cork.

Unbalanced – A wine in which one or more components or elements is excessive.

Vanilla – The smell of new oak in some wines.

Varietal – A single grape variety, sometimes shown on the wine label.

Vin de paille – The French term for a sweet wine whose grapes have been dried on straw mats prior to fermentation.

Vins de pays – The French term for "country wines."

Vin doux naturel – Sweet, French fortified wines.

Vin gris – The French term for a pale, rosé wine.

Vino novello – The Italian term for a new wine, fermented and bottled shortly after fermentation for immediate drinking. (*See* NOUVEAU)

Vinous – A wine with good fruit extract.

Vitis vinifera – A species of European vine that produces most wine, worldwide.

Volatile acidity – Excessive acidity that can produce acetone smells like nail polish or vinegar.

Well balanced – A wine in which all the components or elements are in harmony.

Yeasty – The smell of bread in some wines, especially those made in the champagne method.

SELECTED BIBLIOGRAPHY

I chose the following books because they are great reference pieces that will be a huge part of any wine library. No matter how wine knowledgeable you become, you will still find yourself referring to these classics time and again.

BOOKS

Amerine, Maynard A., and Edward B. Roessler. *Wines, Their Sensory Evaluation*. San Francisco: Freeman, 1976.

Aspler, Tony. *Wine Lover's Companion*. 3rd rev. ed. Whitby, Ontario: McGraw-Hill Ryerson, 1998.

Aspler, Tony, and Jacques Marie. *The Wine Lover Dines*. Scarborough, Ontario: Prentice-Hall, 1986.

Broadbent, Michael. *Complete Guide to Wine Tasting and Wine Cellars*. London: Simon & Schuster, 1984.

Coren, Stanley, Lawrence M. Ward, and James T. Ennis. *Sensation & Perception*. 2nd ed. New York: Harcourt Brace College Publishers, 1984.

Frumkin, Lionel. *The Science and Technique of Wine*. Cambridge: Patrick Stephens, 1974.

Geldard, Frank A. *The Human Senses*. 2nd ed. New York: John Wiley & Sons Inc., 1972.

Johnson, Hugh. *Modern Encyclopedia of Wine*. New York: Simon & Schuster, 1998.

Lembeck, Harriett. *Grossman's Guide to Wines, Beers and Spirits*. 7th ed. New York: Charles Scribner's Sons, 1983.

Lichine, Alexis. *New Encyclopedia of Wines & Spirits*. New York: Knopf, 1985.

Peynaud, Emile. *The Taste of Wine*. San Francisco: The Wine Appreciation Guild, 1987.

Robinson, Jancis. *The Oxford Companion to Wine*. Oxford: Oxford University Press, 1994.

Robinson, Jancis. *Vines, Grapes and Wines*. New York: Knopf, 1986.

Rosengarten, David, and Joshua Wesson. *Red Wine With Fish*. New York: Simon & Schuster, 1989.

Sharp, Andrew. *Winetaster's Secrets*. Toronto: Warwick Publishing Group, 1995.

Simon, André. *Wines of the World*. 2nd ed. by Serena Sutcliffe. New York: McGraw-Hill, 1981.

Vandyke Price, Pamela. *The Taste of Wine*. London: Random House, 1975.

Young, Alan. *An Encounter With Wine*. 2nd ed. Perth, Australia: International Wine Academy Publication, 1986.

Young, Alan. *Making Sense of Wine*. Richmond, Australia: Greenhouse Publications Ltd., 1986.

PERIODICALS
Britain: *Decanter Magazine*
U.S.A.: *The Wine Spectator*
Canada: *Wine Access, Winetidings*

INDEX